West Coast Plays

Greek
Steven Berkoff

Going To See The Elephant
Hensel, Johns, Kent, Meredith, Shaw, Toffenetti

Factperson
Factwino Meets The Moral Majority
Factwino vs. Armageddonman
San Francisco Mime Troupe

The Dream of Kitamura
Philip Kan Gotanda

One To Grow On
Brian Kral

Sand Castles
Adele Edling Shank

PUBLISHED BY THE CALIFORNIA THEATRE COUNCIL
Brian Bennett, Executive Director

© Copyright 1983, California Theatre Council
Winter and Spring 1983

These plays are fully protected, in whole, in part, or in any form under the copyright laws of the United States of America, the British Empire, including the Dominion of Canada, and all other countries of the Copyright Union, and are subject to royalty. All rights, including professional, amateur, motion-picture, radio, television, recitation, and public reading, are strictly reserved. All inquiries should be addressed to the agent named on the first page of each play.

West Coast Plays is published two times a year (Spring/Summer, Fall/Winter) in Los Angeles, California, by the California Theatre Council. Subscriptions are available at $25 per year. Send checks or money order to West Coast Plays, California Theatre Council, 849 South Broadway, Suite 621, Los Angeles, CA 90014.

This project is supported by grants from the National Endowment for the Arts, The California Arts Council, The San Francisco Foundation, The Zellerbach Family Fund, and The Yorkin Foundation.

West Coast Plays prints only plays which have been produced in a theater on the Pacific Coast of the Americas and can consider only those scripts which have been recommended by a member of the advisory board.

Script submissions should be made to Robert Hurwitt, Editor, West Coast Plays, P.O. Box 7206, Berkeley, CA 94707.

ISBN: 0-934782-15-6

THE CALIFORNIA THEATRE COUNCIL

The California Theatre Council is a non-profit service organization whose goals are:

To promote the development and support of non-profit theater in California

To work to increase communication within the theater community and to assist theatrical organizations with funding information, technical advice, and other matters

To provide legislators, arts agencies, and the general public with information on the special concerns of the California non-profit community.

While all the arts have broad areas of common concern, theater has its own special problems, a fact sometimes overlooked by granting agencies and unknown to much of the public. The CTC was formed in 1974 to explore and address the unique problems of the non-profit theater in California and it bases its purposes, goals, and objectives upon the multifaceted needs of the state's theatrical communities. Theatrical activity in California is intense, varied, and reflects the extraordinary ethnic, geographic, and economic diversity of the state. The strongest element in support of the CTC's need and effectiveness is the scope of its membership—organizations spanning the spectrum of California non-profit theater with budgets ranging from $10,000 to $7,000,000 per year. Member theaters encompass every demographic group and geographic area and present traditional, ethnic, alternative, and experimental theater.

EDITOR

Robert Hurwitt

ASSOCIATE EDITORS

Rick Foster
Susan LaTempa

President
BILL BUSHNELL
Los Angeles Actors' Theatre

First Vice President
MARIAN CIRISCIOLI
Merced Regional Arts Council

Vice Presidents
SUSAN HOFFMAN
Peoples' Theater Coalition

RICHARD REINECCIUS
Julian Theatre

SAM WOODHOUSE
San Diego Repertory Theatre

Treasurer
PEG YORKIN
Los Angeles Public Theatre

Secretary
STEPHEN J. ALBERT
CTG/Mark Taper Forum

Board Members
CHUCK CARSON
Theatre Publicist

ARLINE CHAMBERS
UCLA Graduate School of Arts Management

WILSON CHANG
Asian, Inc.

MARIE ACOSTA COLON
San Francisco Mime Troupe

QUENTIN EASTER
Lorraine Hansberry Theatre

NANCY EBSEN
Newport Harbor
  Actors' Theatre

DON EITNER
American Theatre Arts

DAVID EMMES
South Coast Repertory Theatre

PHIL ESPARZA
El Teatro Campesino

ANDY GRIGGS
Bear Republic Theater

THOMAS HALL
Old Globe Theatre

ERIC HAYASHI
Sansei Theatre Company

GILMAN KRAFT
Performing Arts Network

SUSAN LOEWENBERG
Los Angeles Theatre Works

MARCIA O'DEA
Magic Theatre

FAITH RAIGUEL
Lutz and Carr

JAMES REBER
San Jose Repertory Theatre

DUNCAN ROSS
University of
  Southern California

RON SOSSI
Odyssey Theatre Ensemble

EDWARD WESTON
Actors Equity Association

ROZ WYMAN
National Council of the
  National Endowment
  for the Arts

Executive Director
BRIAN BENNETT

Contents

Greek Steven Berkoff	7
Greek: Brave Words for a Victim of "Language" Silvie Drake	45
Going To See The Elephant Karen Hensel Patti Johns Elana Kent Sylvia Meredith Elizabeth Lloyd Shaw Laura Toffenetti	49
Factperson	97
Factwino Meets the Moral Majority	127
Factwino vs. Armageddonman San Francisco Mime Troupe	159
Comics On The Stage Henri Picciotti	185
The Dream of Kitamura Philip Kan Gotanda	191
One To Grow On A Play For Young People Brian Kral	225
Sand Castles Adele Edling Shank	257
What Is A Play Anyway? Raising Some Initial Questions Bernard Weiner	325

The Playwrights

STEVEN BERKOFF *(Greek)* was born in Stepney, London in 1937 and began acting in the City Literary Institute when he was nineteen. After studying acting and mime in London and Paris he founded the London Theatre Group in 1968 in order to direct and perform his own work. Since then he has become recognized as one of England's leading playwrights with adaptations of Kafka's *Metamorphosis* and *The Trial, East, Agamemnon, Decadence,* and, most recently, *West.* He has performed and/or directed his own work in Great Britain, Europe, Israel, and Australia, and his plays and short stories have been published in Great Britain, The Netherlands, and in the United States by Riverrun Press. The Los Angeles production of *Greek* introduced Berkoff's work to American theater audiences.

PHILIP KAN GOTANDA *(The Dream of Kitamura)* is a third generation Japanese American playwright, born and raised in Stockton, California. His plays have been performed in New York, Los Angeles, and San Francisco. He is the author of a musical, *The Avocado Kid or Zen in the Art of Guacamole,* as well as *A Song For a Nisei Fisherman, Bullet Headed Birds, The Wash,* and *American Tattoo.* He received the 1982-83 Rockefeller Playwright-in-Residence grant from the Mark Taper Forum in Los Angeles. Gotanda is currently collaborating with Michael Sesaki on the musical score for a new film by Wayne Wang.

PATTI JOHNS *(Going to See the Elephant)* is a direct descendant of Kansas pioneers and used her own family histories in beginning work on this play. She has worked as an actress at Los Angeles Actors' Theater, Cast, and for four seasons at South Coast Repertory, as well as on television. As a student at Northwestern University she wrote a one-woman show, *Ladies of the Journal,* which was later produced in New York, sponsored by the *Ladies Home Journal.* She has won numerous awards as an actor and a playwright.

KAREN HENSEL *(Going to See the Elephant)* has acted at ACT in San Francisco, San Diego's Old Globe, South Coast Repertory, L.A. Stage Company, and the Mark Taper Forum. She was in the original and Broadway casts of Luis Valdez's *Zoot Suit* and in the long-running Los Angeles production of *Sister Mary Ignatius.* She directed a highly acclaimed production of *Voices* and has won numerous awards as an actress. Hensel is currently on the faculty of the West Coast Academy of Dramatic Arts.

ELANA KENT *(Going to See the Elephant)* is a graduate of the American Academy of Dramatic Arts. She is currently writing a musical and a screenplay while pursuing her acting career.

BRIAN KRAL *(One To Grow On)* is the author of several plays for children and adults, including *Special Cases* and *The Ransom of Red Chief*, both published by Anchorage Press of New Orleans. Selected as the Winifred Ward Scholar for 1982 by the Children's Theatre Association of America, he is completing an MFA from Arizona State University. His most recent plays have premiered at ASU and with the California Young People's Theatre in San Jose, but he continues to live and work in Las Vegas as the artistic director for the Rainbow Company.

SYLVIA MEREDITH *(Going to See the Elephant)* was nominated for a Los Angeles Drama Critics Circle award for her portrayal of Ma Wheeler in *Going to See the Elephant* and received a 1981 Dramalogue award for her role in John Guare's *Bosoms and Neglect*. Meredith made her Broadway debut in *Season in the Sun* and performed throughout the east opposite Bert Lahr in *Harvey*.

THE SAN FRANCISCO MIME TROUPE *(Factperson, Factwino Meets the Moral Majority,* and *Factwino vs. Armageddonman)* was founded in 1959 and has performed extensively on the streets and in the parks and theaters of North America, Europe, and Latin America. Besides a heavy schedule of touring, and occasional winter productions in San Francisco, the Mime Troupe has presented a free show in the parks of the Bay Area every summer for over twenty years. Collectively run, most of its productions are of original works scripted by the company. Other plays by the Mime Troupe are available in *By Popular Demand,* published by the collective, and in *West Coast Plays* #10. Songs from the two *Factwino* plays and from *Americans or Last Tango in Huahuatenango* may be heard on *The Album,* Flying Fish Records.

ADELE EDLING SHANK *(Sand Castles)* has concentrated recently on "The California Plays" series, each play set in a different part of California. The first of these, *Sunset/Sunrise* (published in *West Coast Plays* #4), was co-winner of the Actors' Theatre of Louisville Great American Play Contest. *Winterplay* (available in the Theatre Communications Group's *New Plays USA: 1*), *Stuck, Sand Castles, The Grass House* were premiered at the Magic Theatre in San Francisco, directed by her husband, Theodore Shank, and have had subsequent productions in Lousiville, Los Angeles, and New York.

Shank has received Rockefeller Foundation and National Endowment for the Arts playwriting fellowships. She has an MA in playwriting from UC Davis and teaches playwriting at UC San Diego.

ELIZABETH LLOYD SHAW *(Going to See the Elephant)* came to California from Indiana. Since her arrival she has produced *The Norman Conquests* and *Going Down*, an original play, and has acted in *The Night of the Iguana* and *Tobacco Road* among other plays. She can be seen in the soon to be released films *Fire and Ice* and Alan Rudolph's *Choose Me*.

LAURA TOFFENETTI *(Going to See the Elephant)* is a founding member of the Los Angeles Repertory Theater and appeared in its critically acclaimed production of *Voices*. She has recently completed co-writing another play, *They all rolled over and one fell out*. Tofinetti is also an accomplished singer.

Editor's Note

This is the first issue of *West Coast Plays* to come out under my editorship and, as rewarding as the task has been, it has left me with a greatly heightened admiration for the work of my predecessor, Rick Foster. Inevitably I have made some missteps in my maiden journey, not the least of which was acquiring more manuscripts than could possibly appear in one book. Consequently, Chris Hardman's intriguing play, *Vacuum,* originally advertised for this issue, is being held over for volume 17/18—a decision which will also give us more time to prepare an appropriately striking visual presentation for a work whose visuals are as important as its text. Our plan is to print *Vacuum* in parallel texts to represent the parallel visual and auditory experiences of the play in production.

A few departures from past practice are worthy of note. Brian Kral's *One To Grow On* marks our entry into the realm of plays for young people, an area too long neglected by standard drama anthologies and an increasingly important component of western theater. Given the amount of creative energy being devoted to this area we expect to print at least one such play in each future issue, and I am particularly pleased to be able to inaugurate the practice with a writer of Kral's caliber. This is also the first issue in which we have printed new plays by authors whom we had published before (not counting our ongoing commitment to print Murray Mednick's *Coyote Cycle). Sand Castles* is the latest in Adele Edling Shank's series of wry California plays, a series inaugurated in print with our fourth issue. Also back for a return engagement is the San Francisco Mime Troupe, whose *Factperson/Factwino* plays, which electrified audiences and critics alike, are presented here for the first time as a unified trilogy.

The innovation most likely to raise eyebrows is our printing of Steven Berkoff's *Greek,* the first British play we have published. This is a departure from past practice only in that we have generally concentrated on plays which have had their world premiere on the West Coast, although our stated purpose has been to print important new plays which have had their American premiere in this region, as *Greek* certainly did. But it wasn't just the enormous success *Greek* enjoyed during its two Los Angeles runs, nor even the remarkable quality of Berkoff's text that determined its inclusion in this volume. Rather it was my conviction that its production was an important event in West Coast theater and that *Greek* will have a major influence on the development of new plays in the region. The play's reception in New York, as detailed in this issue by Sylvie Drake, strengthens that conviction. The text printed here differs from the English version (available from Riverrun Press through Flatiron Book Distributors) to incorporate changes made by the author for its Los Angeles production.

Nothing is more remarkable about the remaining plays in this issue than the plays themselves. *Going to See the Elephant* has been a well-deserved, long-running hit in L.A. *The Dream of Kitamura* is another example of the exciting new work coming out of America's Asian Theaters. I am proud to debut my editorship with such a strong issue.

Thanks are due to many people, but most particularly to Rick Foster and Brian Bennett who smoothed my way considerably, as well as to the authors, who have made the task a pleasure.

Robert Hurwitt

Greek
Steven Berkoff

Greek was first presented at the Half Moon Theatre, London, on February 11, 1980, with the following cast:

EDDY and FORTUNE TELLER	Barry Philips
DAD and MANAGER	Matthew Scurfield
WIFE, DOREEN, and WAITRESS	Linda Marlowe
MUM, SPHINX, and WAITRESS 2	Janet Amsden

Directed by Steven Berkoff

Greek had its American premiere on April 30, 1982, at the Matrix Theatre, Los Angeles, produced by L.A. Theatre Works with the following cast:

EDDIE and FORTUNE TELLER	John Francis
DAD and MANAGER	Ken Danziger
WIFE, DOREEN, and WAITRESS	Gilllian Eaton
MUM, SPHINX, and WAITRESS	Paddi Edwards

Directed by Steven Berkoff
Associate director, Carey Perloff
Set and lighting design by Gerry Hariton *and* Vicki Baral
Costume design by Peter Mitchell
Producer, Susan Albert Loewenberg

NOTE

The text, revised by the author, is that of the Los Angeles production.

PLACE: England

TIME: Present

The stage setting is a kitchen table and four simple chairs. These merely define spaces and act as an anchor or base for the actors to spring from. All other artifacts are mimed or suggested. The walls are three quadrilateral white panels, very clinical and at the same time indicating Greek classicism. The faces are painted white and are clearly defined. Movement should be sharp and dynamic, exaggerated and sometimes bearing the quality of seaside cartoons.

©1980, 1981, 1982, 1983 by Steven Berkoff.
CAUTION: All rights strictly reserved. Professionals and amateurs are hereby warned that *Greek* is subject to a royalty. It is protected under the copyright laws of all countries covered by the International Copyright Convention. Permission in writing must be secured before any kind of performance is given. Reprinted by courtesy of Riverrun Press, New York, and John Calder (Publishers) Ltd., London. Performing rights are controlled by Rosica Collin, Ltd., 1 Clareville Grove Mews, London SW7 5 AH, England.

Greek
Steven Berkoff

ACT ONE

The actors are seated frozen at the table. Sound of a TV pattern noise, loud.

DAD: Turn it off son.
EDDIE: *(Shuts off TV.)* So I was spawned in Tufnell Park that's no more than a stone's throw from the Angel/a monkey's fart from Tottenham or a bolt of phlegm from Stamford Hill/it's a cess pit, right... a scum hole dense with the drabs who prop up corner pubs, the kind of pub where ye old ass holes assemble... the boring turds who save for Christmas with clubs... my mum did that... save all year for her slaggy Christmas party of boozy old relatives in Marx and Sparks cardigans who stand all year doing as little as they can while they had one hand in the boss's till and the other scratching their balls... They'd all come over and vomit up Guinness and Mum's unspeakable excuse for cuisine all over the bathroom, adjust their dentures... rage against the blacks, envying their cocks, loathe the yids envying their gelt... hate everything that walks under thirty and fall asleep in front of the telly... So they'd gather in the pubs, usually a smelly corner pub run by a rancid thick as pig shit Paddy who sold nothing but booze and crisps in various chemical flavors to their yokel patrons who play

incessant games of cruddy darts, drink yards of stale gnat's piss beer, and chatter like, "see Arsenal last week... I think England's team's all washed up... what abaht the way he dribbled the... nah nah, he's lorst his bottle... do leave orf..." The stink of the pub rises and the oafs sit in the corner staring out into the dreams they never had...

DAD: Lager and lime. (DAD, MUM, *and* DOREEN *mime drinking.*)
EDDIE: With a drip of snot hanging off the ends of their noses...
DOREEN: My round next time.
EDDIE: And try to make a pint last four hours...
MUM: Lovely.
EDDIE: Start crowding up now (DAD, MUM, *and* DOREEN *make crowd noises.*) and the Paddy starts raving fucking time *(Crowd noise ends.)* and pulling the glass out of your hand while he's bursting your eardrums screaming like a sergeant major his wife attempts to shovel some paint on her evil hate-all face which looks as if it's been applied by a drunken epileptic on a roller coaster... "Allo luv," she foams... staring out of a yellow face with little snot brown eyes like two raisins in a bowl of porridge. And if by chance you lean over the bar too far some bastard monster cunt Alsatian leaps at you, its dripping fangs simply dying to rip your fucking throat out... so I gave up going to the corner pub with its late night chorus of lurchy
DAD. MUM, *and* DOREEN: 'Night all, see ya.
EDDIE: We got wine bars now, handsome. That's much better—sit down, a half bottle of chateau or bollinger, some pate and salad served by a chick who looks as if she's been fresh frozen... you take your favorite woman there, my woman, very nice mate, looks like she's been just minted and sharp as new mown grass, knickers as white as Christmas, eyes like the bluest diamonds/a pair of fiery red rubies for lips, the light hits them and shatters your eyes, she smiles and your heart leaps into your throat and you carry a demon between your thighs and up to your chin/the whole time... I wear shades to protect myself against the brightness of her teeth... no tobacco stains on them boy... breath like an ocean breeze on Brighton Pier... now could you take her to that pub? Could you ever! Nah! It's like a way of death. It's like a death wish personified. It's really for the old fascists singing war songs on the pavement.

DAD, MUM, *and* DOREEN *sing*: Knees up, Mother Brown,
     Under the table you must go

Greek   11

EDDIE: So I go to my wine bar with my bird who's carved out of onyx and marble and laced in the smells of the promise of sex the way you wouldn't believe... I swim in her like I was plunging into the Jordan for a baptism. So anyway one day my dad calls me in the kitchen.

DAD: Come in son.

EDDIE: He says.

DAD: I wanna chat to ya, or we could go down the corner to the pub, I'll buy you a drink.

EDDIE: No! Not that pub I yelp in real and unfeigned terror. I'll throw some tea into a pot instead... Mum's out... the Daily Mirror crossword half finished... some egg on the tits of the center page spread... well it is a bit grotty but homely in a sickly sort of way if you're not used to anything better, it's not like the interior of a zen temple but cozy. A few crumbs on the carpet, some evil photos of my sister on the mantelpiece and a picture of Granny looking like Mussolini in drag which they all looked like in those far off days of prehistory, the poodle's shit again behind the cocktail cabinet... the old bacon rinds sit stinking in the pan and the room renches of lard. I make Dad a cuppa. Mum's at bingo and Sis is meditating in the next room on the squeezing out of some juicy blackheads... her old knickers lie sunny side up... she always left them on the floor for Mum to scoop up while I wouldn't have touched them except with those pincers that pick up radium behind thick walls. So we sit down and he confesses this story to me... pulls out a fag and sits there with his flies half undone (DAD *mimes action as* EDDIE *speaks.*), and the ash of his fag ready to drop all over his shirt. I try not to look at him or his flies. I try to occupy my thought with my latest Stan Kenton. I look out of the window and see the grey clouds of Tottenham stray across the window pane... a tiny sliver of sun is struggling to peep through, sees what it has to shine on and thinks "fuck it—is it worth it" and beats a retreat. So Dad says...

DAD: Look here son.

EDDIE: I says "yes, Dad?" clocking his work-raped face, his tasteless shit heap Burton ready made trousers, and his deadly drip dry shirt that acquires BO faster than shit attracts flies... I clock all this fusion of rubbish and say "yes Dad? What do you want to chat abaht," never hearing much else out of his gob than...

DAD: Send the darkies back to the jungle.

EDDIE: And...

DAD: Hitler got the trains running on time.

EDDIE: You got a lot of Nazi lovers among the British down and out. Lazy bastards wondered why at the end of a life of skiving and strikes Moisha down the road copped a few quid or why the Cypriots had a shop full of goodies not that pathetic shit heap down our street that stocks only Mother's Pride and mousetrap cheese a few miserable tins of pilchards and Heinz baked beans and a dreary cunt inside saying, "No we don't get no demand for that" when asked for something only slightly more exotic than Kelloggs. So Dad did not come out with any of that fascist bullshit which relieved me since the Front were full of dads like this and that cunt in the grocery shop... "Yeah Dad" I said "whats on your bonce?"... his face squeezed up like it's hard to say, like those old ads for Idris lemon squash showing a screwed up lemon and comes out with...

DAD: When you were a nipper/we went to a Gypsy, a fortune teller/a bit of a giggle/an Easter fair/don't laugh/a caper what else/spent a tosheroon on a bit of a thrill/don't talk to me about thrill/so in we went/the Gypsy asks have I a son? "I have," I says, I mean who don't have a son?/his face meanwhile staring into the ball/his eyes all popping/I'm not taking it for gen, straight up a lark/Easter and all/I've got a lovely bunch and all that *(All mime laughter.)* His face gets all contorted and twisted and he says/he sees a violent death for this son's father/do what! But I'm his dad/come orf it/don't get all dramatic/we get on like houses blazing/and I see he says, something worse than death/and that's a bunk-up with his mum/I'll give you a backhand I utter/you're having me on/you been smoking them African woodbines/no he shrieks I see it, and what I see I see/so don't pay me, just scarper/leave my tent/keep your gelt/outside we ran, your mum was white as Persil/I as yellow as a Chinaman with jaundice/course we took no notice/forgot about it like, but not quite/waited till you got to be a bloke and then one day I said, "Dinah/you remember that darkie in the fair who came out with all that filth about Eddie"/one morning in bed just lying there, redigesting bits of past and sucking still the flavor of some juicy memories...

MUM: Not many.

DAD: Our Dinah slurps...

MUM: Not many, I nearly dropped Doreen with whom I was six months pregnant then/funny times...

DAD: Well, I say, that fair is back in town, the same firm fifteen years later... let's bowl down and see that geezer, tell that Hornsey Gypsy what a lot of old bollocks/how he upset my missus with his pack of dirty lies/so off we went. (MUM *and* DAD *come*

downstage; DOREEN *turns back to audience.)* Doubted somehow that he'd still be there, since he was pushing sixty then/you never know, we waited our turn/it was the same name "have your future read/Fantoni's magic crystal gazer"... shall we go in?...
MUM: Do you think we should?
DAD: Why not, it's now or never/we went pale a bit but in we marched same old schmutter on the table, the beads we walked through and the bit of old glass and no, it weren't him, so I said where's the old geezer that we once saw whose handle now you seem to have?"
FORTUNE TELLER: My late old man.
DAD: He said.
FORTUNE TELLER: Five years ago he uttered his last/and fell off the porch/but taught me the trade/imbued his vision in me/I got his powers now/so don't you fret/if he did good by you/donate a quid and I'll do my best.
DAD: So Ed, your mum and I sat down just like before/the years they shrank away/just like a hole fell out the earth and time and space had faded away/we seemed then to have hurtled back those fifteen years/in that small tent/the music tinkling through from the carousel outside and that funny smell/the shouts growing faint just the whiff of stale grass under our feet/and like the tent seemed small/like a trap and suddenly hot and nothing outside just quiet but his face/his face getting all twisted up just like his dad/his mouth all white and tight like an earthquake was going on inside his nut and his lips were straining against it coming out.
MUM: Oh, Ted.
DAD: Dinah sussed but natch we waited/"don't tell me.," I said," you see a son of mine"/his eyes looked up affirmed/no word just that look and his tight mouth/like holding back something worse than vomit/"and you see something worse." I says, "like a nasty accident perhaps"... he nodded, parted his lips enough to mouth the word death which he hadn't the guts to sound. He then stared hard at Dinah/but we had enough and wanted not to hear the other half but fled. *(*MUM *and* DAD *flee from table.)* I turned and snatched the quid back from the table/don't know why/but like before when I got my money back/it seemed to say by taking back the gelt it couldn't happen/his eyes looked like pity/like those sweet pics you get in Woolworths of those kids with a tear just ripe to drop. *(*MUM *and* DAD *sit down at the table.)* I know it's just a fun fair Ed/a laugh, a bit of a giggle/I didn't blame the kid/what do you make of it son/you don't fancy your old mum do you son!

You dont want to kill me do you boy.
DOREEN: Leave off you two.
EDDIE: Doreen!
DAD: Hey!
MUM: Shh.
EDDIE: His face hung there like a soggy worn out testicle/mouth open and eyes like carrier bags/fancy my mum! I could sooner go down on Hitler, than do anything my old man so gravely feared/no Dad/but all this aggro and old wive's tale gone and put you in a tiz/I'll leave home/split and scarper/the central line goes far these days and that's to foreign climes/I'll piss off tomorrow/I needed to escape this cruddy flat and this excuse seemed good as any/tata Ma and Pa. (DAD, MUM, *and* DOREEN *wave.*) They waved to me outside the flats...my mum looked sad/her spotty apron wrapped round her like the flag of womanhood/I never saw her out of it/always standing in the kitchen like some darkie slave behind Dad and me and Sis...

CHORUS

DAD: Bung us the toast
EDDIE: Where's the jam?
DOREEN: Pig!
MUM: More tea love?

Chorus is repeated three times. The third time MUM *alters her line.*

MUM: More taters love?
DOREEN: I'm on a diet.
MUM: More cake love?
EDDIE: No Mum I've had six slices already.
MUM: Go on have some more.
EDDIE: I dont want no more you rancid old boot,
DAD: Hey!
EDDIE: I'd spray affectionately.
MUM: Oh he don't like my cake,
EDDIE: She'd simper... all right bung us another slice and I'll wedge it down wiv a mug of tea to slop it up a bit.
DAD: Bung us the toast. *(All four mime eating.)*
EDDIE: Where's the jam?
DOREEN: Pig!
MUM: More tea love?
EDDIE: And she gazes at us with moist eyes on all of us slurping like fat pigs in a trough/we'd leave a wreck filled table, Ma's washing

Greek

up, how well she knew that washtop/Dad's picking out losers in the worn out armchair—Sis is fitting in her cap for the night's activity cussing and swearing in the next room as she struggles with it...

DOREEN: Fuck it!

EDDIE: And Mum sits in front of the box watching some dozy cretin making cunts out of the cunts who go on to win a few bob/Mum's giggling in her glee/her legs like a patchwork quilt from hogging the electric fire, while I was in my little room plotting and dreaming of ruling the world/take a Charles Atlas course/wondering if the queen gets it often/or planning a dose of robbery wiv violence or glorious bodily charm/so in my little room I plotted/smoked/played Stan Kenton and wanked wiv Mum's cooking oil. Now no more will I escape to my little domain... hearing the sounds of Hughy Phlegm in the next room through the snot encrusted walls. So all in a flash these thoughts slinked like maggots through my bonce as I waved my goodbyes to the fast diminishing figures of my mum and dad wed together in the distance like mould on cheese... my dad was the mould/never mad about him... as I reached the end of the road I could only see the apron and lost the figure/the apron stayed in my mind the longest. When my old lady went to the happy hunting ground I would frame that apron.

MUM: Take good care of yourself.

DAD: Don't forget to write.

DOREEN: Got your photo.

MUM: Be a good boy.

DAD: Send us some money.

DOREEN: Miss yer.

MUM: Love yer Ed.

DAD: Take care on the roads.

DOREEN: Au revoir.

MUM: Bye, boy. *(The sound of a train is heard.* EDDIE *exits.)*

DAD: The toast is burnt.

MUM: Saw Vi the other day. *(A toilet is flushed. Sound of footsteps.)*

DAD: Neighbors don't complain no more.

MUM: Matilda's had six kittens.

DAD: Where's my smokes?

MUM: 'Ere, 'ave you seen the cooking oil?

DAD: I miss our little Ed. *(Sound of explosions.)*

MUM: How will he fare, strikes up and down the country?

DAD: The city sits in a heap of shit.

MUM: Of uncollected garbage everywhere.

DAD: The country's in a state of plague/while parties of all shades battle for power to sort the shit from the shinola/the marxists and the workers' party call for violence to put an end to violence/anyone who wants to kill maim and destroy/arson, murder, and hack are being recruited for the new revolutionary party/the fag libs are holding violent demos to be able to give head in the public park when the garbage strike is over and not to be persecuted for screwing on the top deck of buses.
MUM: Fortes catering is resisting the staff's demand to be paid wages and is recruiting workers from the jungles of South America.
DAD: Yet also strongly resisting the need to clear out the rats for which they are duly famous.
MUM: Most of the stores are closed but Fortnums and Harrods soldier on shrilly packed with screaming advocates of limited nuclear drop on Hyde Park and so rid the country they say of a twisted bunch of rancid and perverted filth.
DAD: The nights in Hyde Park are lit by fires and the sound of tom toms from the Brixton black workers revolutionary gay lib join forces with white is ugly forced abortion/wanking is not a town in China but an alternative to the filthy men female party group.
MUM: Meanwhile the rats head down Edgware Road up to Oxford Street preparing to turn right into Bond Street/get down Piccadilly and raid Fortnums, pick up their mates at Fortes and join forces to make all resistance impossible.
DAD: The rats march across Piccadilly avoiding Soho where the food is dangerous even for rats, heading down to the Strand/collect the Savoy contingent, overfat rats not sleek for battle but just good germ carriers with rotten teeth head across Waterloo Bridge and to the National Theatre... try to wake the theater rats who have been long in coma from a deadly attack of nightly brainwash.
MUM: Those that can be woken streak up Drury Lane to Holborn and on to Kings Cross...
DAD: Avoiding the carcasses of rotting football Scots swollen and putrefying on the streets/those who failed to make the last train and died while waiting for the next one/their flesh is deadly/the rats come marching in.
MUM: Maggot Thatcher is our only hope love. *(Explosions phase out.)*
DAD: If we only had more Maggots to eat through the stinking woodpile. But how is poor Ed going to manage in all this? *(Train sound heard again briefly.)*

Greek

EDDIE: *(Enters.)* The shit has hit the fan as if from a great height. (DAD, MUM, *and* DOREEN *make siren noises.*) I walked and walked/the sirens like wailing banshees from black marias tear along the garbage filled London streets, chock full of close shaved men in blue and clubs in black/stacked full of teeth hate-clenched/wiv fists all hungry for their daily exercise...the Scotties line the curb face down in vomit which swishes down the rat-infested gutters... dumb Jocks down for their dozy game of football/some excuse to flee their fat and shit-heap Marys in the tenements/they wear funny little hats with bobbles on and rotten teeth, they belch into the carbon air their rotgut fumes and sing a lurchy tune or two about owning some pox-ridden scab heap called Glasgow when they don't own a pot to piss in. Then one blue-eyed bobby lays a skull or five (well aimed, son) wide open.

DAD, MUM, *and* DOREEN: SMASH... SPLATTER... CLOBBER. *(Repeated three times.)*

EDDIE: Take that you tartan git...

DAD, MUM, *and* DOREEN: CRASH...SHATTER. *(Repeated twice.)*

EDDIE: Lovely...

DAD, MUM, *and* DOREEN: 'Ere you are, wot the fuck you doin'...

EDDIE: Shut up...

DAD, MUM, *and* DOREEN: KERACKKK!!!

EDDIE: The whores descend and drain their filthy wallets. With their con of fuck...

DOREEN *and* MUM: Hello cheeky.

EDDIE: And as the Jock steps inside for fantasies of London pussy.

DAD, MUM, *and* DOREEN: KERACK!

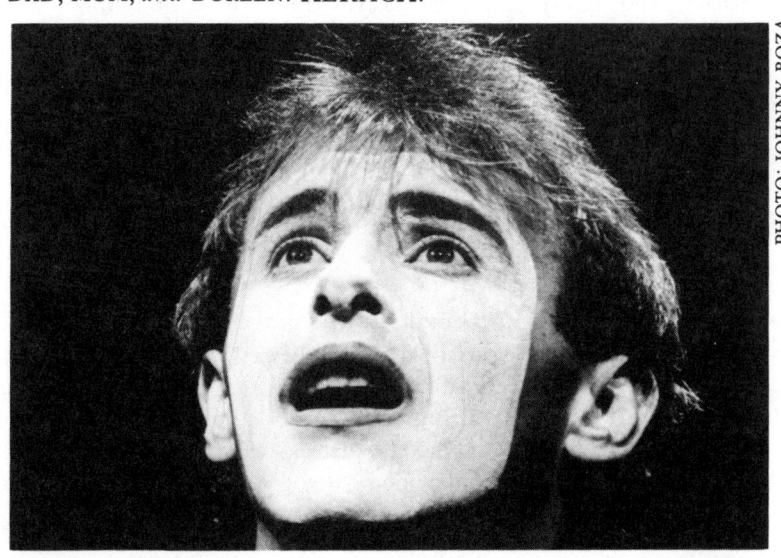

PHOTO: JOHNNY ROZA

EDDIE: A villain hard faced doth distribute a bit of sense with bars of iron/so on they go, the foul ignoble mob/they watch the match the wrong way round so pissed as newts and then they stagger (DAD, MUM, *and* DOREEN *mime drunkenness.*) into Euston Station driven by a blind sense of instinct or smell to join their fellow tartans on their journey back.

DAD, MUM, *and* DOREEN: Ay ad a loovely taime. *(They mime vomiting.)*

EDDIE: Meanwhile and spewing up the Mall down which I walked to escape the deadly gas from ten day haggis freshly heaved upon our silver London streets. When what do I espy (DAD, MUM, *and* DOREEN *mime holding guns, moving them slowly from left to right.)* but fuck and shit MacDougal and his Paddies from helfast and raring to blow up anything that moves.

DAD, MUM, *and* DOREEN: Hate, hate, throw the bomb. Hate, hate, throw the bomb.

EDDIE: Thick eared with hands like bunches of bananas/their voices from afar were like a pack of baying hounds. They were an army dressed in blue eyes and liquid gelignite stuffed in their macs and little bombs in innocent sandwich bags... armpits concealing stinking sweaty guns ready to blow some mother's son's head off and spray the dusty Strand with thick rich ruby/knock off some chick who god forbid could be some sweet of mine/or take the legs off some poor cunt who happened to be hanging about/and then they get all stinking in their pubs and roar with leprechaunish glee...

DAD: I've only got six Guinnesses...

EDDIE: And fight to say who was the one to toss the bomb...

MUM: Whose round is it now?

EDDIE: How many tommies did you spray apart?...

DOREEN: My fucking husband's in the pub again...

EDDIE: How many boys were drowning in their blood/who that very night had kissed the loving girls farewell...

DAD: Jesus, Mary, and Joseph.

EDDIE: How many mothers' daughters copped a face of shrapnel/lost an eye...

DOREEN: Fuck my fucking husband, fuck it!

EDDIE: How many mothers douse the graves of kids of eighteen/ wives and widows chatting to a piece of earth while you, you crock of gonorrhea in serge wolf back another gallon, leer home to your Bridget alone and waiting with six kids, and unwashed climb aboard dragging across her fleshy wastes your skimpy shred of dirty prick/poke it about a bit and come your drip of watery spunk

Greek

ten seconds later/she's lying there like a bloated cow/never known what coming is/only read about those soft explosions in the groin/heard rumors like/the only explosions Paddy here can make are ones that make you scream in fucking agony and pain awash in blood not ecstasy and spunk. What a fucking obscenity that is... FUCK FUCK FUCK AND SHIT.

DOREEN: MY FUCKING HUSBAND'S LYING ACROSS THE ROAD/HIS LEGS ON ONE SIDE AND HIS TORSO ON THE OTHER. OH GOD HELP ME.

ALL: OH!

EDDIE: MAGGOT SCRATCHER HANG THE CUNTS/HANG THEM SLOW AND LET ME TAKE A SKEWER AND JAB THEIR EYES OUT/LOVELY/GREEK STYLE/... Hanging's no answer to the plague madam/you'd be hanging everyday/I'm a human like us all/we're all the same linked/if you kick one his scream will hit my ears and hurt my mind to think of some poor cunt in shtuck/the way a kitten crying in the night will make you crawl out of your soft pit say what the fuck's up little moggie/free Guinness that's the answer and sex instruction initiated by luscious English birds well trained in fuck and suck then instead of marching down the street with weapons of war and little people on the side waving flags *(All mime flag waving.)* they'll march down with cocks at full alert and straining proud and strong/and promptly get arrested. Still you can't help it/you're drowned in aggro since a kid and Dad has fed between your flappy lugs not love but hate/has fed the history of ye old past to give you causes/something to do at night/has woven a tapestry of woe inflicted on him from the distant foggy patch called past. So what else can you do/your tired soggy brain awash with Guinness laced with hate... I jumped into the bushes and watched the curly mob in a storm of dust go past...

DAD, MUM, *and* DOREEN: Hate, hate, throw the bomb.

EDDIE: The palace was on alert... the sturdy chiselled chins fresh shaved of our fine and brave John English ready to defend the queen and all her minions who represent all that is fine in this drab slab of grey/this septic isle...

DOREEN *and* MUM: *(Sing.)* Rule Britannia, Britannia rules the waves...

EDDIE: Eventually jumped on a train. *(Train sound;* DAD, MUM, *and* DOREEN *mime passengers.)* Found one whose carriage wasn't entirely smashed and wrecked and rode in peace to London's airport skidrow alone and reflective in my thoughts except for some Paki in the carriage getting a right kicking for some no doubt vile offence like inadvertantly catching the eye of some right gallant son of Tottenham, the kicking lent a rhythmic ritual to my thoughts which were beginning to get formed to take some mighty fine decisions that would shoot me on my path to riches and success sweet smelling pussy and golden arms and lashing tongues. I fell into a kind of reverie. *(Train sound and mime ends.)* I fell asleep and dreamed... I saw a dozen pussies on a bed nestled between some soft and squeezy thighs, like little gentle kittens suckling on a mother's teat/their sweet and ivory columns hanging loosely fell apart revealing flowers in a garden that you water and like a randy bee I buzzed from one to t'other/their petals gently opened wide/sent forth their perfumes in the air/and as I left they'd close again/and then the next and each one subtly different/each like precious luscious plants/each like a grasping toothless mouth hungry like open beaks of little birds while I, like mother, into their open throats would drop my worm which hungrily and devouringly they'd grasp. Then I awoke *(Train sounds and mime again.)* and rudely saw the world just as it is and started on my adventures thrust all young and sweet into the seething heaving heap of world in which I was just a little dot. (DAD, MUM, *and* DOREEN *make chorus of airport sounds and noises.)* All this confused me/who needs to go/do I do you do he/I decided to stay and see my own sweet land/amend the woes of my own fair state/why split and scarper like ships leaving a sinking rat/I saw myself as king of the western world/but since I needed some refreshment for my trials ahead, I ventured into this little cafe... everywhere I looked... I witnessed this evidence of the British plague.

Cafe. Chorus of kitchen/cafe menu sounds and phrases.

MANAGER: Kidney pie, cooked all week
WAITRESS 2: Cheese roll, greasy chips
WAITRESS: Cold tea, bacon's off
EDDIE: Excuse me. One coffee please and croissant and butter.
WAITRESS: Right. Cream?
EDDIE: Please. Where is the butter so I might spread it lavishly and feel its oily smoothness cover the jagged edges of the croissant?
WAITRESS: Aint got none. There's a plague on.
EDDIE: Then why serve me the croissant knowing you had no butter?
WAITRESS: I'll get you something else.
EDDIE: I'll have a cheesecake, what's it like?
WAITRESS: Our cheesecakes are all made from the nectar of the gods

PHOTO: HARITON-BARAL

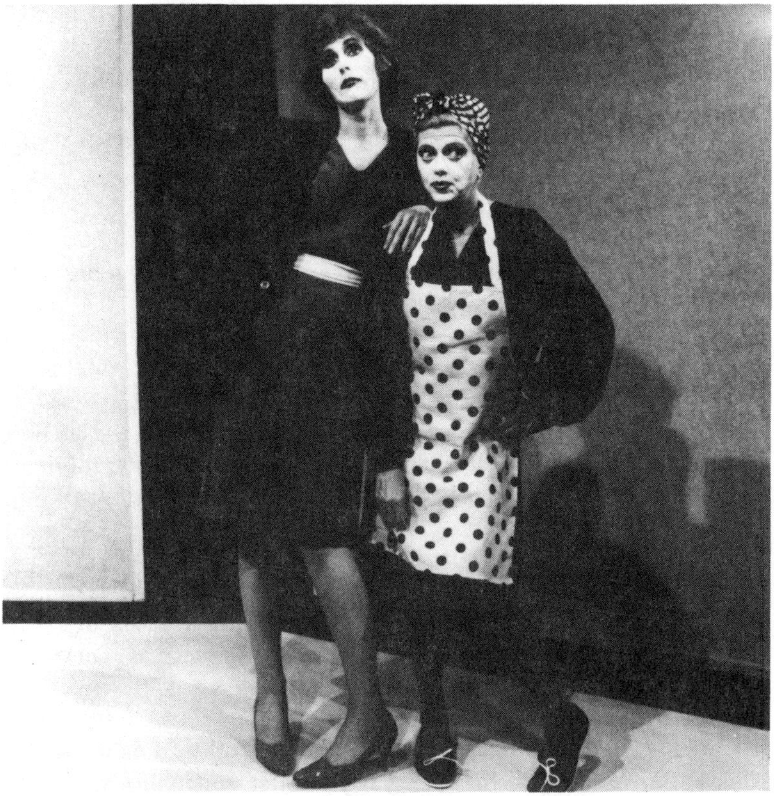

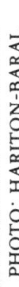

mixed with the dexterous fingers of a hundred virgins who have been whipped with bullrushes grown by the banks of the Ganges.

EDDIE: Ok, I'll have one. *(She brings it.)* I've finished the coffee now and won't have any liquid to wash the cake down with.

WAITRESS: Do you want another coffee?

EDDIE: Not want but must not want but have to/you took so long to bring the cake that I've finished the coffee, so bring another.

WAITRESS: Alright.

EDDIE: But bring it before I finish the cheesecake or I'll have nothing to eat with my second cup which I only really want as a masher for the cheesecake.

WAITRESS: OK. *(To other* WAITRESS.*)*...so he came all over your dress...

WAITRESS 2: Yeah.

WAITRESS: Dirty bastard.

WAITRESS 2: It was all thick and stringy it took ages to get off/he was sucking me like a madman when my mum walked in.

WAITRESS: No! What did she say?

WAITRESS 2: Don't forget to do behind her ears/she always forgets that.
WAITRESS: I wish my mum was understanding like that/I haven't sucked a juicy cock for ages, have you?
WAITRESS 2: No, not really, not a big horny stiff thick hot pink one.
WAITRESS: What's the biggest you've ever had?
WAITRESS 2: Ten inches.
WAITRESS: No!
WAITRESS 2: Yeah, it was all gnarled like an oak with a great big knob on the end.
WAITRESS: Yeah?
WAITRESS 2: And when it came, it shot out so much I could have wallpapered the dining room.
EDDIE: Where's my fucking coffee? I've nearly finished the cheesecake and then my whole purpose in life at this particular moment in time will be lost/I'll be drinking hot coffee with nothing to wash it down with.
WAITRESS: Here you are, sorry I forgot you!
EDDIE: About bleeding time an' all.
WAITRESS: Oh shut your mouth, you complaining heap of rat's shit.
EDDIE: I'll come in your eyeballs you putrefying piece of army gang bang.
WAITRESS: You couldn't raise a gallop if I plastered my pussy all over your face, you impotent pooftah bum boy and turd bandit.
MANAGER: What's the matter, that you raise your voice you punk and scum/fuck off!
EDDIE: No one talks to me like that
MANAGER: I just did.
EDDIE: I'll erase you from the face of the earth.
MANAGER: I'll cook you in a pie and serve you up for dessert.
EDDIE: I'll tear you all to pieces, rip out your arms and legs, and feed them to the pigs.
MANAGER: I'll kick you to death and trample all over you/stab you with carving knives and skin you alive.
EDDIE: Come on then.
WAITRESSES: No, no, no, no, no, no, no, no, no
EDDIE: Hit   hurt   crunch   pain   stab   jab. *(The two men mime fighting, standing at opposite sides of the stage and then moving closer together but without ever touching.)*
MANAGER: Smash   hate   rip   tear asunder   render
EDDIE: Numb   jagged glass   gouge out
MANAGER: Chair breakhead   split   fist   splatter   splosh crash

EDDIE: Explode   scream   fury   strength   overpower   overcome
MANAGER: Cunt   shit   filth   remorse   weakling   blood soaked
EDDIE: Hemorrhage, rupture, and swell.   Split and cracklock jawsprung and neck break
MANAGER: Cave-in   rib splinter   oh the agony   the shrewd icepick
EDDIE: Testicles torn out   eyes gouged and pulled   strings snapped   socket   nail   scraped
MANAGER: Bite   swallow   suck   pull
EDDIE: More   smash   and more power
MANAGER: Weaker and weaker
EDDIE: Stronger and stronger
MANAGER: Weak
EDDIE: Power
MANAGER: Dying
EDDIE: Victor
MANAGER: That's it
EDDIE: Tada.
WAITRESS 2: 'Night Jackie. *(She exits.)*
WAITRESS: You killed him/I never knew words can kill.
EDDIE: So can looks.
WAITRESS: You killed him/he was my husband.
EDDIE: I didn't intend to I swear I didnt/he died of shock.
WAITRESS: He was a good man, solid except in his cock but he was good to me, and now I am alone/who will I have to care for now who to wait for at night while he cleans up our cafe or while he's at the sauna getting relief/who to cook for or brush the dandruff from his coat and the grease from his hat or the tramlines from his knickers/who to comfort in the long nights/as he worries about me/who will put the kids to bed with a gentle cuff as he frolics after coming home all pissed from the pub and smashes me jokingly on the mouth/whose vomit will I clean up from the pillow as he heaves all over my face on Friday nights after his binge? Whose black uniform will I press in readiness for his marches down Brixton with the other so noble men of England/ whose photos will I dust in the living room of his heroes, Hitler, Goebbels, Enoch, Paisley, and Maggot not forgetting our dear royals? Is it worth it anymore?/I married a good Englishman/ where will I find another like that?/See what you did/and all over a stupid cheesecake.

EDDIE: Wars, my dear, have been fought over less than that.
WAITRESS: I'll never find another like him.
EDDIE: Yes you will.
WAITRESS: Where?
EDDIE: Look no further ma'am than this. *(MANAGER exits.)* Your spirit's won me/cast thy gaze to me/my face/and let thine eyes crawl slowly down/that's not a kosher salami I'm carrying/I'm just pleased to see you/sure I can do like him/polish my knuckle-duster/clean *my* pants/I'll give you a kicking with the best if that's what you really want/you'll have my set of proud photos to dust/I'd rather treat you fair and square and touch your hair at night and kiss your sleeping nose/I'll not defile your pillow, but spread violets beneath your feet/I'll squeeze your toes at night if they grow cold and when we through rose gardens walk I'll blow the aphids from your hair/I'll come straight home from work at night not idle for a pint and all my spunk I'll keep for thee to lash you with at night as soft and warm as summer showers/I'll leak no precious drop in the Camden sauna for a fiver ("don't be long dear, others waiting") but strew the silver load in these to dart up precious streams/I'll heave my scepter into thee/your thighs I'll prize apart and sink like hot stone into butter/into an ocean of ecstasy for that's what you are to me/an ecstasy of flesh and blood and fluted pathways softest oils and smells never before uncapped/I'll turn you upside down and inside out/I'll strip you bare and crawl under your skin/I'm mad for you/you

luscious brat and madam, girl and woman turned into one/I'll kiss your bum hole like it was the lips of cherubs/I'll take you love for what you are!

WAITRESS: You've eased my pain you sweet and lovely boy/I thought I'd miss him desperately but now I can when looking at you hardly remember what he looks like. You look so familiar to me though we have never met/so strange perhaps the true feeling love brings to your heart. The familiar twang.

EDDIE: I feel the same for you.

WAITRESS: You remind me of someone or something.

EDDIE: What, ducky?

WAITRESS: Oh, nothing.

EDDIE: Confess my dear the quandary that doth crease your brow and make the nagging thought stay in your head, the way an Irish fart hangs in the air long after its creator wends his weary way to Kilburn High Street.

WAITRESS: 'Tis nothing sweet but this/I had a kid, just two he were, sweet and blue-eyed just like you/a darling, then one day disaster struck/and don't it just/an August trip to Southend for the day... (MUM *and* DAD *enter and freeze.*) all hot and sticky (EDDIE *and* WAITRESS *begin a slow, stylized waltz.*) with floss and smiling teeth/hankies and braces/start off at Tower Pier excitement, sandwiches, and loads of fizzy Tizer. (MUM *and* DAD *hide behind the two chairs at upstage side of table.*)

EDDIE: *(Aside.)* Strange, I love Tizer.

WAITRESS: Then two or three miles out we hit a mine that slunk so steadily up the Thames, like some almighty turd that won't go down no matter how often you flush the chain, so this had stayed afloat, it showed its scarred and raddled cheek from its long buffets round the choppy seas and just by luck as if the fates had ordained us to meet it blew us at the moon/at least it made a hole so large that suddenly the Thames resembled Brighton on a broiling day with heads a bobbing everywhere, my Frank swam back and I clung to a bit of raft but little Tony, for that was his fair name, ne'er did surface up... I hope his end was quick.

EDDIE: No chance that some local fisherman may have snatched him from the boiling seethe?

WAITRESS: No word, no sign, not even his little corpse did show/I stuck around all night, then as the dawn arose I saw his little oil soaked teddy bear, as if heaved up from deep inside the river's guts. It lay admidst the condoms on the junk filled strand. I took it home and washed it.

EDDIE: That's a sad tale/and I feel grieved for you my dear that woe should strike at one who was so young and fair/and let the others more deserving of fates lash to get away with murder.

WAITRESS: Fate never seems to give out where it's meant but seems to pick you out as from a hat/like bingo and if your number's on it boy you've had it.

EDDIE: That little bear you mentioned, sweet... may I see the precious relic?

WAITRESS: You really want to?

EDDIE: Yeah, let's have a butcher's. *(She goes and brings the bear in.)* 'Tis strange but often times I dreamed of such a thing a little Rufus just like this/I never had one, yet seemed to miss the little furry cuddly thing as if my body knew the feel whereas my mind could not/since then I've always liked small furry things. Come, love, you've had your share of woe and so have I and if fate heaps the shit it also heaps the gold and finding you is like a vein I never dreamed of, so fate's been kind this time/I think we're fated, love, don't you?

WAITRESS: I do, my precious, for once I bless the stars that this time made me such a man/you've got the same eyes as my Tony—green and jadey like the sea.

EDDIE: Your eyes are like the sunlight in the sea that speckles on the rocks so deep below/all blue and gold.

WAITRESS: Your face is like all Greek/and carved from ancient marble.

EDDIE: Your body feels all soft like puppies, strong as panthers.

WAITRESS: Let's go to bed my sweet.

EDDIE: Ok. *(EDDIE and WAITRESS exit. MUM and DAD's heads appear behind the chairs.)*

PHOTO: HARITON-BARAL

DAD: Do you think that it could happen
that the curse could come about
that Ed could kill his own dad,
pop into his mother's pants, I had to kick him out.

MUM: That's something we will never know dear
until the day, when suddenly
you'll see quite a different Ed
than the one that's known to me.

DAD: You're right, dead right...
Oh Dinah what did we do
that such a curse should be blasted
on the heads of me and you?

MUM: Who knows my dear what evil lies in store
that we are unaware of, did we cause some
grief somewhere, inflict some unhealed sore?

DAD: I've done nothing all my life
I've been an honest Joe
Shit on that fortune teller
and his vile and evil joke.

MUM: It's funny that twice we heard it Ted
It's funny that a second time
Another face years later should
sound the same old horrid warning line.

DAD: Perhaps we should have told him Dinah
perhaps we ought to tell
our son should know the secret
or we may end up in...

MUM: Hell you mean, you make me laugh
it's over now, it's past,
it can't be now undone with words
fate makes us play the roles we're cast.

Heads slowly disappear behind the chairs as lights fade.

ACT TWO

EDDIE: Ten years have come and gone, scattered their leaves on us/drenched us in blazing sun and rain/toughened my sinews to combat the world. I improved the lot of our fair cafe by my intense efforts, aided of course by my sweet mate/got rid of sloth and stale achievement/which once was thought as normal/I made the city golden era time/the dopes just died away when faced with real octane high power juice/the con men that have tricked you all the while with substitute and fishy watery soup/ went out of business and people starved for nourishment brain food and guts just flocked to us/the fat faced bastards you saw sitting on expense accounts and piles too long defied the needs of our gnawing biting hunger/real food and drink/real substance for the soul/not those decayed and spineless wonders who filled the land/strutting and farting pithy anecdotes at boring dinner parties on profits made by con and cheap/they thought they were the cream and not the sour yuk they really were/we showed them the way/they died in trying to keep us with us/they faded in a heap. (DAD, MUM, *and* WIFE *mime clapping, soundlessly.*)

WIFE: Ten years have flown away as Apollo's chariot hath with fiery stride lit up our summers, thawed our frosts and kissed our cheeks/ten winters hath the hoary bearded god of ice encased our Earth in pinch hard grip of chill/to be kicked out in turn by spring's swift feet of Ceres, Pluto, Dionysus/and April brooks do glisten giggling over rocks and reeds so pleased to be set free/ten years this splendid symphony of life hath played its varied song/hath saddened and elated/hath drawn the sap of life into the fiery poppy and frangipani and gripped them in its autumn sleep again/whilst we my man that is and me, for three thousand three hundred and sixty five times did celebrate our own ritual in nights of swooning.

EDDIE: While I each day and year have scored another niche into this world of ours/have moved about and jostled/cut a throat or two metaphoric of course...

ALL: HA HA HA.

EDDIE: And shown how what this world doth crave is power, class, and form with a dab of genius now and then. (DAD, MUM, *and* WIFE *giggle.*) We cured the plague by giving inspiration to our plates/ came rich by giving more and taking less/the old style portion control practiced by fat thieves went out with us/we put the meat back into the sausage mate.

DAD, MUM *and* WIFE: Hallelujah! Hallelujah! Hallelujah! Hallelujah!

EDDIE: Now once more the world will taste good/no more the sawdust and preservative coloring and cat shit that you could beter use to fill your walls than line your stomachs.

DAD, MUM, *and* WIFE: Blech!

EDDIE: So foul that nations overseas would ban them from their fair stalls and shops...

MUM: *(In French.)* No, no, no, no, absoluement pas!

WIFE: *(In Italian)* Terribile, terribile!

DAD: *(In German)* Das ist Scheisser.

EDDIE: Lest their strong youth should fall into the listless British trance so often seen in Oxford Street or on the Piccadilly Line at 8 am. *(Others mime listlessness.)* A nation half asleep and drugged with foul and bestial things poured out of packets. *(Others make noise and mime action of machines.)* Massed up by operators who conspired with commies thick in plot to weaken our defences/feed the nation shit and mother's crud and watch them crumble down in heaps upon the pavement/then the cunning reds just blow them over skittle like. *(Others mime machine guns.)* But now in our great chain we energize the people, give soul food and blistering blast of protein smack/sandwiches the size of fists chock full of juicy smile filled chunks. *(Others smile broadly.)* The nation blinks and staggers back to work on this/not fast/it takes a while to use those muscles starved so long/limp with only holding Daily Mirror race results/and eyes so dim from weekly charting of the pools/we'll get them back to work, no fear though they may die of shock upon the way/we'll drag them out of pubs, *(MUM and DAD grab table.)* their fingers still gripping on the bar they know so well, like babies reluctant to part with mother's tit/it's us that has to do it/rid the world of half-assed bastards clinging to their dark domain and keeping talent out by filling the entrances with their swollen carcasses and sagging mediocrity/let's blow them all sky high, or let us see them simply waste away as the millions come to us.

ALL SING: Jerusalem, Jerusalem,
    Lift up your heads and sing,
    Hosannah in the highest.
    Hosannah to our King.

Song ends in a hum.

WIFE: The plague is not quite over yet. There's still a plague around this city darling that will not go away, caused by some say some evil deed that has not purged itself, but continues to rot away inside the wholesome body of our state/people are dropping like flies/armed killers snipe from the shattered eyes of buildings and death stalks in the foul and pestilent breath of friends whose eyes are drunk with envy and greed at your success/people shake your hand with limp grips as if afraid to catch it. The illness of inertia, and should I shan't I, the country's awash in chemicals that soup the brain to dullness to dull the dullness of grinding hips long bored with ancient habit and lovers are afraid to stroke each others groins lest new laws against the spreading of the plague outlaw them. Masturbating shops line every High Street and the pneumatic drill of strong right wrists ensure a girl a fat living, the country's awash in spunk not threshing and sweetening the wombs of lovers but crushed in Kleenex and dead in cubicles with red lights. Meanwhile men in white are penetrating the holy crucible where life may have slipped in, and armed with scalpels and suction pumps tear out the living fruit and sluice it down the river of sewage, the future Einsteins, Michelangelos, and future Eddies. The blood and plasma of creation is swept and flushed away with gasps of don't inside the tender packages not yet fulfilled.

EDDIE: That's the plague at work all right, there's something rotten in the city that will not die/a Sphinx I read stands outside the city walls tormenting all that pass they say and killing those who cannot answer her strange riddle/no doubt she helps to spread the canker and the rot and yet no one can destroy her.

WIFE: I heard that too, and yet she can at will dissolve herself to air.

EDDIE: I'll go and sort her out.

WIFE: Be careful darling/you are all I have.

EDDIE: Don't fret, if I've come this far, survived the worst that fate can throw, I'll come through this as well. Don't wait up I may be late but if I'm not back by dawn, I'll meet you in heaven, if not we'll meet in hell! *(They kiss.* EDDIE, WIFE, *and* DAD *exit separately.)*

MUM: *(Sings as she takes off headscarf and proceeds to wipe table with it.)*

    We'll meet again
    Don't know where, don't know when,
    But I know we'll meet again some sunny day.
    Keep smiling through...

She climbs on table, then suddenly drops her head forward into a wig to become SPHINX, *sitting up suddenly in a strong, red overhead light.* EDDIE *enters.*

SPHINX *outside the walls.*

SPHINX: Who are you, little man/pipsqueak scum/drip off the prick/mistake in the middle of the night/you've come to answer my riddle/the riddle of the Sphinx/fuck off you maggot before I tear your head off/rip your eyes out of your head and roast your tongue/you nothing, you man/you insult of nature go now before I lose my cool.

EDDIE: I'm not afraid of you... you old slag/you don't scare Eddie cause Eddie don't scare easy/I've beaten better than you in Singapore brothels/you can only frighten weak men not me/why do you exist to kill men you heap of filth/you detestable disease/because you can't love/loveless you can only terrify man no one could love you/who could even kiss that mouth of yours when your very breath stinks like a Hong Kong whorehouse when the fleet's in.

SPHINX: You make me laugh you fool man/you should know about brothels, they exist for you to prop up your last fading shreds/men need killing off before they kill off the world/louse, you pollute the earth/every footstep you take rots what's underneath/you turn the seas to dead lakes and the crops dying are from the plague that is man/you are the plague/where are you looking when you should be looking at the ghastly vision in the mirror/the plague is inside you. You make your weapons to give you the strength that you lack/you enslave whip beat and oppress use your guns, chains, bombs, jets, napalm, you are so alone and pathetic, love from you means enslavement, giving means taking, loving is fucking, helping is exploiting, you need your mothers you motherfucker, to love is to enslave a woman to turn her into a bearing cow to produce cannon fodder to go on killing/can you ever stop your plague/you're pathetic, unfinished, not like me, never like us, a woman, a Sphinx. Women are all Sphinx. I have taken the power for all, I am the power/I could eat you alive and blow you out in bubbles/I devour stuff like you... oh send me strong men you scrawny nothing/look what they send me/mock up heroes/plastic movie watchers/idolizer of a thousand westerns/punk hero/flaccid man/macho pig/rapist filth and shit/oh nature's mistake in the ghastly dawn of time/when women were women, androgynous and whole and could reproduce themselves but somewhere and some time a reptile left our bodies, it crawled away and became man, but it stole our little bag of seed and ever since the little reptile has been trying to crawl back, but we don't want it anymore, all we need is your foul little seed, you gnat... something that takes you thirty seconds of your life and us nine months we create build nourish care for, grow bigger and fat and after we suckle and provide. While you dig in the earth for treasure, play your stupid male games/go you biped of dirt/just a prick followed by a heap of filth, I feel sorry for you/I really feel for you/I've eaten enough men this week/so go/fuck off/stink scum dirt shit/go, before I tear you to pieces/go and plot and scheme, hurt, exploit, and rape, oppress and wound, make a few more evil laws you shrivel of flesh, you poor unreliable penis. You have not even our capacity for passion... I could come ten times to your one/wanna try big boy? You are from my rib mister/me from you? What a joke/woman was Adam/she was the Earth, woman is the tide/woman is in the movement of the universe/our bodies obey the phases of the moon... our breasts swell and heave and our rich blood surges forth to tell us we are part of the movement of nature/what signs do you have? Do you bleed/do you feel the kicking in your womb/does a mouth draw milk from your soft breast/can you tell the future/can you do anything? What signs do you have/a date with death/the hour you must attack/unable to create you must destroy/I am the earth/I am the movement of the universe/I am liquid, fire, and all elements/my voice rises octaves high and communicates with the spirits of the dead/my skin is soft and velvet and desirable to those with rough faces and bodies hard and muscled to labor, to toil across the face of the earth for us/the goddess of life/woman/we/sex/Sphinx, the grand and majestic cunt, the great mouth of life/the dream of men in their aching lonely nights/the eternal joy that men die for and envy and emulate/what they sicken for and crave for and go insane for/so go, you are small, insignificant, piss off you worm or I'll break your teeth and pull out your fingers/go fuck yourself or stick a bomb up your fucking asshole you heap of murdering bastard shit filth... go, you make me vomit.

EDDIE: Without me you are nothing/without me you wouldn't exist without me you are an empty screaming hole.

SPHINX: You what! You think I need you. I need milk but do I go to bed with a cow. I'll farm and fertilize you and keep you in pens where you will do no harm/now go boy, I am getting aroused, be grateful that for some reason I feel for your pathetic attempts at heroism.

Greek   33

EDDIE: I want to answer your riddle.
SPHINX: Then you must know that those that can't answer it die, and then if you can't I will kill you, I will tear your cock off with my teeth before I eat you up.
EDDIE: With pleasure/if I answer it/what do I gain?
SPHINX: You can kill me.
EDDIE: Then I will cut off your head for women talk too much.
SPHINX: I agree. You're a brave little fart. So here goes: What walks on four legs in the morning, two legs in the afternoon, and three legs in the evening?
EDDIE: Man! In the morning of his life he is on all fours, in the afternoon when he is young he is on two legs, and in the evenings when he is erect for his woman he sprouts the third leg.
SPHINX: You bastard, you've used trickery to find out the riddle.
EDDIE: No, just reason. All right, sorry to have to do this, I was growing quite fond of you.
SPHINX: I don't care any more/to tell you the truth I was getting bored with scaring everyone to death and being a Sphinx/ok cut it off and get it over with. (EDDIE *mimes cutting off her head and tucks her wig under his arm. Light returns to normal.*)
MUM: Carton of fags for the ole man, two jars Marlade, one kipper sandwich, twenty Woodbines.
EDDIE: Anything else?
MUM: Could I have my hat back? (*Takes wig and exits.*)
EDDIE: She would put you off women for life/but not me/I love a woman/I love her/I just love and love and love her/and even that one/I could have loved her/I love everything that they possess/I love all their parts/I love every part that moves/I love their hair and their neck/I love the way they walk across the kitchen to put the kettle on/in that lazy familiar way/I love them when they open their eyes in the morning/I love their baby soft skin/I love their voices/I love their smaller hands than mine/I love lying on them and them on me/I love their soft breasts/I love their eyelashes and their noses/their teeth and their shoulders/and their giggles/and their desperate passions and their liquids and their breath against yours in the night/and their snores/and their leg across yours and their feet in the morning and I love their bellies and thighs and the way each part fits into mine/and love the way my part fits into her/and love her sockets and joints and ball bearings/and love her hip bone and her love soaked parts that want me/I love her seasons and love her sleeping and love her walking and speaking and whispering and loving and singing

and love her back and her bum nestled into you and you become an armchair/and love her for taking me in/and giving me a home for my searing agonies/my lusts/my love/my dreams/my sweetness/my honey/my peace of mind/and love her waiting for me and love her soothing me as I tell her about my day's battles in the world—and love and love and love her and her and!

WIFE: *(Enters.)* Well done my sweet, now all will be well/my hero... yes you are/my brave and shining knight/my lion, yes! And I'm your mate/my brave and gentle lion/and now to celebrate let's have your dear old pa and ma to dine and reconcile the fairy tales and woes of past and be all gooey nice together in family bliss.

EDDIE: I have to laugh when I think of my soppy mum and dad/locked up in council bliss/and forty pounds a week.

WIFE: Invite them over Ed *(*MUM *and* DAD *enter.)* to share just once our color TV, hi-fi, home movies showing us in fair Ibiza and Thebes, of you diving in the bright blue cobalt sea, your smiling new capped teeth all sparkling in the brilliant sun, invite them to partake of our deep leather sofas/succulent wines/show our video that records those programs that you wish to view when after working late at night in selfless graft you sit with dog and slipper by your feet... let them enjoy the comfort of central heated bathroom... no more the cold ass on a plastic seat but wool covered and pipes all steaming hot, of stairs thick gloved in pile so soft that each tread is like a luscious meadow. Would they not like a slumberdown or even our soft waterbed which thrusts our pelvises so sweetly swished together, needlepoint shower. Show your mum the joys of kitchen instant disposal waste, no washing up, just time to enjoy our super apple pie.

EDDIE: I'll send the chauffeur down to pick them up/that's if my dad has rid himself of that old hoary myth that like a louse ate inside his nut, to tell him of patricide and horrid incest/or subtitled could be called the story of a motherfucker/a tale for kiddiwinks to send them mad to bed and cringe at shadows in the night, and in their later years to bung good gelt to shrinks in Harley Street.

WIFE: When you told me that story Ed/I could not believe that grown ups still could set such store by greasy Gypsies in a booth/and to kick you out all young and pink into the seething world while you were wet behind the lugs/maybe 'twas a ruse to get you out the nest.

EDDIE: Who knows my dear the wily minds of cruddy mums and dads whose head chock full of TV swill, the pools, and read your own horrorscope/so what, it put me on the springboard young and lively and I learned how to jack knife into the surging tide with all the best.

WIFE: You're tuf that's what my love/you're a survivor in the swilling mass of teeth and knives and desperate eyes all anxious to carve out their pound of flesh/you did it and you're still a beaut/still lovely brown and svelte/success has not paunched you or stuck a fat ass on your hips or burnt an ulcer in your gut/or made your mouth a stinking ashtray where fat cigars hang like a turd that cannot be expelled/but hangs on till the end/your sweet and honey breath/your tongue's not coated with the slime of ten course meals taken with other con artists who flash their gaudy rings and thick as pig shit wives who sit at home and wank or play some bridge with other dozy bags whose only exercise is stretching out an arm to screech out taxi outside Harrods/you're sweet and your body's like a river, flowing flowing into me/it moves like a flowing river... your streaming muscles carry me along your river, along your soft and hard and flowing river/when I'm in your arms I'm carried along this endless stream and then I reach the sea, I'm swept up by your sea, I'm carried by a wave, I'm threshed up in your wave and then set down again only to be regathered up as your volcanic wave gathers me as a piece of ocean, as your sweet lustful pangs gather up its morsel I'm swept up, I'm gathered up, I'm sucked up and spun along a raging storming river... I love your body, I love your fingers round and round and tearing and gripping and finding and searching and twisting and gathering me for your sweet lustful pangs... and then and then and then... your body is like a tree... like branches twisting and breaking... like a wave like a wind, like an animal like a lion... ferocious and sweet lustful pangs grow bigger darling... as they grow bigger to make your sweet spunk flow... they grow bigger and the lion's breath is hot and the grip on me is growing tight and more ferocious and then and then I know... that you tremble, you shake, quiver, you shake, you thrash... oh the river flows, oh... it flows, oh it floods through me... as you tremble your quiver is shot into me... oh I am flowing with the river in the wet and warm and succulent flow... you turn me into a flow and flood me... and the shivering and the quivering and the shaking and the trembling, softly softly... softly goes as the storm passes slowly... goes... slowly... rumbling into the distance... slowly goes... the breath less hot, but soft and silky and sweat on your back and silky on your thighs and warm between our thighs... oh/life my love/oh love my precious/oh sweet my honey/oh heaven my

angel/oh darling my husband. (MUM *and* DAD *make sound of car screeching to a stop.)*
EDDIE: But soft my darling wife/what noise is that/it must be my cruddy mum and dad/who interrupt your lovely flow of gob rich thick and pearly verbs that send my blood a racing to my groin so I might manufacture love wet tides.
DAD: Bing bong.

MUM *and* DAD *enter. Greeting sounds.*

DAD: Look how he's got on/you really got on well son/I'm proud of ya. He's got class and qualities drawn from me.
MUM: From me more, his mum whom he did love not this wet fart that calls himself his dad.
DAD: Don't talk like that in front of Eddie's wife you sloppy titted, slack assed lump, you raving scrawny dried up witch.
MUM: Don't talk to me about my body/age has withered my soft beauty but you will need cremating since your poisoned flesh would cause pollution in the earth and make widespread crop failures you're death on two varicosed legs and a hernia belt.
DAD: I've got no words for you Dot... since you were gang banged by that bunch of drunken darkies... a dozen it were, if I counted right, whose swollen truncheons flashed their golden sprints of foam into the sulfurous and heavy night, since that bad time you've not been right in ye old bonce... I know that night was dark for you in double horror and I fear that it may be the cause of your unseemly evil tongue that like a poisoned snake doth linger under filthy damp and rotting stone.
EDDIE: Hello Dad, hello Mum—good to see ya again...
MUM: Oh Ed, it looks really lovely, and this is your lovely wife/oh! how lovely, oh she's nice.
WIFE: Why thank you, I think you're very charming yourself.
MUM: Oh thank you you are nice, bless you, you're welcome, have a nice day.
WIFE: Please feel free, make yourself at home, how very nice to meet you. Have you had a good journey? How is everyone at home? Isn't the weather cold now? It will soon be winter. You're looking so young. You really look well. You've lost weight. Are you going away this summer? Do you use Fablon in your kitchen?
MUM: You've a lovely home, it's really lovely, just lovely. Some people are lucky, some people have all the fun. Some mothers do have 'em. Mind you, I mean, it goes to show, well it does. Idle hands make wicked thoughts. He's all right, really, underneath...

Greek

when you get to know him, he's lovely. Have you been away this year? Water off a duck's back dear.

EDDIE: So what's the news my folks/my flesh and blood/chip off the old/apple of your/say what goes on in my old neighborhood/where once rank violence stalked the dirty streets and filthy yobbos hung round the corners of old pubs like flies on dead carrion. Move out that council flat where urchins' piss does spray the lift which takes you to your aerie on the 25th floor and move in with us, or do you still fear that old curse/that bunch of Gypsy bollocks, that you so avidly did gulp/though secretly methinks you used that as a ruse, to clear out the womb and save yourself some loot/you always said I'd eat you out of house and home/round here only the poodles drop their well turned turds in little piles so neat. And *au pair* girls go pushing little Jeremys into the green and flowery parks/no ice-cream vans come screaming round this manor/all's quiet/just the swish on the emerald lawns close cropped like the shaven heads of astronauts. So come and stay. You're welcome and bring the cat as well, we've always got room for Moggie.

DAD: Nah son but thanks and double ta. You're very kind to us... how thoughtful/bless you, you're welcome, have a nice day, but we're used to wot we got, can you teach an old dog new tricks, a bit long in the tooth, you're as old as you feel, and I feel like a worn out old fart... we know the familiar faces/our rotten neighbors/the geezer who collects the payments on the fridge and on the telly every week/meals on wheels that daily calls now that we're getting older, all familiar trappings that have trapped us/now that our useful working life has been sucked dry by the state we get a little pension and some security for which I sign/now that my boss god bless him sits back fat and greasy/not that I mind, he got it by hard graft and cunning/good luck to him/he gave me fifty quid when I retired, handsome and a watch with fifteen jewels/right proud I was/so what I got asbestos in my lung/so what I got coal dust in my blood/so what I got lead poisoning in my brain/so what I got shot nerves from the machines/so what I lost two fingers in the press/so what I'm going deaf from the steel mills/so what I lost a lung for our old king in Dunkirk/I'd do it again/yes I would I tell ya/so what I got fuck all for it from our fair state/so what they're gliding past in their Rolls Royces/and their fat little kids come tumbling out on piggy little legs/so what they thieve and murder and get away with it/so what our lovely royals pay no tax/they're figureheads mate/so what I starve waiting for your check which sometimes you forget to send if you are busy entertaining, when you forget your old ma and pa... son!

MUM: Don't listen Ed, he's gone a bit in the nut since they retired him/all he does is grouse and quail. When you complain remember others worse off than you/I think of mothers whose sweet fruit of their most holy wombs/those warm and precious sacks of giggling joy, who have been snatched by sex mad fiends. They stalk around the town... there are so many around you/you cannot pick up the daily snot picker these days without seeing between the tits and race results the photos of the burns and scalds and broken limbs... the staring eyes of kids/how one is burnt by fag ends/others punched black and blue/screams in the night/neighbors too scared or fastened to Hawaii Five-O to receive the bloated cries that stab through the walls like an open hand saying help me/others, babies with broken lips, their little ribs all smashed by dads who have caught the British plague that cements their heads and puts vitriol inside their hearts/some kids chained to their beds for hours at a time and others crawling in shit and piss... and whack and zunk goes mum and splatter back hand crack goes dad... one kid's nipples almost burnt off... what about the dad who picked up his small innocent and smashed his head against the wall until his brains seeped out... what dreams did that kid have as his grey thoughts ran down the wallpaper... and then the judge says... "Off you go, you are basically a good character"... and then he's off to celebrate in the nasty pub with his old lady... and up and down the length and breadth the straps are out and babies, bairns, and kids are straightened out, lashed out, whipped, and made to obey, the nation's full of perverts if you ask me/the plague still flourishes mate.

EDDIE: The plague Mum/the plague is still about? You never did nuffin like that to me/you only gave me muffins and jam/swaddles of lovey love and spoiling and cuddling and story telling. And swishing my pillow *(The others sway, softly singing "Underneath the Arches.")* and a ride on Dad's back and chase around the garden, and a three wheel bike. You only gave me ten slices of toast every morning and Marmite after school... I looked all bisto like, and like those kids whose shoes have a long way to go I was put on a path called bliss with jammy mouth and sticky doughnut fingers/a dad who put me on the crossbar of his bike and never once introduced the back of his hand to my bonce not once opened his eyes wide and hatefilled and sought to venge some filthy taste for coloring my flesh in chartreuse green or bruisy blue. No! We'd race across the municipal lido. How long can you stay under? Dandy and the Beano each week and even the Film Fun as well.

DAD: You were loved son/we wanted to give you love/we loved ya kid. You know... like open hands gripping your shoulders and a squeeze at the end... palm on your head and ruffling your hair, a clenched fist and a slow tap on the chin... like chin-up when you didn't pass your eleven-plus 'cause you were a dummy... I didn't want you to hate us.

EDDIE: Hate? I never used that word my folks. Do you mean to say you loved me because you were afraid I'd hate you? 'Cause the Gypsy's curse rang in your ears? Let's smother him with spoiling and cuddling so he won't want to hurt his old dad, you make me laugh... you would have loved me the same without the rotten curse/I'm your flesh and blood, it's natural.

DAD *and* MUM: But you're not our son, son.

EDDIE: SHIT GIVE UP THE GEN/SPILL YOUR GUTS/OPEN YOUR NORTH AND SOUTH AND LET ROLL THE TURDS BEFORE I PONEY MY Y FRONTS. IN OTHER VERBS OPEN YOUR CAKE-HOLE AND UTTER. LET ME EARWIG YOUR HOBSONS. NOT YOUR SON. OH BOLLOCKS AND CRACKLOCK.

WIFE: Don't say that he ain't your real produce of your blood swept thighs, not shoved out of your guts in warm sticky afterbirth, not the sparkle in his dad's eye in the glinting night when his pa heaved apart his woman's limbs and unloaded a binful of hot spunk, not eyed her like a lodestone or a star, or a jewel in the

corner of his eye not breathed hard or pulse raced to produce this lovely hunk of super delicious wondrous beefy darling spunky guy/not seen you walking from behind and wanted to grasp your arse and deliver the mail up your wet and wondrous letter-box?
MUM: Nah! Fraid not!
WIFE: Oh fuck.
EDDIE: So what if I'm adopted/who gives a monkey's tit?
DAD: Like this it was. Cries and groans, shouts and shrieks. I was fishing by Wapping, just down from the Prospect of Whitby... a peaceful Sunday (you were fished out, what a find, what I prayed for, a son) threw my line, the big steamers going out to Southend. The old Tower Bridge opening up to allow the steamer's funnels through like some big lazy East End tart from Cable Street opening her thighs... on the deck in the sun the people of Bow, Whitechapel, and Islington in their cheese cutters and chokers, all doing a bit of a dance on the deck, the streamers flickering, the Guinness pouring... *(EDDIE, WIFE, and MUM wave with both hands.)* Us waving from the shore as the old steamer cuts through the scummy old Thames and sends the swell over to us and makes our little boats kneel and bob as she passes by. When all of a sudden boy/the sun's up high, Hitler's just topped hisself. It's hot. Churchill's in command, there's peace at last. Twenty million dead/including my two boys, the radio plays we'll meet again and *(Sings.)* mares eat oats and does eat oats and little lambs eat ivy, remember. Well all of a sudden in that hot August afternoon no bananas in the shops and coupons for four ounces of sweets each week, pictures of Auschwitz just come out/thousands of bodies like spaghetti all entwined/all done in the name of Adolf/all of a sudden in the hot blue day... they're all swimming look at them, look at all that blood and oil, bad mix, the sky turned black. What a terrific hell of a bang, and soot is dropping all over us plus bits of people, all the fish dropped dead from shock, hey let's shlap them out. Look let's get some help, they're all in the water, some Jerry ball of hate stacked full of painful promise and carrying the names of the future dead blew the Southend tripper to the moon and down they fell in a deadly mesh of Guinness and gold flake... come on mate... "I'll give you a hand." We pulled them in all night, the others just bloated up like funfair freaks. Come on mum, don't fret, 'ere have a cuppa, where's your little Johnnie?... now, now he'll be all right, can he swim? No... oh. We'll find him... won't we lads... we'll find the little bleeder... shine your torch over here Bert, yeah, there's an old lady, give us your hand

love, I'll pull you in... oh no, just a stump, she left it in the water... what bastard could do this... more blankets... bring more tea... there's just not enough of us... there's not enough people to help, who does this to people? What sick perverted bastard started all this shit... if he was in front of me, I would take a butcher's fucking knife and carve him slowly bit by fucking dirty piece and feed it to the river rats and any cunt that supports him, I'd fucking throw them in acid baths... when all had gone and the dawn arose we saw what seemed a little doll clinging to a piece of wood but on closer butchering revealed a little bugger of about two he were, struggling like the fuck and gripping in his other paw a greasy old big bear, which no doubt helped to keep him up. We threw the bear back in the slick, and lifted the toddler out all dripping wet and covered in oil looking like a darkie so, no one about we took him home and washed him/he was a beaut/and Mum was double chuffed to see a little round soft ball of warm goo goo/don't want to give him up quoth Dinah, must we she said. Nah, I said his mum will think he's dead anyway/so let her go on thinking it/but...

MUM: Think...

DAD: Our Dinah rightly slurps...

MUM: Of how its real mum will fret and pine and waste away and mourn for her sweet lovely soft flesh of her own.

DAD: All right I says we'll keep him for one day only and then give him back. A day turned into two/then after a week we thought the shock now would be too great and that the true mum would be adjusted to her sad loss.

WIFE: Oh shit and piss and fuck. I just pissed in my pants. *(She screams and faints.)*

EDDIE: My dearest wife and now my mum, it seems, this lady was the very one whose baby you snatched/she told me the selfsame and bitter tale of how she lost her Tony and if you found him then I am he, he whom you found that belonged to her was me. The he you stole and gave to her did once belong to she... so I am the squelchy mass of flesh that issued from out the loins of my dear wife/oh rats of shit/you opened a right box there didn't you, you picked up a stone that was best left with all those runny black and horrid things intact and not nibbling in my brain. Ta ta Ma, ta ta Pa. Have a nice day.

DAD: We thought the curse was for our stealing you from your real mum, and you'd revenge yourself on us if somehow you'd find out... and when we heard the curse the second time. We thought

it's time for you to go (tonight I had to tell you 'cause it's choking on my tits/I can't stand it any more...
MUM: Get it off your chest...
DAD: Quoth Mum...
MUM: He's big enough.)

MUM *and* DAD *exit singing "Pack up your troubles in an old kit bag and smile, smile, smile..."*

EDDIE: So the man I verballed to death was my real pop/the man to whom my words like hard edged shrapnel razed his brain/was the source of me, oh stink/warlock and eyes break shatter, cracker, and splatter...!/who laughs? Me who wants to clean up the city/stop the plague destroy the Sphinx/me was the source of all the stink/the man of principle is a motherfucker/oh no more will I taste the sweetness of my dear wife's pillow... no more... no more... So I left my cozy and love filled niche now so full of horror/foul incest and babies on the way which if they come will no doubt turn into six fingered horrors with two heads/poor Eddie. Oh this madness twisting my brain/I walked through the plague rot streets and witnessed the old and the broken/the funny faces staring out of the dead vinyl flats/the flickering shadows of the TV tube/I sat in cafes and thought of my desirable lovely succulent and honey filled wife and as I sat and stared at the rheumy faces and the dead souls with their real wives who were plastered forever in casts of drab compromise, my own wife seemed like a princess/I fastened her face on the horizon like the rising moon and stared forever into space/and when the cafe closed I sat and stared forever and forever, ran through in my mind every combination of her face and smile and eyes and twists and curves of her lips, I sat and projected her picture on the moon and poured through every page of our life together like a great holy bible of magic events. I examined every feature of her landscape and ate up every part of her and loved every part whose sum total made up this creature, my wife. And then the moon turned as red as blood/the clouds raced across her face and became her hair and then her eyes and the wind pulled her hair over her face/like it did when we walked together through the fields and the forests, when the trees shivered and the sun kissed us and the universe wrapped us round in a cloak of stars and rain and crushed grass and ice-creams and teas and clenched fingers/hold on to me/hold on to me and I will hold on to you and I'll never let you go, hold on to me, does it matter that you are my mother, I'll love you even if I am your son/do we cause each other pain, do we kill each other, do we main and kill, do we inflict vicious wounds on each other? We only love so it doesn't matter mother, mother it doesn't matter. Why should I tear my eyes out Greek style, why should you hang yourself/have you seen a child from a mother and son/no. Have I? No. Then how do we know that it's bad/should I be so mortified? Who me? With my nails and fingers plunge in and scoop out those warm and tender balls of jelly quivering dipped in blood? Oedipus how could you have done it, never to see your wife's golden face again, never again to cast your eyes on her and hers on your eyes. What a foul thing I have done, I am the rotten plague, tear them out Eddie, rip them out, scoop them out like ice-cream, just push the thumb behind the orb and push, pull them out and stretch them to the end of the strings and then snap! Darkness falls. Bollocks to all that. I'd rather run all the way back and pull back the sheets, witness my golden bodied wife, and climb into her sanctuary, climb all the way in right up to my head and hide away there and be safe and comforted. Yeh I wanna climb back inside my mum. What's wrong with that? It's better than shoving a stick of dynamite up someone's ass and getting a medal for it. So I run back. *(Runs in place.)* I run and run and pulse hard and feet pound, it's love I feel it's love, what matter what form it takes, it's love I feel for your breast, for your nipple twice sucked/for your belly twice known/for your hands twice caressed/for your breath twice smelt, for your thighs, for your cunt twice known, once head first once cock first, loving cunt holy mother wife/loving source of your being/exit from paradise/entrance to heaven.

Blackout. Explosions.

GLOSSARY

Paddy	Irish person
lost his bottle	to lose one's courage
grotty	disgusting
Hughie Phlegm	(Hughie Green) well-known British TV interviewer
skiving	avoiding work
copped a few quid	made money
what's on your bonce?	what's on your mind?
nipper	small child
tosheroon	English money
African woodbines	dope
aggro	aggravation
scarper	quick exit
sussed	suspected or understood
pic in Woolies	picture in Woolworth's
carrier bag	paper shopping bag
picking losers	picking losers in horse races
wanked	masturbated
cap	diaphragm
glorious bodily charm	grievous bodily harm
bung	give
cuppa	a cup of tea
gob	mouth
gen	information
a bunk up	sexual intercourse
schmutter	clutter
haggis	a Scottish sausage of sheep intestines
spunk	semen
moggie	cat
Enoch, Paisley, and Maggot	Enoch Powell, extreme right-wing politician; Ian Paisley, a militant Protestant Irish Politician; and Margaret Thatcher
Fizzy Tizer	soda pop
let's have a butcher's	let's see
council bliss	subsidized housing
yobbos	young thugs
11-plus	school tests at age 11 to determine your academic future
poney my Y fronts	lose control of one's bowels
cake-hole	mouth
earwig your hobsons	let me hear what you have to say
Southend tripper	day pleasure boat

Greek: Brave Words for a Victim of "Language"
Silvie Drake

Writing from New York City, theater critic Sylvie Drake described the reception accorded Greek *by New York critics in the June 15, 1983 edition of the Los Angeles* Times.

New York—Writer director Steven Berkoff's *Greek*, a show considered Los Angeles' best shot last year, has come to this town and gone, shot down in a hail of bad reviews that left producers no choice but to close the show Sunday night.

"I was prepared for anything but this," said Susan Loewenberg, artistic director of Los Angeles Theatre Works, which mounted the show in Los Angeles last year and co-produced it here with Mark Beigelman at the Actors' Playhouse.

"Somehow I had never anticipated that reviewers would miss the whole point of the text. It's one thing to object to a poorly presented show, but that was not the issue. Most reviews praised the production. They just never got past Steven's language."

"Steven's language" was, indeed, Greek to reviewers here. A primary stumbling block. Not one—not even reviewers who liked the show, such as *Newsday*'s Allan Wallach, Howard Kissel of *Women's Wear Daily,* or the Newhouse chain's William Raidy (who called *Greek* "an artful spitball...a striking, audacious piece of theater")—saw the piece as an anti-war play.

Not one perceived it as an angry invocation for the power of love to triumph over the obscenity of violence—or saw its barrage of vulgarities as a deliberate juxtaposition designed to drive the point home. Few, in fact, seemed aware at all of its pervasive, if unconventional lyricism.

Sylvie Drake has been a theater critic and columnist for the Los Angeles *Times* for the past twelve years. This article is copyright 1983, Los Angeles *Times;* reprinted by permission.

The New York *Times'* Mel Gussow acknowledged that "now and then there are moments of earthy lyricism," but called the script "a cesspit of scatological imagery...twice too long, four times too repetitive and infinitely self-indulgent," while John Simon of New York magazine found it "a consummate emetic."

"Two surefire ways to spot a theatrical stinker," Simon shot off as an opening salvo, "are (1) actors wearing clown makeup, and (2) critical and audience adulation in Los Angeles."

"There is a 'show me' attitude, a real paranoia, about a hit from Los Angeles," producer Beigelman said Tuesday. "Without summoning the venom of East/West rivalry, you have to wonder at the intensity of the negative response. I think it's a tragedy. I'm obviously very proud of the show."

In fact, the New York production of this updated East London version of the Oedipus legend was every bit as precise and powerful as the Los Angeles staging. Its two new cast members—Mary Denham and Georgia Brown—proved that the show is not dependent on individuals so much as on their ability to disappear into a carefully synchronized ensemble. They did so exceptionally well.

So, insofar as one can every gauge intangibles, why the dismal reception?

"It was a glorious production that was offered and just turned down." Beigelman said. "Certain kinds of shows simply rub people the wrong way. There are also periods in time when people don't want to deal with certain subjects.

"We discovered that we had a small group of people who were fervent supporters (playwright Megan Terry, who saw the show Saturday, called it 'blinding in its perfection'), but it didn't add up to longevity. As far as we could tell, word of mouth was mixed. We worked hard to see what it would take to build the show up to break-even, but the figures were astronomical. Closing the show was the only intelligent decision."

Beigelman acknowledged that the initial $100,000 raised to bring the show to New York is a total loss. The show was brought in for $85,000, lost money during its run, and closing expenses are taking care of the rest.

"Money wasn't—is never—the problem," said Beigelman, who as general partner has the last word, financially. "You can always raise more if you have something to go on. But the smart commercial producer has to acknowledge the facts. With bad reviews in the major papers and poor word of mouth, it would have been foolish to go on."

Greek: Brave Words for a Victim of "Language"

"You have a fiduciary responsibility," Loewenberg echoed. "You can't, in the face of overwhelming evidence, throw investors' money away. Gordon Davidson (artistic director of the Los Angeles Mark Taper Forum), who thought the show was brilliant, told me it would be folly to take it to New York." (Davidson recently suffered a similar Off Broadway defeat with Michael Cristofer's *Black Angel*.)

"But I wanted to do *Greek* here and I'm not sorry," Loewenberg added, "only sorry we didn't make more of an impression. I'm proud of the production. Steven's an important playwright. His newest show, *West*, just opened in London to rave reviews. Irving Wardle (critic for the London *Times*) called him 'a lone warrior of the British stage.'"

Loewenberg toyed with the idea (more practical, perhaps) of bringing the show to a subscription theater. It would have guaranteed a run.

"We had an opportunity to do it," she said, "but it wasn't the right situation. So we gambled and lost. Chalk it up to a different sensibility. I'm still amazed that the top New York reviews came in at a level of perception close to the worst reviews we received in Los Angeles. Next year, I'm going to bring Steven back to direct his play *Decadence*."

In Los Angeles, of course.

"*Greek* is a show that challenges your assumptions," she said, "something most people aren't willing to do. Perhaps New Yorkers weren't ready for that."

Going to See the Elephant

Karen Hensel
Patti Johns
Elana Kent
Sylvia Meredith
Elizabeth Lloyd Shaw
Laura Toffenetti

Going to See the Elephant was first presented on August 6, 1982, by the Los Angeles Repertory Theatre at the DeLacy Street Theatre, Pasadena, California, with the following cast:

SARA	Laura Toffenetti
MAW	Sylvia Meredith
ETTA	Patti Johns
MRS. NICHOLS	Karen Hensel
MR. NICHOLS	Drew Deighan

Directed by Karen Hensel *and* Carl Reggiardo
Set design by Vaughn Armstrong *and* Janet Davie
Costumes by Zale Morris
Lighting by Beverly Smith
Sound by Elizabeth Shaw
Music arranged by Laura Toffenetti
Stage manager, Beverly Smith

The play was a collaboration by six authors who made the following contributions: original writing and structure, Karen Hensel and Elana Kent; character development and dialogue, Patti Johns, Sylvia Meredith, Elizabeth Lloyd Shaw, and Laura Toffenetti; concept, Patti Johns.

SETTING

Somewhere in Osborne County, Kansas.

TIME

Act I: 5 pm on July 3, 1870.
Act II: Later that evening and the next morning.

©1983 by Karen Hensel, Patti Johns, Elana Kent, Sylvia Meredith, Elizabeth Lloyd Shaw, Laura Toffenetti.
CAUTION: All rights strictly reserved. Professionals and amateurs are hereby warned that *Going to See the Elephant* is subject to a royalty. It is protected under the copyright laws of all countries covered by the International Copyright Convention. Permission in writing must be secured before any kind of performance is given. All inquiries should be addressed to the author's agent, Michael Imison Playwrights Ltd., 150 West 47th Street, Suite 5F, New York, NY 10026.

NOTES ON CHARACTERS

BELLE "MAW" WHEELER is somewhere between sixty and death; she has a worn face, a womanly bosom, and a great deal of energy. She is a cheerful tyrant, willful and self-educated. She is never unpleasant, merely domineering, sure of her own moral and intellectual superiority. It is important to the impact of the piece that the actress who portrays her be genuinely old; there are character lines in a human face that say more than the playwright can.

SARA WHEELER is Maw's daughter-in-law, married to Josh and mother of Jake and Marthie (six and two respectively). She is attractive in a wholesome way, between 26 and 28 years old, and very shabbily dressed. She should have long hair, preferably brunette. She must be able to sing well, as she does so several times in the piece. She is the living embodiment of sincerity and kindness, not overly intelligent; what was once known as "the salt of the earth."

ETTA BAILEY is the youngest, the least educated, the one who has lived all her life on the prairies of Kansas. She is simple in the good sense of the word: unaffected and child-like. She has lived through a terrible trauma, but has accepted the stoicism of her milieu. There is definitely something strange or otherworldly about her, and she should be no older than 22, with very short hair (cut off by her family six months before), preferably dark.

HELENE NICHOLS is a lady; gracious and refined, or trying to be, under brutal circumstances. She would have been fine had she stayed in New York and presided over tea parties, but here her personal resources are strained to the point, not of actual madness, but hysteria. The role requires a balance between vulnerability and strength. At the very point when Mrs. Nichols thinks she is weak, she has a terrible, savage strength. This is a Victorian woman, graceful, intelligent and preferably pretty, ideally fair-haired. She should be visibly older than the young women, say 35.

NOTE ON THE SET

The original set for this play was based on photographs readily available of actual soddies of the 1870s. These homes were crude, low-lying constructions of mud and straw. Our set consisted of a representation of the front of such a home, with one door stage center, hung with an Indian blanket, and one small window. Our research indicated that in the warm months, and this play takes place in July, tables, chairs, and stoves were moved outdoors because of the stifling nature of a dwelling that only had one window and a door. Downstage of the door we placed a crude dining table, surrounded upstage left, right, and center by ladder-backed chairs, and downstage by a large wooden crate. Downstage and right of the table we placed a small stove (designed for wood burning but here, in Kansas, fueled with buffalo chips) accompanied by a crate covered with pots, pans, and various cooking utensils. To the right of the door was found a bench and a large water barrel from which water is constantly drawn with a tin cup. Hanging from the eaves of the house were lines of dingy wash, through which entrances and exits are made. To stage left of the door, under the window, a worn horse collar which belongs to Mrs. Nichols, and which is one of the articles she takes with her in the climax. Also to be discovered on the walls of the house: ropes, harnesses, and halters. We simulated dirt by distressing carpet padding salvaged from the trash bins of carpet stores. This worked out very well, visually and in deadening the sound of feet realistically. We covered the entire floor of our stage with this material. The sod bricks were simulated by carving styrofoam, texturing it, and, as a final touch, using pieces of this same carpet padding to represent straw between the cracks. To be authentic, colors must be uniformly dirt brown!

Going to See the Elephant
Karen Hensel
Patti Johns
Elana Kent
Sylvia Meredith
Elizabeth Lloyd Shaw
Laura Toffenetti

ACT ONE

As lights go up on stage we see the font of a small, sod house with one window and a low door. After no more than a beat of silence, we begin to hear singing offstage. The song is "Housewife's Lament" (see Appendix) and after a verse or two, an extremely old woman, somewhere between sixty and death, appears in the doorway with an armload of books. She moves to the downstage table, places her books on its surface and looks out, her eye caught by some movement out on the prairie. She stands transfixed in an animal alertness, as the young woman enters, still singing, carrying an enormous tub and pushing her way through the lines of wash. This attractive but weathered housewife abruptly drops the song and joins the older woman in scrutinizing the horizon. They stare in silence for almost a minute.

SARA: What are we looking at?
MAW: I dunno, saw a little dust come up.
SARA: Wolves?
MAW: I dunno. I thought...someone walking maybe.
SARA: No one would be out there alone.
MAW: Could be mistaken.
SARA: Probably. *(But they continue to look anyway.)* I'm gonna take these down and put them in the house. What are you gonna do?
MAW: I'm gonna set here for a minute; maybe ten.
SARA: Suit yourself. Can I take these indoors or is your patient sleeping? *(Referring to dry clothes from line.)* Is Mr. Nichols awake?

MAW: What? Oh, go on in. He won't notice much today. *(SARA does, while MAW reads aloud from her book.)* Mad...a...gas...car. Hummm. Khartoum.

SARA: *(Returning.)* I'm gonna wring out these, but I'm not doing any more laundry for at least two days. My holiday's about to begin. Someone will have to see to that beast out there. *(No response.)* It has to be done. *(Pause.)* All right. *(She stalks off stage left.)*

MAW: *(Not noticing her absence.)* Did you see this book he gave me? It's full of maps, there's a map of the whole world in here. *(From SARA's direction we hear a cow moo and a clatter.)* The Kingdom of the Congo.

SARA: *(Returning.)* Now that's all I'm going to take. I quit. Maw, you'll have to help me with that beast out there or she will be roast beef for dinner. *(Shouting out to cow.)* And that's a promise, Jezebelle! Maw?

MAW: Yes. *(Not looking up.)*

SARA: I said I can't handle the cow.

MAW: Well, everybody knows a milker won't stand for being touched by a woman that's expecting. They won't stand and the cow won't give. Everybody...

SARA: Knows that. Yes. Well then you'll have to take over that chore because there's no one else here to do it 'til Josh comes home. There's no milk. I got half of Kansas coming to my house tomorrow afternoon and not a spot of butter. Are you listening?

MAW: Look how they have every country a different color and everything that belongs to England marked out in the prettiest red.

SARA: Will you do the milking for me today or not?

MAW: In a minute. You know, I never realized how small England is, it's just a speck of an island. You'd think something that important would be bigger.

SARA: Did Mr. Nichols give you that?

MAW: Yes, maps of the whole world. They say the sun never sets on British soil. Of course they got a woman running things which seems sensible to me.

SARA: Do you mean to tell me that you've been nursing a sick man day and night for five days and all he give you was a book of maps?

MAW: That's what I wanted and what I asked for. I wouldn't take his money. He give me these other books, however.

SARA: Sometimes you are like a selfish child. You mighta thought of some one else, you mighta thought of us. We could've used some money...or one of their horses...even two pounds of coffee...but books?

MAW: So many places I'll never see. That bothers me. A person can't seem to live long enough to see even a part of it. Don't it ever bother you Sara that you'll never see France or Italy or...Madagascar?

SARA: Why would I want to go to France or Mada... They don't even speak English there. Why would I want to leave my own home and go somewhere where I couldn't even talk to people.

MAW: Just to see the elephant I guess.

SARA: Huh. The point is... *(She hangs up sheet.)* those people ain't thinking about me. They're not sitting on their front porch on a hot summer day saying, "Wish I could go over to Osborne County Kansas and watch Sara Wheeler do her laundry," are they? No. And I don't blame them a bit. Guess I'll rinse out the bucket. She stepped in it that vicious old so and so...

MAW: Can't you just set for a minute, girl?

SARA: Belle Wheeler, I would love to set if I could get *someone* to milk that cow.

MAW: All right. I'll do it. But *now* I want to talk. *Set.*

SARA: Now?

MAW: Yes.

SARA: Do you think I could sit and wring out a little wash while I get this geography lesson? *(She goes to tub on bench.)*

MAW: Girl, there's lots you could learn and it wouldn't hurt you neither.

SARA: Such as what?

MAW: Well, did you know that there are places where the people ain't even Christians? Like Turkey and China?

SARA: I've heard of China. I'm not as ignorant as you imagine.

MAW: They say they're dainty little people, kind of yellow, with slanty eyes and all they eat is rice.

SARA: I guess I'd eat rice too if I could get my hands on some. Is Kansas on that map? I'm more interested in where I am then where I'm not.

MAW: Kansas just ain't big enough to show up much on the world map.

SARA: It looks pretty big from where I sit.

MAW: You gotta try to see things in their proper perspective, Sara. Kansas just ain't much.

SARA: Well, my pisspecktive is that for all the good it does me, the *world* might as well end about forty miles down that road.

MAW: Here, page 29, "Map of the United States of the Americas and the Territories Attendant Thereto."

SARA: I'll look at that. *(She moves to table and looks over MAW's shoulder at the book.)* What's that little foot dangling down there?

MAW: Florida.

SARA: And those little tear drops; them lakes?

MAW: Yes... The Great Lakes, Michigan, Huron, Erie...

SARA: How is it you know so much about it?

MAW: Because my whole life is spread across that map. Look, North Carolina. My great grandmother came there from England *(Points out beyond the edge of the table.)* and married a Frenchman, or so they say, but my daddy was awful dark so I figure there's a nigger in the woodpile so to speak.

SARA: But I thought you was from Kentucky?

MAW: Well, my grandparents wanted to better theirselfs so they come across the Cumberland Gap with Daniel Boone. Walked most of the way and my granny pregnant at the time. They did good in Kentucky; cattle, crops, and slaves. You didn't marry into trash.

SARA: Yes, as you have many times reminded me. Funny how many southerners was rich before the war.

MAW: There were plenty poor ones in the hills of Kentucky where my daddy did his doctoring. Now I was born here in Elizabeth Town, but when I married that no good Jack Wheeler, he brought me to Booneville, on the river.

SARA: *(Reverently.)* The Mighty Missoura.

MAW: Yes, but for Jack Wheeler it was more like the River Babylon. Gambling, whoring. That's where my little Desiree was born. Born and died, on the river.

SARA: And Josh?

MAW: Can't find it. There, Brunswick. Then Jack took us to Fort Scott, Kansas. That was a time; border ruffians, abolitionists, John Brown hacking people up. The blood was running. Then that husband of mine dragged us to Oscaloosa.

SARA: *(Laughs.)* Nobody ever dragged you anywhere.

MAW: True. I never went back. I never saw Kentucky again.

SARA: Why is that?

MAW: That would be like beginning my life's book all over again instead of turning the pages forward to see what dandy things are happening next.

SARA: Where are we now?

MAW: There. Middle of Kansas. Osborne County.

SARA: End of the line. *(She goes back to her wash.)*

MAW: I don't know that I like the sound of that. Sounds pretty final to me.

SARA: Well, all journeys must come to an end. This is the end of mine and glad of it.

MAW: *(She looks at* SARA*'s back for a long moment, then takes a letter out of her apron pocket, a tattered letter.)* Sara.
SARA: Yeah?
MAW: You could handle this claim without me, couldn't you? Sure you could.
SARA: I don't know... Why should I have to? *(Stops with her back still to* MAW.*)* Why? *(Turns.)* What are you saying? Are you sick?
MAW: *(Amused.)* No, I ain't gonna die, not just yet anyway. Actually, I was just thinking of moving on, that's all.
SARA: That's all? What do you mean?
MAW: Well, I got this letter from Mrs. Custer, the General's wife. It come about a month ago. She's recruiting nurses for the Colorado Territory. It pays well, and she don't want any young pretty ones. They all get married right off. She says here that she wrote to an agency in St. Louis last year and they sent her, at her request, the ugliest buck-toothed women they could find, bow-legged and cross-eyed, but when they got to Colorado, they was all married within three weeks! Who knows what might happen to me?
SARA: What are you saying? At your age.
MAW: My age? I'm not dead, Sara, just old.
SARA: That's why you been pawing over that map all day. That's what all this talk about maps and travel is, isn't it? You're gonna leave your family to go husband hunting in the Rockies.
MAW: You could come too, except you already got a husband. Oh, Sara, I'd just be of more use out there sewing up soldiers. But you could come too.
SARA: No. This is my home, at last. I won't move from this spot for the rest of my life.
MAW: Who's an old woman now?
SARA: You must be joking. I can't believe you'd desert us.
MAW: I won't be so far, and I won't go 'til that baby's born.
SARA: Thank you kindly, and then? What happens to me and my children, your grandchildren? We need you here, and wasn't that the agreement, that you would spend the rest of your life here with us?
MAW: Rest of my life, end of the line. I'm still alive. Don't bury me so quick. That kind of talk kills people just as quick as the fever does.
SARA: But I don't understand, why would you want to go to Colorado?
MAW: It's not Colorado, don't you see? I wouldn't stay there neither. I'd stay for a year, save up some money, work my way across. Children always think their parent's life is finished when their children is grown. But my life isn't finished, not until the last breath leaves my body.

SARA: Has Mr. Nichols put these ideas in your head? All those long talks you two been having? What's he been saying to you?

MAW: Nobody has to put these ideas in my head. I was already restless. Look at Queen Victoria, they got a picture of her in this book. She's a widow like me. Hell, she even looks like me. Look at that, small but tough. We both been through trouble, but at least she rules the world. She owns India for Crissake. If I had been born somewhere else, someone else, I coulda done that. I woulda been a helluva queen, and if I'd been born a man, I coulda been president.

SARA: But you weren't.

MAW: Yeah, but I still rule the days I got left.

SARA: I don't understand you.

MAW: I don't expect you to, your dreams are awful small, Sarree.

SARA: But what did you expect would happen?

MAW: Considerable more than did. I just somehow got this feeling that there was supposed to be more, something I was supposed to do, to have.

SARA: It's Mr. Nichols. You've never talked like this to me before. It's his books, and his nice manners and his fancy wife stirring you up, making you unhappy. There's so many things in this country we can't count on. The only thing we can count on is each other. Don't take that away! If you leave... It's not just the work. I'll be alone, alone with no woman to talk to but a two year old girl.

MAW: There's Etta.

SARA: For how long? How long does any girl stay single here, even Etta?

MAW: I might come back. Don't carry on so. I'll come back.

SARA: No. We'll never see you again. *(She sits at bench with tub again.)*

MAW: Oh, don't be so sure. I think I'll live to be a hundred. No, a hundred and ten. There was a slave on my daddy's place was that old. She worked in the fields every day and had a lover was only fifty-five. That's what keeps you alive, work, love, and curiosity. You gotta keep turning those pages to see what happens, for better or worse. Well at least my conscience is clear. Please tell Joshua for me. Tell him he won't have to look at my confederate face much longer. Guess I'll take a looksee at that cow. You really got to learn to flatter her. Cows is very vain. You must talk pretty to her. *(All this as she moves offstage with stool and pail.)* Jezzie? Jezebelle? Haul yourself over here you sweet thing.

SARA *starts to wring out the last of her sheets with a vengeance, back to the audience, singing "Old Joe Clark." After a moment,*

ETTA, *a young girl with short hair and mannish clothes, walks on front downstage center, sweating, and looking harried. She silently walks up behind* SARA *and puts her hand on* SARA's *shoulder.*

SARA: AHHHHHHHHHHRRRRRRRRRGGGGGGGGGG! Etta! Where'd you come from? You like to scare me bald, sneaking up on me. Where's your brothers?
ETTA: *(Very serious.)* What are the "Plagues of Egypt?"
SARA: Huh?
ETTA: What are the "Plagues of Egypt?"
SARA: Did you walk five miles to ask me about Bible stories?
ETTA: No, but I been thinking about it all the way here. What are they? There's hail, boils, lice, darkness... *(She works her way downstage.)*
SARA: Uh, locusts... Does Willi know you're here all alone?
ETTA: Yes, and sea of blood...
SARA: Sea of blood. We didn't expect you until tomorrow.
ETTA: Rats? *(Sits downstage of table on the crate.)*
SARA: No, flies. That was a damn fool thing to do.
ETTA: Frogs?
SARA: No, toads. And murain.
ETTA: What's that?
SARA: Something like hoof and mouth. Etta!
ETTA: But there's something else, something bad we've forgotten.
SARA: Death of the first born.
ETTA: Yes. Are you glad to see me?
SARA: Of course I'm glad to see you. I'm always glad to see you, Etta, but you frightened me, truly you did. What will your father say?
ETTA: I like to walk. I can't spend the rest of my life in the house, shut up in that house. I'm not afraid.
SARA: Well you should be. We've had trouble with the wolves. You shoulda waited and come with one of your brothers. Do they know you're gone?
ETTA: I left a note. They're watching me all the time, looking at me. I can't abide their sad looks. I need some cheerful female company. Besides, George MacReady come by the house and said you had guests. I'd walk twenty miles to see a new face.
SARA: Oh Etta, I am glad to see you, but are you all right?
ETTA: Yes.
SARA: Well, for God's sake, sit down and let me bring you some water. You look to be burning up. Take that towel there and wipe down your face. *(SARA goes to the barrel,* ETTA *looks out to prairie.)*

ETTA: Do you know what the plagues of Kansas are?
SARA: What? Of Kansas?
ETTA: I figured it out and it's just the same; locusts, flies, disease in the cattle, sometimes a sea of blood... and death of the first born.
SARA: Yes, that's true. Now add boredom, loneliness, and bad coffee, and you got the whole list.
ETTA: *(Picking up a doll.)* Where are they, Sara? When I walked up and I didn't see a child or a horse I thought... Where are they all?
SARA: It's all right. They've gone to town, Joshua and the children. They've gone to get us some real food for the party tomorrow, and Joshua thought as he might get some fireworks, too, if he has enough money. He's bringing me some sugar. I haven't had white sugar in this house in...it must be two months.
ETTA: That's not why. You wouldn't send the children to buy fireworks. That's two days, one day there and one day back.
SARA: Well, Maw needs medicine...and...well, it's these people, Etta. The man is awful sick. I just thought I'd try to get Marthie and Jake away from him for awhile. I've had the angel of death sitting on my roof all week long. *(Goes back to the washline and clothes.)*
ETTA: *(Looks up.)* Oh.
SARA: Why d'ya think I'm hanging wash on a weekday? We gotta wash his sheets because Maw says, "It ain't healthy." I swear it ain't healthy for me to be doing so much laundry, but she likes Mr. Nichols a whole lot. She's determined to work one of her miracle cures on him. Part of the cure seems to be clean sheets. She rips them off the bed with no thought of the washing. I don't begrudge him his health but we're in the middle of a dry summer and I'm running out of soap. I was hoping to make it to September when we butcher the hogs, but now I don't know...
ETTA: When George MacReady come by our house he said that they was easterners.
SARA: Yeah. New York State. You don't get any more east than that, I guess. They're smart people, but not in any practical way. They washed out after six months, had to leave their claim. They've got a wagon full of books. She sits and *reads*. I'm not surprised they didn't make it. You gotta have your mind on what you're doing to survive here.
ETTA: Still, is she pretty? Does she have nice clothes?
SARA: Oh my yes. She's got some nifty dresses I wanna tell you. I haven't felt so shabby in years. Here I am making my boy pants outta flour sacks. He's got "Tyler's Best" written across his

backside and this woman walks in with clothes like new and shoes. I had forgotten there was a world where women looked so nice. I think my husband had too.

ETTA: That's just what I wanted to know. I got me some new material with the last of my rescue money and I hope we could start on a dress. Maybe she knows how.

SARA: What did ya get? Calico? *(Comes down to table to see material.)*

ETTA: No. Better than that. I'll show you, I've brought it with me.

SARA: *(Wonderingly.)* A new dress. *(They reverently hold and smell the cloth.)*

ETTA: Yeah, but you got to help me because I got no women over to my house and I do believe that Willi and John would make a mess of it.

SARA: Don't let them even breathe on that material!

ETTA: When was the last time you had a new dress?

SARA: Lemme see. I had a nice yellow dress when I got married, but as I recall we sold that to buy the window frame. My mother sewed me three calicos when I left Oscaloosa. I still have those. No, I haven't had a actual new dress in...five years. *(Pause.)* Why a new dress Etta? What's the occasion?

ETTA: I brought some gifts, some candy for the children and Maw, some ribbon for you. Let me put it in your hair. I'll put it in your hair. Where's your comb?

SARA: Etta, I been doing chores usually done by five people all day. I'm not clean. I'm not fit for ribbon. Maybe tomorrow.

ETTA: But I brought it for you.

SARA: I told you my hair is not clean.

ETTA: You just said you was tired of looking shabby. I bought it with my rescue money.

SARA: All right, you can play with my hair. My brush is there on the window sill. *(As ETTA combs her hair.)* Why a dress, why a new dress now?

ETTA: George is coming to the party tomorrow.

SARA: I know.

ETTA: He wants an answer.

SARA: Does he?

ETTA: I'm gonna tell him yes.

SARA: Are you?

ETTA: Yes, He's a good man. I like him.

SARA: I like him too but...You've only been back six months. It's too soon.

PHOTO: DWORA DREILINGER

ETTA: I would give something to have hair like yours.
SARA: If you marry George, where will you go?
ETTA: He's bought some land in Rooks County.
SARA: That's far. Oh Etta, that's far.
ETTA: Yes. If I go, do you think Pa and my brothers will be all right without me?
SARA: They'll do fine. Men ain't sentimental. They can cook and do chores and will when they realize no woman's gonna do it for them. Just as soon as they get hungry enough. It's not your men I'm worried about.

Going To See the Elephant

ETTA: *(Twisting SARA's hair up into a ridiculous "do" during following exchange.)* They won't remember to water my geraniums. They'll dry up and die. There won't be any geraniums once I'm gone.

SARA: Well, those are things that only matter to women. We bring them when we come, they die when we leave. When you marry there's no looking back. Ouch! What are you doing there?

ETTA: Wait a minute. There's something here...

SARA: It's not lice is it? Oh Lord, I hope it isn't lice.

ETTA: Gotcha! No. Just a flea.

SARA: Thank God. Maw has the most awful smelling cure for lice. Just terrible; kerosene. Makes me sick.

ETTA: Well, if it ain't the lice, it's the fleas. And if it ain't the fleas, it's mosquitos: the plagues of Kansas. You been having trouble with the drought? You know our roof's so dry, big chunks of it have been falling from the rafters. I can't hardly cook indoors anymore without picking big clods of dirt out of the pot.

SARA: That's why we've moved the stove out here, that and the heat.

ETTA: It's a strain. It falls on everything and we can't spare the water or the time to patch it up proper. I woke this morning and there was dirt all over the blanket, all over my face.

SARA: Well girl, maybe you should sleep under a parasol. Talk about a strain on your nerves, I had to have Maw milk Jezebel. That old guernsey and me are at war. She's started kicking me again.

ETTA: Oh?

SARA: Yeah, she just won't leave me be, won't let me touch her. She walks out of her way to step on me.

ETTA: Uh huh.

SARA: Remember when she done that before, coupla years ago?

ETTA: I guess.

SARA: Well, she's doing it again.

ETTA: Oh.

SARA: It's like trying to put socks on a rooster. She's really mean.

ETTA: Are you trying to tell me you're expecting?

SARA: Took you long enough.

ETTA: Are you glad?

SARA: Do I have a choice? It couldn't come at a worse time as it turns out. Another baby born in the middle of winter. But it's not like I can wish it away. God's will.

ETTA: There's more to it than God's will, isn't there, Sara?

SARA: Etta!

ETTA: Well, there is. You talk as if you found babies under a cabbage leaf.

SARA: What do you mean?

ETTA: I mean there's Maw, and Marthie, and little Jake, and you, and Joshua all living in this little house, sleeping side by side, night after night. It seems to me you could avoid God's will if you wanted to.

SARA: You don't know anything about it.

ETTA: Don't I? *(Strained pause.)* Are you afraid of the pain?

SARA: I don't remember the pain in-between. Only when it starts. Then I think, "Aha. That's why I didn't want to do this again."

ETTA: You make jokes but you could die.

SARA: I know I could die. I know that better than you, but I'm not gonna dwell on it. I got two healthy children and I aim to have a third, that's what I think about. But I wouldn't mind it much if just once Josh could do the pregnancy for me.

ETTA *is finished with the "do."* MAW *returns with a full pail and cheerful.*

MAW: Now, all that little princess needed was a little curtseying, and "Thank you, Mams," and she was gentle as a lamb. Etta! What are you doing here? The party ain't til tomorrow. Your calendar's off. Where's Willi and John?

SARA: They're not here. She came alone. took a little walk.

MAW: A little walk?

ETTA: I heard you had visitors. George said you had strangers. I came to see.

MAW: You did huh? I should charge admission if new folks is such a novelty. *(To* SARA.*)* What happened to your hair?

MRS. NICHOLS *appears in the doorway. She is very well dressed, her hair arranged fashionably, and generally exudes an air of sophistication and intelligence.*

MRS. NICHOLS: Mrs. Wheeler, may I speak to you for a moment?

MAW: Is he worse?

MRS. NICHOLS: No, not exactly. I simply would like you to look at him again.

SARA: Mrs. Nichols? This here is my friend Etta. She walked five miles especially to meet you.

MRS. NICHOLS: Oh. What was the name?

SARA: Etta, Etta Baily.

MRS. NICHOLS: How do you do Miss Baily? I believe they mentioned you to me before. You and your family are the only neighbors, aren't you? (ETTA *is dumbstruck;* MRS. NICHOLS *extends a hand but is ignored.*) It's a pleasure to meet you I'm sure. (*Still no response from* ETTA.) If you will excuse me I'll take Mrs. Wheeler into the house. (*She takes her inside.*)

SARA: Well?

ETTA: She has nice manners.

SARA: Which is more than I can say for you. You gawked like she was a giant pickle.

ETTA: She's not like us. I didn't know what to say.

SARA: Mebbe you're right. "Better to keep your mouth shut and be thought a fool than to open it and remove all doubt." Here, help me take this tub back to the pump. (*They do.*)

ETTA: How does she do that with her hair?

SARA: Do what?

ETTA: Get it to curl like that?

SARA: I don't think she does anything. I think it's natural.

ETTA: Oh Lord. She looks so, you know.

SARA: I think it's because she still cares about how she looks. She's got a mirror. I seen her use it.

ETTA: Did you use it? Did you look at yourself?

SARA: Me? Not on your life. I don't have the time for that... I don't have the inclination... I don't have the courage. Some things I'd rather not know.

We hear cries from inside the soddy which stop SARA *and* ETTA *cold.* SARA *mimes to* ETTA *that this is* MR. NICHOLS *and that he has a stomach ailment.*

MAW: (*Offstage.*) Frederick, lie down...Mrs. Nicholson, hold his head.

MR. NICHOLS: Let me up. I'm so hot...let me have something to drink, Helene.

MRS. NICHOLS: Frederick, you must lie down.

MAW: Drink this... Not so much. Mrs. Nicholson, hold his head.

MR. NICHOLS: I'm on fire. Helene, please let me go outside. Let me breathe.

MRS. NICHOLS: Stop it, stop it and lie down.

MR. NICHOLS: I'm sorry. I'm sorry Helene but I'm so hot.

MRS. NICHOLS: Oh God, there's blood, Mrs. Wheeler.

MAW: Calm down.

ETTA: Blood. She says there's blood.

SARA: Don't Etta. (MR. NICHOLS *continues to mumble incoherently and cry.*) Maybe I should go inside and help.

ETTA: No. Don't go in there, there's blood.

MAW: Sara!
ETTA: Don't go.
SARA: What Maw?
MAW: Get me some cool water, now.
MRS. NICHOLS: I've got to get him to Abilene. I've got to get him out of here.
MAW: Sara! Get that water! There ain't nothing they can do for him that I can't do here... Take off his shirt.
SARA: I'm going to get the water.

As ETTA *hears the following dialogue, she sings "Golden Ring" (See Appendix).*

MR. NICHOLS: I'm sorry Mrs. Wheeler. I'm sorry Helene, but it hurts.
MAW: That's all right. You just gotta lie down now and let your body heal itself.
MR. NICHOLS: But I want to help. I can't just lie here. I've got to get up. Helene?
MRS. NICHOLS: Yes?
MR. NICHOLS: I'll be better tomorrow. I'll get up tomorrow, then we can go, I promise.
MAW: You're not going anywhere just yet. You gotta face that fact.
MR. NICHOLS: Where's Eric? Don't let Eric outside. Eric? Eric?
MRS. NICHOLS: Eric isn't here. He's dead. Don't call for him.
MR. NICHOLS: Where is he? Where is he?
MRS. NICHOLS: Stop it, stop it right now.
MAW: There, let him rest now. Let's go outside and leave him rest.

SARA *comes out of the house and touches* ETTA *on the shoulder to stop her singing.* SARA *exits with soiled sheet.* MAW *and* MRS. NICHOLS *enter.* MAW *carries bowl with towel over it.* MRS. NICHOLS *carries* MA's *medicine bag.*

MAW: He's mighty weak and I don't think we should move him.
MRS. NICHOLS: No, we have to keep moving. We should probably leave tomorrow.
MAW: You can't take a man sick as that in a wagon.
MRS. NICHOLS: You really don't think he can travel, or are you being cautious?
MAW: Over that rough ground? In the sun? No.
MRS. NICHOLS: Well, we'll see how he is this evening. Maybe by morning...
MAW: What will you do if he gets worse while you're on the road?

MRS. NICHOLS: I think he's stronger than he looks... He wants to go...hasn't he gotten better since we've been here? *(SARA enters.)*
MAW: I wouldn't say so, no. He's still passing blood. Here, Sara. Take this for me. And be sure to bury it. No sense attracting wolves. *(SARA exits.)* I wouldn't say he was better. You can't take someone on a cross-country trip whilst they're passing blood.
MRS. NICHOLS: I think we should reserve judgment until tomorrow.
MAW: I can tell you ahead of time what's going to be tomorrow... *(She is toying with bottles in her bag.)* Etta, fetch me a cup of water from the barrel... I been doing this for more years than I care to remember. He'll be a little bit better but not well enough to travel, no. *(She takes out a mortar and pestle and grinds.)*
MRS. NICHOLS: We'll see.
MAW: I don't think you want to see, Mrs. Nicholson.
SARA: *(Enters.)* Tell her about some of the people you nursed. She just don't know your record is all.
MAW: Why do you think they call me the medicine woman? I'm the only medicine between here and Abilene. And the man that calls hisself a doctor in Abilene is no better than a broken down dentist. You ever nursed anyone, Mrs. Nicholson?
MRS. NICHOLS: Yes. I have. I nursed my whole family. They were all sick, and my neighbors too.
MAW: Where was this?
MRS. NICHOLS: Jewel, near Jewel.
MAW: What was wrong with them? Did you get it?
MRS. NICHOLS: The same thing, whatever it is my husband has. I really do believe he will feel better if we...How many days can it be to Abilene? Two, three?
SARA: More like four, but you should wait 'til the men come.
MRS. NICHOLS: Yes. I should have gone with your husband to Delphos. I really think... There are days when he feels better; when we were coming here, he sat up front with me in the wagon. I really think he will be all right once we are on our way home, back to New York, where we belong. Perhaps, Mrs. Wheeler you can teach me, show me what to do to keep him comfortable, and I could nurse him myself. Tell me, what has he got?
MAW: Oh I know what he's got.
MRS. NICHOLS: What?
MAW: An inflamed gut.
MRS. NICHOLS: Do you mean the dysentary?
MAW: You can call it that, but I call it a damn sick gut. His insides is all worn down and bleeding. With good nursing, mebbe, maybe he'll be all right in two weeks.

MRS. NICHOLS: No, I can't wait.

MAW: Was you planning on arriving with a live man?

MRS. NICHOLS: It comes and goes, really it does. These past few days it's been worse, but it's a pattern.

MAW: Well, I'll tell you what, Mrs. Nicholson, we won't talk about it. I know what I know, and I hope you know what you don't know.

SARA: I really would listen to Maw, Mrs. Nichols. She has healed so many. She's got healing power in her hands. It's the gift of God. Tell her, Maw.

MAW: I don't like to do any bragging. I ain't a bragger. I don't need to be.

SARA: But it's interesting.

ETTA: She delivered triplets once and they lived. *(Everyone looks at her.)* Once she put a silver dollar in a man's head.

SARA: Yes, that's a good one, Maw, tell her.

MAW: Well, it was the spring of sixty-eight...

ETTA: She was called to this man's home and saw this hole in his head.

SARA: He busted it in an accident, you see...

ETTA: And she thought, well, what am I gonna do with all these brains coming out of this man's head?

SARA: His children was sitting there in the room, staring her down...

ETTA: Yes, staring her down...

SARA: So she took this silver dollar she had in her bag...

ETTA: Somebody gave it to her...

SARA: Yes, somebody gave it to her for a rough birthing. And she took a hammer and hammered this silver dollar out flat and put it over the hole in his head...

ETTA: In his skull...

SARA: And pulled the skin around it, sewed it up tight, and prayed.

ETTA: And that man is still walking around these three years later.

MAW: Yes, but he's still not quite right. *(SARA and ETTA laugh through the following exchange.)*

MRS. NICHOLS: Yes, I know Mrs. Wheeler. Your medical reputation preceded you. That's obviously why I came ten miles out of my way to see you.

MAW: How much education you got?

MRS. NICHOLS: I... Well, I went to New York University at Albany for two years.

MAW: And did they teach you anything about the human body at New York University at Albany for two years?

MRS. NICHOLS: As a matter of fact I did take human anatomy, yes.

MAW: And what did they teach you about the gut in college?

MRS. NICHOLS: I didn't bring my notes with me, Mrs. Wheeler. I don't recall.

SARA: Well, let's leave it be for now. I'm sure Mrs. Nichols will think better of it later.
MAW: Well, talking of medicine, did you tell your husband to get me kerosene and alum? I've bound his head in a cold cloth, and wrapped his feet in cabbage leaves, which may seem barbaric to someone who went to medical college...
MRS. NICHOLS: I never said I went to medical school...
MAW: But which I assure you is a great tonic for the summer fever. Sara will make some sage tea. Oh Sara? Will Joshua buy soda this trip? Baking soda?
SARA: I don't know Maw. Why didn't you ask him yourself?
MAW: What?
SARA: You coulda told him yourself. It seems to me your mouth is working just fine today.
MAW: No.
SARA: Stubborn.
MAW: I don't know as I like hearing that from you. Sounds mighty fresh to me.
SARA: Here we are, three grown people and two small children living in the same house, one small room, and she won't talk to her own son because of some argument they had over the war. Foolish old woman!
MAW: I got my reasons...
SARA: That war is over, over for six years. Let it go and good riddance.
MAW: Only five years...
SARA: Let it go.
MAW: We lost everything we had, everything; our land, our cattle, our slaves who we loved like children... our dignity.
SARA: I don't want to hear about it. Josh don't need to have it brought up again and again. He's not been the same since. It's a sore subject.
MAW: My own son a damn Yankee. All he has to say is, "Maw, I am sorry I done this to you."
SARA: It's done. Let it go.
MAW: Well he shouldn't have gone.
SARA: He's not going to admit it was wrong even if it were, which it weren't. He's a man and he's proud. He's your son. He's not going to say "sorry." You been pouting about it for five years.
MAW: Well I won't be here much longer, so you needn't fret.
SARA: Oh hell.
ETTA: How's that, Maw?
MAW: Come next spring I won't be here and no one will hafta worry about what I say or what I don't say. *(She enters the house with bag.)*

ETTA: Where are you going Maw?...Sara, what does Maw mean she won't be here next spring? Maw, are you ailing? Is there something you haven't told us?

MAW: *(Returning to hand* ETTA *the silverware.)* No. *(She moves back into house.)*

SARA: Maw is taking a little...uh...honeymoon trip to Colorado.

ETTA: What?

SARA: Yea, she's going to elope to the hills of Colorado. Say, Mrs. Nichols, mebbe you should try Colorado if you don't take to Kansas.

MRS. NICHOLS: No, thank you. I'd rather not.

ETTA: What do you mean, elope?

MAW: Well, shall we get the rest of this meal on the table and sit down to eat like Christian people?

ETTA: *(As they complete the table set up.)* What did you mean?

SARA: Oh don't ask, Etta, don't ask. *(Enters the house for lamp.)*

MAW: Where is the pitcher and the bowl?

ETTA: Did you want the milk?

MAW: No, my cleansing bowl. Etta, run over to the stove and see if there's some water boiling. Then put it in the pitcher that's on the shelf, the one with the cloth over it. Oh and there's a bowl too. Bring them both out with a towel.

ETTA: *(Uncomprehending.)* Alright. What are you making?

MAW: Hygiene.

SARA: *(Enters—hands lamp to* ETTA.*)* Oh Lord, I'll get it. Set Etta. *(Returns to house for cleansing bowl and re-enters.)*

MAW: You don't have to believe in it Sara, so long as you do it. I have read in the *Lancet Magazine* about this man named Lister, and he says that germs, little things we can't even see, are causing most disease and if we're going to prevent it we must wash.

SARA: That's why I'm toiling over those sheets day and night, Etta.

MAW: Now, everyone, Mrs. Nicholson, will hold out their hands over the bowl, soap them, and I will rinse with the hot water.

SARA: Couldn't we just go to the pump?

MAW: A lick and a promise won't do it. It's hot water and soap or nothing. There's sickness in this house. Do you want your children to catch it? No. So we will wash.

ETTA: This would go over pretty with my brothers I can tell you.

MAW: *(Is the last to wash and does so very elaborately.)* There. Now that didn't hurt anybody and believe me, it's important. Now I will say grace. Clean hands and a clean conscience..."I will say of the Lord, He is my refuge and my fortress, my God. In Him will I trust. Surely He will deliver thee from the noisome pestilence. He

Going To See the Elephant

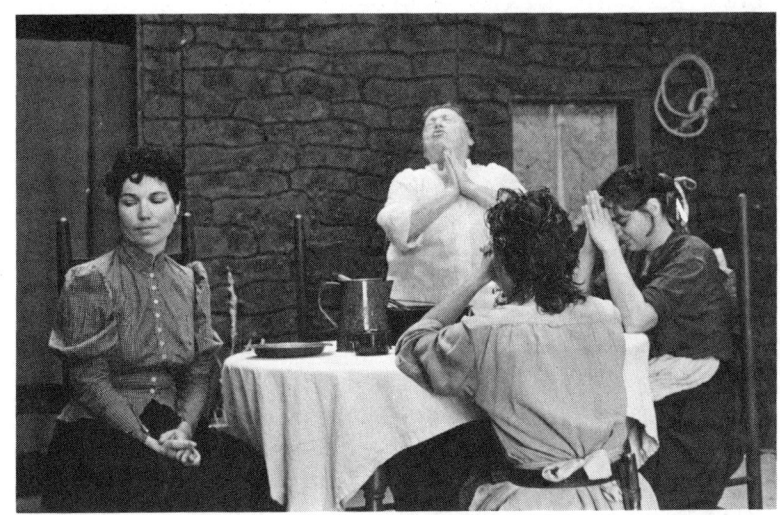

shall cover thee with His feathers, and under His wings shalt thou trust. Thou shalt not be afraid for the terror by night, nor for the arrow that fliest by day, nor for the pestilence that walketh in darkness. A thousand shall fall at thy side, and ten thousand at thy right hand, but it shall not come nigh thee. Amen."

ALL: Amen.

MAW: As guest, would you like to say something over supper, Mrs. Nicholson?

MRS. NICHOLS: "Small cheer and great welcome makes a merry feast."

MAW: I don't believe I recognize that prayer. Is that from Psalms?

MRS. NICHOLS: No, Shakespeare.

ETTA: I am so hungry I'll eat anything that doesn't eat me first.

SARA: This if good, Maw. You did well by this.

MAW: Well, it's the last of that old rooster, may he rest in peace. But I'm sorry to say the coffee is so weak, I'll have to help it out of the pot.

SARA: That's fine by me. I don't like to cut my coffee with a knife like you.

MAW: Where's the cornbread?

ETTA: *(Who has watched* MRS. NICHOLS *put chicken back in the pot.)* Don't you like chicken, Mrs. Nicholson?

MAW: Mrs. Nicholson is a vegetarian, Etta. She don't eat meat in any form.

MRS. NICHOLS: My name is Nichols. *(To* ETTA.*)* Nichols.

MAW: Ain't you never heard of that, Etta?

ETTA: You don't eat any meat?

MRS. NICHOLS: Not if I can help it.

MAW: That's what she chooses to be.
ETTA: The Cheyenne don't eat anything but meat.
MAW: Out to the Donner Pass, the people et each other.
SARA: Maw! Not at the table.
ETTA: Do you eat eggs?
SARA: Etta, leave it be.
MRS. NICHOLS: Yes, occasionally.
MAW: There's different kinds. Some will eat eggs, some will eat fish.
ETTA: You don't eat chicken?
MAW: No.
MRS. NICHOLS: No.
ETTA: You don't eat sausage?
MRS. NICHOLS: Well, sausage is probably the worst thing for you, Etta.
ETTA: Well, no wonder you were all sick. How'd you keep your strength up?
SARA: Eat up, Etta, and don't worry Mrs. Nichols.
MAW: So, sausage is the worst thing, huh? Well, I've lived a long time eating sausage and I ain't ready to go to my rest yet. I've had a long time on this earth and...
ETTA: How long, Maw Wheeler?
MAW: I been eating beef *and* pork *and* sausage...
ETTA: How long you been on earth?...
SARA: Eating sausage? *(They laugh, as does* MAW.*)*
MAW: Wouldn't you two like to know. A woman who'd tell her age would tell anything. You'll never hear it from my lips.
ETTA: But Mrs. Nichols, how long's it been since you ate meat? Have you always been a vege...table?
MRS. NICHOLS: Vegetarian. Well, my husband and I were very influenced by Thoreau.
MAW: That's a Yankee writer, Etta. He was an abolitionist.
MRS. NICHOLS: Yes, well anyway, Thoreau says, "No humane being will wantonly murder any creature which holds its life by the same tenure that he does." Which means, really, that it's more than that meat is bad for your body, it's that eating other creatures is...Well, it's a violation of Christian principles. In a sense, bad for your soul. Because they feel pain as we do. They are not without feeling. *(Other women stare without understanding this explanation.)*
SARA: I hope Jezebel feels pain because she gives me one.
ETTA: Didn't God put them on this earth for us to eat? I mean, why else are they here?
MRS. NICHOLS: Oh, I can hardly argue the logic of it with you, Etta. It's a conviction... A feeling you either have or you don't have.

SARA: This group you come with, was they all vegetarians too?
MRS. NICHOLS: For the most part. And if everything we had been promised had been provided, we would never have gotten sick, or left, because I assure you, Etta, the life of the vegetarian is a healthy one. We were healthy in New York. But a steady diet of corn bread and nothing else...
SARA: What did they promise you? I mean what were you expecting?
MRS. NICHOLS: Oh, there was a contract. A prospectus. They sent us a brochure when we invested our money, our life savings. You see, we thought we were buying into a community, a going concern as it were. There was supposed to be a mill, a meeting house, even a church. All built and waiting for use. There in Jewel.
MAW: And what did you find?
MRS. NICHOLS: Nothing. Nothing had been done, not one building built. It broke my husband's heart. We had absolutely no way to recover our money. We had been shorn like lambs.
SARA: Was anyone else there?
MRS. NICHOLS: Oh yes, several families, practically starving to death. We had to share what food we had brought. We were so unprepared.
SARA: I don't understand. Excuse me for prying, ma'm, but what I don't understand is why'd you come here? I mean, you got an educated husband. I guess you had a house and all. Why would a woman like you and a man like your husband come here?
MRS. NICHOLS: Why did *you* come? Why does anyone come? We thought... Our dream was to build a new life. My husband dreamed of owning property, working the land himself. Thoreau says, "Simplify...simplify..." We believed that most of the luxuries, and even many of the comforts of life are hindrances to the elevation of mankind. They destroy the spirit. They corrupt the soul.
ETTA: Do you really believe that?
MRS. NICHOLS: I don't know any more.
SARA: Well, if I do without life's comforts, not to mention the luxuries, it's not because I don't want them. I don't think having nice shoes would work any great corruption on my little children. We come here because there was nothing to hold us at home. I can live without nice things if I hafta, but I don't necessarily want to.
MAW: Well, that's the price you pay for going to see the elephant.
MRS. NICHOLS: I beg your pardon? What elephant?
MAW: Ain't you never heard that expression?
MRS. NICHOLS: No.
MAW: It means going over the hill, going to see what's on the other side, to see the wonders. Whatever fancy reasons we give for

coming, I really believe it's just that at heart; pure restlessness and human curiosity. Human people is born believing the grass is greener on the other side, like you. You was living in comfort but you just had to come and have a looksee. Me, I've never been cured of it.

SARA: Ain't that the truth. Well, just because you washed out in Jewel don't mean you can't stay here, Mrs. Nichols. I mean, there's a abandoned house not five miles from this spot. You could settle there; I know you could start a school! I know there are plenty would subscribe for something like that. I would for one.

MRS. NICHOLS: No, thank you. I cannot get back to New York State fast enough.

MAW: That's clear.

ETTA: Didn't you ever like it here?

MRS. NICHOLS: Oh yes, at first. We were disappointed of course, but it was exhilarating, beautiful. The spring.

SARA: The spring is something else.

MRS. NICHOLS: I had never seen nature so raw and wild. The prairie was, well, like they say, a sea of grass, an ocean of flowers and sweet smells moving in waves to the horizon. Magnificent.

ETTA: Yes.

MRS. NICHOLS: I grew stronger, the work, the walking. The fresh air was like a tonic. I never got sick, you see. Somehow I was spared. We were sleeping outside, well, virtually outside. There was an abandoned Indian dwelling...

ETTA: A lodge.

MRS. NICHOLS: No, more like a dug out. Except the roof had collapsed. It was only three walls. When I lay down at night I could see the sky. I would look up at the stars until...until it seemed that I was really looking down at them, that I would fall into the sky... Anyway, we were so desperate that we were using the broken bowls and tools that the Indians had left behind. It was humiliating.

MAW: Did you get a crop in, plant anything?

MRS. NICHOLS: Almost. That would have saved us. I think we might have been able to hold on if there had been the hope of a crop in the fall, but the plow broke. (SARA *having heard something, looks out to the fields.*)

ETTA: That's a tragedy.

SARA: Just about the worst thing that can happen to you.

MRS. NICHOLS: I didn't understand the significance at first. I didn't believe, I didn't know that one tool could make the difference between success and failure, between life and death.

ETTA: Did someone die?

SARA: What's that? *(She stands and sees something.)*
ETTA: Did one of your family die?
MAW: Hush, Etta, hush for a minute.
MRS. NICHOLS: What is it?
MAW: Shhhhhhhhh . Don't talk.
SARA: Is it Joshua coming back?
MAW: No.
ETTA: Is it?
MAW: No. But don't anybody move sudden. Let's keep on as usual. Sara, sit.

SARA: But...
MAW: Sit.
ETTA: I don't see anything. *(Pause. We hear howling.)*
MAW: They're in the cornfield.
SARA: *(Trying to act normally.)* Etta, why don't you ask Mrs. Nichols about New York State.
ETTA: Huh?
SARA: Ask what she done for fun in New York.
ETTA: *(Very half-heartedly.)* What didya do for fun in New York?
MRS. NICHOLS: *(Scared to death.)* We would go shopping...or...to the theater.
ETTA: I've never seen a play. Is it nice?
MRS. NICHOLS: I used to think it was quite exciting. *(More howling, barks.)*
MAW: Sara, my gun is just inside the door to the right. Get up slow and reach in there.
ETTA: My mother always said that the theater was a scandal and that no decent woman would go there.
MAW: Tush. Queen Victoria always goes to see the plays and she's decent. I guess if Queen Victoria goes it's all right. *(We hear a plaintive moo.)* Jezebelle knows they're here.
SARA: Good.
MRS. NICHOLS: What is it? For God's sake who is it?
MAW: I don't quite know. Etta, is that wolves, or is that...Cheyenne.
ETTA: *(Listens; everyone frozen.)* No. It's just wolves.
MAW: Good. Animals I can handle. Etta, get a pie pan and a spoon, a metal one, and when I say go, ladies, I want you to jump and shout, shout to save your souls, and Etta, hit that thing like you mean it. *(Pause.)* There they are! Go! *(All yell except* MRS. NICHOLS *who is too frightened. After everyone else has stopped yelling,* ETTA *laughs.)*
SARA: I've seen them before but they've never come this close!
MRS. NICHOLS: What would make them so brave as to come that close in daylight?
SARA: Maybe they know the man is gone.
MAW: Maybe.
MRS. NICHOLS: Do you think they're gone for good?
MAW: I do not.
MRS. NICHOLS: But surely they've been frightened away... Why didn't you shoot?
MAW: Because I want to save my ammunition.
MRS. NICHOLS: Will they be back?

SARA: Yes.
MRS. NICHOLS: Why?
MAW: Because they smell sickness, Mrs. Nicholson. They smell blood, and they smell...
MR. NICHOLS: *(From inside the house.)* Helene? Helene, are you alright?
MRS. NICHOLS: Yes, Frederick. *(She moves to the door.)* Everything is fine.

Lights down.

ACT TWO

SCENE ONE

Evening of the same day. Sun is setting.

Lights up on SARA *sitting at the table alone, singing "Dear Companion."* MRS. NICHOLS *appears at the doorway halfway through the song to listen. When* SARA *finishes, she speaks.*

MRS. NICHOLS: That was pretty.
SARA: Oh, I was just singing at that sky. This is my favorite time of day. Somehow I always wind up singing sweet sad songs. Josh don't like it, he likes footstompers. I know New York must be lovely, they say Chicago is something to see, but there can't be nothing there to compare with these sunsets. God's presence is so strong here. It's like He's saying, "No matter how hard your days may be, I still love you enough to show you My pleasure."
MRS. NICHOLS: Yes, it's beautiful.
SARA: When I was a little girl in Missoura my mama used to sit and watch the sunset every night. We had this two story house and my daddy built her a porch on the second floor so she could have a clear and open view. Every night she'd call us up and we'd just set and watch. That was Missoura. I wish she could've seen it here, seen these skies. When there's no mountains, and no trees, that sky seems so awful big. Those clouds billowing up like that and the bright, bright colors. It makes me feel small. Safe, but small.
MRS. NICHOLS: Yes, small... Sara, I have offered your mother-in-law some money, she refused. I would try to offer you some but I have a feeling you wouldn't take it either. *(She picks up a suitcase near door and holds it.)*

SARA: *(Embarrassed.)* No, that's alright.

MRS. NICHOLS: I only thought we would stay a day or two. Somehow it's turned into five. And I know it has been a burden. You have been very kind.

SARA: We only did what anyone would do. What I would expect you to do.

MRS. NICHOLS: Since you won't take the money, I would like to offer you these clothes. They're boys' clothes, and I think your little Jake could wear them.

SARA: Oh. Well, yes. God knows he don't have much and he grows like a weed.

MRS. NICHOLS: *(Opens the suitcase and starts to remove clothes.)* Good. There are three pair of pants here. Do these look as if they'd fit? Oh, there's a rip in this knee.

SARA: That's nothing. I can fix that. They're better than he's used to.

MRS. NICHOLS: There may be some tears. You may have to mend them. This was an active boy, and strong. But it's good quality gabardine. So, would you want these? *(Hands SARA some clothes.)*

SARA: Yes. Thank you. *(She looks at them with pleasure.)*

MRS. NICHOLS: These are shirts, and here's a jacket. This blue shirt is especially nice. I think my mother bought it in Boston, very good quality. Look at the seams, and the buttons. *(She brings the suitcase to the table, sits.)*

SARA: *(As MRS. NICHOLS puts blue shirt on table.)* What a nice color blue.

MRS. NICHOLS: Yes, Eric looked quite handsome in this shirt with his blue eyes...I'm afraid the trousers are a little long perhaps for your boy, but you can take them up. I nearly forgot, there are some shoes, they're in our wagon. I'll get them tomorrow. I'm sure your boy could use shoes for the winter. They all run around barefoot in the summer...but in winter...

SARA: Mrs. Nichols...

MRS. NICHOLS: I've been carrying these around with me for months. I'm glad someone can use them. The shirt is good-looking, isn't it? He was so handsome in this, such the little man...

SARA: About your boy...

MRS. NICHOLS: *(Pulls a little jacket out of the suitcase.)* This is a Sunday suit. I almost buried him in this suit, but somehow I couldn't bring myself to do it. I had to leave him. Yes, it's time I gave away these things. I don't know why I've brought them this far.

SARA: *(Trying to avoid a painful scene.)* Thank you, Mrs. Nichols... Helene.

MRS. NICHOLS: I had to bury him in a cardboard box. We didn't have anything else. I did it myself. Everyone else was sick by then. My husband was ill and too weak to help, always too weak to help. I was the only one still on my feet. And so it was me...and my dead child.

SARA: I am truly sorry.

MRS. NICHOLS: I washed him with lavender soap and combed his hair but somehow I could not bear to dress him in his clean Sunday suit. I just didn't know if the box would hold. It was only a cardboard box. I was afraid it wouldn't keep out the dirt, keep out the dirt. I wrapped him in the cleanest sheet I could find and laying against the white sheet he looked...so beautiful, so... No. I don't think I can part with the suit...Did I dig it deep enough. Did I do it right? Is he safe out there? I don't know...I don't know...I don't...know.

SARA: *(After a considerable silence.)* I lost my first baby here. She come at Christmas, that awful cold winter of '64. She was healthy, we thought. First three weeks she was fine and fat; face nothing but cheeks. And then she just started ailing, couldn't keep the milk down, got so weak. Maw had come out for the birthin'. She suffered so, not being able to help. But in the end there weren't nothing she could do. God's will. I guess the good Lord decided my baby was just too fine for this wicked world.

MRS. NICHOLS: What did you do?

SARA: I wrapped her in my wedding shawl. Best piece of cloth I had, and we put her in a big tin cracker box and buried her in the snow. We were housebound that winter, trapped inside. Josh had to dig a tunnel to the shed in January, it was that deep, the snow. I couldn't sleep, thinking about my little girl laying out there in the cold. And my breasts so full with no one to nurse. I couldn't sleep and my husband couldn't stay awake. He slept all day sometimes. All that winter, there was a terrible silence in this house.

MRS. NICHOLS: This country, this God forsaken place.

SARA: With the first thaw, we buried her proper under that sapling there, and Josh threw himself into the land. He worked like a man possessed and the work healed him. Me, I started walking. After the morning chores Maw would send me out of the soddy with a blanket wrapped around me and I'd walk, walk 'til I couldn't walk no more. And then, one day I walked out to the fields where Josh was working and I put my arms around him. We knew then we was all right again.

MRS. NICHOLS: *(Attacking her.)* I don't see how you could go on, how you could stay in this nightmare land. Death is everywhere, everywhere you look, waiting for you to turn your back so that it can snatch your children. Even hope dies here.

SARA: But the next year we had Jake, and then my little Marthie. I have two healthy children, Helene. It ain't the land that takes our babies, it's the Lord. You've got to make peace with this country, there's so much beauty here, and sometimes great abundance. We're the trespassers. You can't blame the prairie for fighting back at times.

MRS. NICHOLS: *(Retreating.)* Perhaps.

SARA: The feeling I get when I see new plowed fields, land that's never been touched before, never made fruitful before, it's holy somehow. And every loved one we bury here makes the land more ours. *(She is touching the shirt;* MRS. NICHOLS *gently pulls it away from her.)*

MRS. NICHOLS: I envy you your husband *(Taking up shirt and suit.)* and your pretty children, Sara, and I hope you can use the clothes. *(Goes to stove to pour cup of coffee but is stopped by the voice of* ETTA, *which startles her badly.)*

ETTA: *(At door.)* Dark!

SARA: Yes.

ETTA: This is what it must be like to be blind.

SARA: It's the light Etta. Now if I was to blow out the light, we'd all disappear.

MRS. NICHOLS: Please don't blow out the light.

ETTA: Maw says to tell you your husband is sleeping Mrs. Nichols.

MRS. NICHOLS: Thank you...You might as well call me Helene.

ETTA: Oh...fine... She also said to ask, "Have you heard anything?"

SARA: Nothing much so far, I think my singing has frightened them off.

ETTA: No Sarie, you sing good.

MRS. NICHOLS: Etta, I have given Sara some...clothes for her children. I found these buttons, and a bit of lace, and I thought you might be able to use them. *(*ETTA *stares uncomprehendingly.)* Well, don't you sew occasionally? I also have a magazine, *Godey's Ladies' Book,* it's about a year old...

ETTA: There must be a dozen buttons here.

MRS. NICHOLS: Please take them.

ETTA: I don't know what to say.

SARA: Thank you would do just fine.

ETTA: Oh yes, thank you m'am, uh, Helene...you see I'm getting married. I'm gonna sew a dress, this is...could I show you my material? Would you look at it and suggest something?
MRS. NICHOLS: Of course. Are you marrying soon, Etta?
ETTA: *(Engrossed in book with* SARA.*)* Yes. *(She and* SARA *gasp audibly.)*
SARA: Do you sew Helene?
MRS. NICHOLS: Oh yes.
ETTA: Did you sew your wedding dress?
MRS. NICHOLS: No, my poor mother labored over it for months.
ETTA: Your mother... What was it like, your wedding dress?
MRS. NICHOLS: I don't know that I remember, that must have been ten years ago at least, yes ten years. I do remember that I had lots of lace and a very long veil... Who are you marrying Etta?
SARA: Did you have a crinoline?
MRS. NICHOLS: Of course, I had an enormous skirt, several petticoats, a crinoline underneath it all. Let me see, a tight bodice with lilies at my waist and in my hair...They were wearing everything off the shoulder then and my skin was so white and soft, I was terribly vain about it. *(Laughs.)*
SARA: Why do you laugh?
MRS. NICHOLS: Oh, I don't know, I suppose I was quite ridiculous, so young...
ETTA: It sounds like a fairy story. Was there dancing?
MRS. NICHOLS: Yes.
SARA: How many people?
MRS. NICHOLS: *(Offhand.)* Two hundred.
ETTA: Two hundred? That's a crowd.
SARA: Was you rich?
MRS. NICHOLS: No, just a large family, nothing spectacular, a very small orchestra, refreshments, sparkling wine, dancing, hardly unusual in our circle.
SARA: *(Exchanges look with* ETTA.*)* What did you dance?
MRS. NICHOLS: *(Turning dramatically.)* The waltz! I danced with all the men. *(Waltzing for them.)* And Frederick danced with all the ladies, I remember that, he was very handsome. He was perfect and I was perfect, the perfect couple everybody said so...What are your plans?
SARA: Well I don't think we will be showing her such a time as that.
ETTA: If I have a new dress and a sugar cake I will be very lucky.
SARA: Oh Etta, we'll have a sugar cake, somehow. I won't let you eat cornbread on your wedding day.

ETTA: I suppose my brother can play his harmonica.
MRS. NICHOLS: The wedding means nothing Etta, the size of it, the dress, nothing. I've been married ten years, and in the end...it's just...when the wedding party goes home it is you and that man for the rest of your life and the only thing that matters is, are you in love with that man; are you?
ETTA: Yes.
MRS. NICHOLS: Then that's all you need, isn't it?
ETTA: Yes.
SARA: Well, weddings are a party and I do love a party. Mine was a corker. People passed out from dancing too hard, too long, and a lot of drinking and horseplay. That's the way they do things in Missoura.
MRS. NICHOLS: When will you be marrying, Etta?
ETTA: I don't know...I only just made up my mind. He doesn't even know I'm gonna, but I want to... I'll talk to him at the party tomorrow.
SARA: I was married in the spring, which is a good time, and I had to wait two years Etta, before we got married, but I have no regrets.
MRS. NICHOLS: None?
SARA: No.
MRS. NICHOLS: And Ma...Mrs. Wheeler, did she approve?
SARA: Yes, it was practically her idea, she knew I was good for him and she was right. I am the best thing that ever happened to that man. He wandered into my daddy's store one day and I knew he was the one, just like that. I let him chase me 'til I caught him...but then the war came, he volunteered for the Union army, and he was gone two and one half years.
MRS. NICHOLS: That's really why you came here, isn't it? The war?
SARA: Well, he come back with kind of a shadow on him, he was quiet but restless. He started talking homesteading so I said "Let's go!" and we wound up here.
MRS. NICHOLS: And how did you meet your young man, Etta?
SARA: He's a good man, George, has ten head of cattle.
MRS. NICHOLS: Ten head of cattle. My, I suppose that is the measure of a man here.
ETTA: He's got a nice laugh.
MRS. NICHOLS: Will you live here after you are married?
ETTA: No. He's got some land over to Rooks County and he wants to move, so do I. *(Looks at SARA.)*
MRS. NICHOLS: And how did you meet this fine man who has ten head of cattle?

ETTA: Further west...I met him west of here.
SARA: He's a fine fellow, is George. Josh thinks the world of him.
MRS. NICHOLS: I don't understand, how is it you met him?
ETTA: *(Pause, looks to* SARA.*)* He was with the cavalry. I mean he wasn't *in* the cavalry, he was with an expedition. And...I met him.
MRS. NICHOLS: What kind of expedition?
ETTA: Against the Indians...there was...trouble with the Indians. In the summer of '68. There were a number of...atrocities...and he was with the cavalry...
MRS. NICHOLS: Oh... Was he fighting the Indians?
ETTA: Yes.
MRS. NICHOLS: But surely *you* weren't fighting the Indians?
ETTA: No.
MRS. NICHOLS: And yet you ran into him in the middle of an Indian war.
ETTA: No...I...
SARA: Please leave it be, Mrs. Nichols... *(All freeze as the howling of wolves is heard again.)*
SARA: Maw!
MAW: *(Entering.)* I know, I heard. Give me the gun, dim the light. Sara, you got the hoe with you?
SARA: Yes.
MAW: Good. We'll circle back of the animal sheds... They'll try for the stock...Etta, go in the house.
ETTA: No. Don't want to. Don't want to be trapped in the house.
MAW: Mrs. Nicholson, can you use a gun?
MRS. NICHOLS: No.
MAW: Damn! Then Etta, take the revolver. I don't think they'll try the house but...you know how to use this?
ETTA: Yes, ma'm.
MAW: Fine. Don't until you have to.
SARA: Whatever you do, don't shoot me. *(*MAW *and* SARA *exit.)*
MRS. NICHOLS: Etta...How long...I mean...
ETTA: It don't pay to fret Helene, we just got to wait it out.
MRS. NICHOLS: Aren't you frightened?
ETTA: It's best not to think about it.
MRS. NICHOLS: How can you not think about it? How can you pretend it doesn't exist? Tonight it's wolves...tomorrow it could be...
ETTA: Everybody's scared...even the Indians.
MRS. NICHOLS: *(Pause.)* How is it you know so much about the Indians?
ETTA: I ain't ashamed or nothing.
MRS. NICHOLS: What?

ETTA: I ain't ashamed but...I'm not supposed to talk about it. I almost forget and then...I have seen the elephant, Mrs. Nichols. I lived with the Cheyenne for a year and a half. I was captured.

MRS. NICHOLS: Oh my God. How? I mean when?

ETTA: August. A hot Thursday in August. I was weeding in the kitchen garden and these three Cheyenne come up to the house. That weren't unusual 'cause every so often they'd come by begging for food, but this day, *this* day my mama called to me. Willi and John were haying in the field with my pa, so I went up to the house so's she wouldn't be alone.

MRS. NICHOLS: She let them in the house?

ETTA: We'd never had any trouble before. They sat down to lunch with us. They ate with us and when they finished, they stood up... *(Howl.)*

MRS. NICHOLS: And?

ETTA: Stood up and started breaking up the furniture just like that and Mama screamed and I laughed, I laughed! But he got me by the hair and I stopped...I had real long hair then and I thought, "He's gonna cut it all off, he's gonna cut my head off," but he didn't, he just dragged me outta the house...and pulled me up on this horse and rode away. He never let go of my hair the whole time.

MRS. NICHOLS: You laughed. Why did you laugh?

ETTA: I can't tell you why, I don't know. Didn't you ever do nothing like that?

MRS. NICHOLS: No. Not that. No.

ETTA: It's not like I thought it was funny...After I lived with them...I saw they weren't that different. They're just as hungry and twice as scared. You can't imagine the panic when they hear white soldiers are coming, "No-Txe-Ve-Ho," they cry, white soldiers, "No-Txe-Ve-Ho"...We were always moving, running. The days passed, I did chores. The women beat me sometimes, not much.

MRS. NICHOLS: *(Whispered.)* Etta, oh Etta...

ETTA: I never cried. *(Proud.)* Not once, not once. He respected that, he thought I was brave, but I wasn't, I just couldn't feel anything, like this table.

MRS. NICHOLS: Etta, this man, did he...did he?

ETTA: Once the Cheyenne girls painted my face brick red, they thought I would like that, I pretended I did. *(We hear howls.)*

MRS. NICHOLS: *(Seeing* ETTA *panic.)* Etta, are you alright?

ETTA: Yes. I was just remembering. Sometimes you think you won't but you do. I had a dream while I was there, I dreamed this person or something came and took my hand and said, "Etta, just do your best, just do the best you can." I felt better after that. I waited, I had faith in that voice because...it sounded like my mother. I waited and in the end they came.

MRS. NICHOLS: Who?

ETTA: Custer. Custer's troops; they come and got me. That's where I met my George. He passed a hat, took up a collection among the soldiers for me. They all gave something. I got fifty dollars silver and I got my George.

MRS. NICHOLS: Your family...

ETTA: My pa was there and my brother, they took my things, my Indian clothes and my moccasins, and they burned them. They even cut my hair. *(Pause.)* I wish I still had my moccasins.

MRS. NICHOLS: And your mother?

ETTA: Dead. She cried herself to death after I was taken...and for no reason because *here I am. (Offstage there is a gunshot.* ETTA, *panicky and holding gun, screams.)* MAW! *(Then softly, trying to locate both* MAW *and the gunshot.)* Maw...Maw...Maw! *(There is another gunshot and* ETTA *loses control, shouting.)* Maw!...Maw!

MRS. NICHOLS: *(Simultaneously under* ETTA'S *cries.)* Etta, don't shoot ...Etta.

ETTA: Maw...Maw!

MRS. NICHOLS: Etta, what do you see? What do you see?

ETTA: *(Screaming at the top of her lungs.)* Maw!

MAW: *(Entering and seeing what is going on.)* Etta!

ETTA: *(Relieved at the sight of* MAW.) Maw.

MAW: Give me the gun. (ETTA *does.* SARA *re-enters. To* MRS. NICHOLS.*)* What happened here?

MRS. NICHOLS: I don't know. Etta was telling me about the Cheyenne, and we heard shots.

MAW: We don't talk about that, you shouldn't have asked her. What's painful to remember is best forgot.

MRS. NICHOLS: No, if you forget the pain you forget the lesson, and this is a bad place to have a short memory.

SARA: Either way it don't help.

ETTA: I heard shots.

MAW: They got to Jezebel. I got one of 'em though. The rest run off. I figure they're gone for now.

ETTA: I heard two shots.

MAW: Yeah. I had to shoot Jezebel. She was all tore up...so I...Mrs. Nichols, take her to bed will ya?

ETTA: Are you going to stay out here? I want to stay out here with you.

MAW: No child, you go on to sleep...tomorrow will be a better day.

ETTA: Sara?
SARA: Go to bed. We'll talk tomorrow. *(MRS. NICHOLS takes ETTA in, gently.)*
MAW: *(After a moment of tired silence.)* I'm gonna light a small fire next to...the carcass; I reckon we'll hafta sit up most of the night.
SARA: Yes.
MAW: Come first light I'll start the butchering. In this heat she won't...
SARA: Yes, I know. *(MAW starts to go.)* Maw, do you really mean it? Will you go?
MAW: When the baby's born, yes.
SARA: *(A very sincere question.)* Why?
MAW: Why? I told you. Why bring it up now?
SARA: It's been a hard day. Before I lose anything else, I'm gonna know why and feel right about it.
MAW: If I don't start that fire, they'll be back. *(She turns to go.)*
SARA: Give me an answer I can understand, one that I can live with. I'm afraid. I don't know if I can handle it without you.
MAW: You will because you have to. It's time.

SCENE TWO

The next morning. Lights up on SARA onstage. She is washing hands and face. The shotgun is near her at all times. As she washes blood off her hands in the basin, ETTA enters quietly from house carrying material.

We hear MRS. NICHOLS arguing in house.

ETTA: Could we cut my dress out now?
SARA: *(Startled.)* Etta! You gotta stop sneaking up on me that way.
ETTA: What way?
SARA: Oh never mind. Anyway, we don't have time to work on your dress today; girl I've got people coming to my house today and my husband coming home. *(ETTA continues to smile winningly at her.)* Oh, alright, we'll have a look at it when I've finished this.
ETTA: Good. I'm not gonna fight.
SARA: That's nice. *(Double take.)* Fight? Fight who?
ETTA: Helene and her husband are having words in there. I won't ever fight with George.
SARA: Humph, that's what they all say...What are they fighting about?
ETTA: I hope we can get all these buttons on the dress, and all the lace...
SARA: Well, we'll try.

ETTA: *(Opening the Godey's book.)* Are you gonna make the sleeve like the one in the book?

SARA: If I can, honey. I've never made a sleeve like that before.

Enter MRS. NICHOLS, *crossing downstage, disturbed, in traveling clothes.*

ETTA: *(Seizing the book from* SARA *and rushing up to* MRS. NICHOLS.*)* Can you make a sleeve like this one?

MRS. NICHOLS: What? Now?

ETTA: *(Grabs material and thrusts it at* MRS. NICHOLS.*)* I want to use all the buttons you give me.

SARA: *(Embarrassed.)* She wants to get a start on it. She'll change her mind if she don't...

MRS. NICHOLS: This is a nice piece of cloth. It smells like civilization... They were wearing them very low this year, cut quite low in front.

ETTA: How low?

MRS. NICHOLS: How much have you got?

ETTA: How much what? *(Looking at bosom.)*

MRS. NICHOLS: Material?

SARA: *(Laughs.)* It looks to be about six yards.

ETTA: It goes around me three times. Look, one, two, three... *(She wraps it around herself.)* I seen this sleeve. *(Points to book.)*

MRS. NICHOLS: No, you'd need a pattern to make a sleeve like that.

SARA: We don't cut patterns out here, don't have the paper, but if you show me, I got a steady hand.

MRS. NICHOLS: *(Not really interested in any of this.)* Do you have some pins? I'll pin up one side of the skirt. *(To* SARA.*)* Fold it on the bias. (SARA *does.)* Now turn...Yes...Good. (SARA *is doing all the work.)*

SARA: You shoulda washed before we done this, Etta.

ETTA: She thinks she's funny.

SARA: No, I think you're funny, Mrs. Society Sleeve.

MRS. NICHOLS: *(Pointing to back of skirt.)* Pin it there, and there...

ETTA: Ouch!

MRS. NICHOLS: That's only the first of many little pains that marriage will bring you, Etta.

MAW: *(Offstage.)* Sara.

SARA: Oh Lord, I knew we shouldn't have started this now.

MAW: Sara, come quick!

SARA: I've got fifteen people coming to dinner and she wants to sew.

MRS. NICHOLS: Go ahead, I'll do it.

ETTA: Are you excited?

MRS. NICHOLS: About what?

ETTA: Biggest day of the year...Fourth of July. Everyone I know in the whole world will be here...Sara, Josh, Marthie, Jake, Willi...

MRS. NICHOLS: What do we celebrate on the Fourth of July, Etta, can you tell me?

ETTA: There'll be food, and lots a talk and even dancing probably. Mr. Brunick will come, *and* the Braden Brothers...will you dance?

MRS. NICHOLS: No. *(She unpins* ETTA *and takes down the material.)*

ETTA: Are you shy? If you're shy I can have George dance with you,

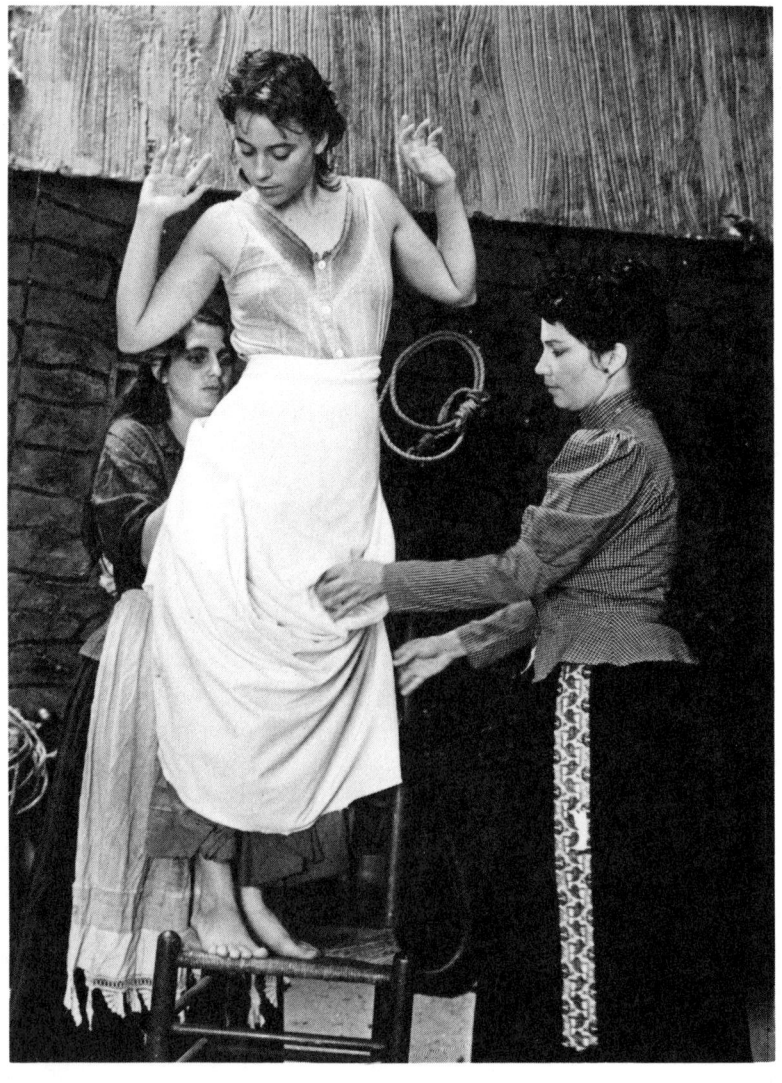

cause he ain't.

MRS. NICHOLS: What do we celebrate today, do you know?

ETTA: The war.

MRS. NICHOLS: Which one?

ETTA: The one that made us free?

MRS. NICHOLS: And are we free? *(No answer.)* I can't stay Etta. I can't stay for the party. I have to take my husband home. You understand that, don't you? *(Pause.)* I think you do. *(Starts to leave.)*

ETTA: But you can't go, your husband's sick.

MRS. NICHOLS: He's much better today. *(She sees* MAW *enter and exits quickly.)*

MAW: *(Entering in a blood soaked apron, holding a cleaver,* SARA *follows.)* Who's much better today?

ETTA: Is it finished?

MAW: Yes. Look at me, I am a sight, just like old John Brown himself after he hacked up everybody in Osawatomie. *(Starts to wash in basin.)* We've burned the damn wolf, and I've buried whatever we couldn't render of the cow. Help me clean up here, Etta. I'm not tall enough to hang the meat, so we'll have to hope Josh comes home real soon.

SARA: He has to. God, he has to. Still I'm glad the children didn't have to see us hack up that poor cow.

MAW: They'll see worse things before they're grown. Today we will have a feast like we haven't seen since I don't know when. Real beef on the table. But all in all, I'd rather have the milk, and Jezebelle.

SARA: I won't eat any, not today anyway...not today. Poor Jezzie.

MAW: I know how you feel, but it don't pay to be sentimental about a dumb animal. *(She sniffles a little.)* Etta, don't scrub so hard.

ETTA: It won't come off, somehow blood never does come clean.

MAW: Sara take this apron out there and throw it on the fire, burn it. *(*SARA *exits.)*

ETTA: Is Mr. Nichols gonna die?

MAW: Huh? No, not if I can help it. But if it's God's will, then...it's God's will. What brings that up?

ETTA: Maybe she'd wait if she thought he would live, if she thought he'd recover.

MAW: Who? Mrs. Nichols?

ETTA: I waited, and I lived. Was that God's will do you think?

MAW: Everything is. What's this about Nichols?

ETTA: She's not staying for the party, she's...they're leaving today.

MAW: Never mind what that woman says. I do believe it was God's will to put that woman on this earth to upset my digestion. Where is she now?

ETTA: In the house.

MAW: If she's going somewhere with that man she'll have to walk over me to do it. *(Calling loudly.)* Mrs. Nichols, may I speak to you? Helene? I know you're in there, come on out.

MRS. NICHOLS: *(In doorway.)* Yes?

MAW: Was there something you wanted to say to me?

MRS. NICHOLS: Yes. Etta, will you leave us alone?

MAW: No, she won't. Spit it out.

MRS. NICHOLS: We've none of us slept all night. I know I'm tired, I suppose it's possible that even you are. So let's keep this simple. I've already packed my wagon, my husband is dressed. We're leaving this morning. You've been very kind, all of you, and I'm grateful to you for nursing my husband back.

MAW: To what?

MRS. NICHOLS: He feels much better today. He's well enough to move on. I know it's rude to leave before the party, but I'm sure your guests will understand. There'll be that much more food for everyone. I would like to make a small contribution to the festivities to defray the costs. *A gift,* not a payment.

MAW: You already tried to buy me off once woman and I've told you no. Now you said I nursed him back. Back to what? He's barely half alive. He couldn't walk to the well much less make it to Abilene.

MRS. NICHOLS: You haven't seen him today, he's much better. *(Trying to remain calm.)*

MAW: Between you and Abilene there's more than eighty miles of *nothing.* Heat, wolves, ruffians. If you go he'll die, and I haven't nursed him this far to see you bury him out on that prairie.

MRS. NICHOLS: It doesn't concern you, it's our decision.

MAW: "Our decision?" He's in no condition to make choices like that.

MRS. NICHOLS: No, he's not. But then he never has been. Whose decision do you think it was that we would be vegetarians? Here in a country where the only thing between us and death just might be a good piece of meat? His dreams, *his* dream to own the land...well look at it, you can't own that land, nobody can. Does the flea own the dog? No. And we're no more than that to this country. I've suffered all I'm going to for his decisions. So if you'll excuse me... *(Begins to exit.)*

MAW: So you're gonna keep on running away?

MRS. NICHOLS: *He has!* He has escaped, lying in there beyond decision, no responsibilities. He's free because he's dying. Well damn him for trying to die on me, *damn him! (She's visibly hysterical now.)*
SARA: *(Who has entered during this tirade.)* You be quiet, he'll hear you.
MRS. NICHOLS: Oh he hears me, don't you, Frederick?
MAW: She's lost her reason.
MRS. NICHOLS: After six months in hell, I suppose I have. If I've lost my mind, it's because I've tried so very hard to stay sane. I don't suppose a woman like you would understand that, Mrs. Wheeler. You're in your own element out here, you're in control because you never allow yourself to doubt. You are just like my husband, you dream carelessly on, dragging others down with your vision. *(Starts to break.)* Oh dear Jesus. Everytime I needed to lean on him he collapsed in a heap, got sick, cried. And when it finally fell apart, when Eric died, he quoted Thoreau. *Thoreau.* Believing is not enough, Mrs. Wheeler, you can't mend a broken plow with philosophy, and you can't feed a sick child with ideas.
MAW: Now that's where he's right and you're wrong; vision is food for the soul, it's the *dream* that keeps you alive. He's a good man, maybe not strong, but you've no right to make him pay for what's done.
MRS. NICHOLS: Yes I do. Oh yes I do. My baby paid for his dream. Now I am taking him today, to the train at Abilene, and if he dies on the way...then...he dies.
MAW: Why, you're nothing but a savage, Mrs. Nichols. For all your fine manners and fancy words, you're nothing but a vengeful savage. Why, you're so busy trying to get back to civilization, but you ain't even civilized. Well, you can go to hell in a handbasket if you've a mind to, but not with him. *(Blocks doorway.)*
MRS. NICHOLS: *(Seemingly calm again.)* Why is it you cannot let him go, "Maw?" Afraid to lose your captive audience? Well unfortunately, he's my husband and you can't have him. And you can't heal him either, because it's his conscience that's killing him. *(She finds revolver on the table, fondles it, picks it up.)* Now he wants to go with me. Ask him; he owes me that, go ahead and ask him. *(Points gun at* MAW.*)*
MAW: You don't know how to use that. Don't make a fool of yourself.
MRS. NICHOLS: *(*ETTA *starts and frightens* MRS. NICHOLS; *she backs away from them.)* Let me go, just let me go and take him, and no one will be hurt...
SARA: You'll be killing yourself and for no reason, it's not your fault the boy died, but it's not *his*!

ETTA: It's God's will.

MRS. NICHOLS: *(Swinging gun to point at* ETTA.*)* What?! God's will? You people see God in everything; Sara sees his very face in the sky. *(Looks up.)* I do too, but it's not the same God, because the one I see is not making pretty sunsets for my amusement. He's smiling alright, but it's a hungry grin and he's going to swallow me up... He's staring down at me at night with those loveless eyes, watching, and waiting, and I have nowhere to hide, because there is nothing here to hide behind...nothing...nothing... *(Points gun at* SARA.*)* Sara knows. Don't you Sara? Don't you lie awake at night and wonder who will die next? I know you do. Please say it.

SARA: Helene, you're not gonna leave that fear behind you when you go. It's inside of you. It's not Kansas, it's *you*.

MRS. NICHOLS: How many more babies will you bury underneath that tree, Sara?

MAW: *(Moving quietly between the gun and* SARA.*)* Don't listen to her Sara, don't listen...

MRS. NICHOLS: And if they don't die, if they're lucky and they don't die, will they end up like Etta? Half a person with only half a mind? (MAW *slowly and unobtrusively takes the revolver from* MRS. NICHOLS' *hand, as* MRS. NICHOLS *focuses completely on* SARA.*)* You know what I mean; inside you're just like me, Sara, I know you are, you just won't say it. You just won't speak your fear. Now you say it, Sara... Damn you, you *say it*. Someone, please say it?

MAW: Woman, you came here wanting something, I don't know what. A better life? But then you never really believed in it. Building something big will always break your back, and your heart too, from time to time. But there's satisfaction simply in surviving, and pride in living it. Nothing's ever finished out here, you gotta take your pleasure in trying. Life is just the best you can make it wherever you are, that's the only truth I know. What do you want from us? Pity? Tears? Woman, the worst thing I could do for you is to sit and weep with you. That's a luxury neither one of us can afford. It's not that I don't feel the pain, it's just that I don't have the time... I'll say this to you and then I'll say no more. Embrace your fear. Run towards it, not away from it. If you really loved that boy you wouldn't bury his mother with him. You wouldn't let him die for *nothing*. *(Pause.)* Now, go alone or stay, it's the same to me. Come on Sara, we've got work to do.

MAW *and* SARA *exit into house.* ETTA *starts to move, warily behind* MRS. NICHOLS *towards the door.*

MRS. NICHOLS: *(Stopping* ETTA *with the words.)* I'm right Etta, I am. There's no hope. There's no peace here.

ETTA: *(Moves to* MRS. NICHOLS, *puts hands gently on her head.)* No. There's no peace here.

MRS. NICHOLS: *(Laughs involuntarily, not humorously, stops herself, then turns to look at* ETTA. MRS. NICHOLS *gathers up her ropes, halter, and suitcase and walks to the prairie. She stops.)* I'm sorry for you. I'm sorry for all of you.

ETTA: Don't be. (MRS. NICHOLS *exits to prairie;* ETTA *watches her for a moment and then suddenly remembers.)* Thanks for the buttons!

MRS. NICHOLS *does not respond.* ETTA *looks one last time and then exits into the house. Silence, empty stage, lights down.*

APPENDIX

HOUSEWIFE'S LAMENT

Oh life is a toil, and love is a trouble
Beauty will fade and riches will flee
Pleasures they dwindle and prices they double
And nothing is as I would wish it to be.

One day I was walking, I heard a complaining
And saw an old woman the picture of gloom
She gazed at the mud on her doorstep, 'twas rainin'
And this was her song as she wielded her broom

Oh life is a toil, and love is a trouble
Beauty will fade and riches will flee
Pleasures they dwindle and prices they double
And nothing is as I would wish it to be.

Traditional Western Ballad

OLD JOE CLARK

Old Joe Clark is a mean old man
The very first day he was born
He took a rail outta my rail fence
And tore up all my corn

Fare thee well old Joe Clark
Fare thee well I say
Fare thee well old Joe Clark
I'm a going away

The awfulest thing I ever did see
Was two old women fighting
One hollered out, "Now that ain't fair"
The other was a biting

Fare thee well old Joe Clark
Fare thee well I say
Fare thee well old Joe Clark
I'm a going away

Traditional Western Ballad

GOLDEN RING

Golden ring around my Susan girl
Golden ring around my Susan girl
Golden ring around my Susan girl
All the way around my Susan girl

Dosey doe my Susan girl
Dosey doe my Susan girl
Dosey doe my Susan girl
All the way round my Susan girl

All the way home my Susan girl
All the way home my Susan girl
All the way home my Susan girl
All the way round my Susan girl

DEAR COMPANION

I once did have a dear companion
Indeed I called his love my own
Until a black-eyed girl betrayed me
And now he cares no more for me

> Just go and leave me if you want to
> Far from this lonely world I'll flee
> For in your heart you love another
> And in my grave I'd rather be.

Last night you were so sweetly sleeping
Dreaming in some soft repose
While I a poor girl broken-hearted
Was listening to the wind that blows

> Just go and leave me if you want to
> Far from this lonely world I'll flee
> For in your heart you love another
> And in my grave I'd rather be

Traditional Ballad

Factperson
Factwino Meets the Moral Majority
Factwino vs. Armageddonman

San Francisco Mime Troupe

Factperson was first presented on August 9, 1980, in Mission Dolores Park, San Francisco, with the following cast (including cast substitutions made during the summer):

RITA, a waitress, later FACTPERSON	Andrea Snow
A COOK, briefly Rita's employer	Lonnie Ford/Phil Walker
A BAG LADY, later revealed to be the SPIRIT OF INFORMATION	Audrey Smith
Two CUSTOMERS at a diner	Joaquin Aranda, Bruce Barthol
MILTON FRIEDMAN, rightwing economist	Barry Levitan
An unemployment claims INTERVIEWER	Wilma Bonet
Three VICTIMS of unemployment	Paty Silver, Joaquin Aranda, Brian Freeman
An IMMIGRANT	Audrey Smith
Two draft-age YOUTHS	Audrey Smith, Joaquin Aranda
An ULTRALEFTIST	Esteban Oropeza
A third draft-age YOUTH	Lonnie Ford/Phil Walker
MRS. GALLO, Rita's landlady	Wilma Bonet
GEORGE and	Barry Levitan
EDNA, a middle-American couple	Wilma Bonet
An unemployed TEACHER	Joaquin Aranda
CHAIRWOMAN, a rich lady, campaign volunteer for Reagan	Paty Silver
CONNIE, a bar owner	Wilma Bonet
JUDY, a barmaid	Audrey Smith
Two STEELWORKERS	Lonnie Ford/Phil Walker, Joaquin Aranda
A BANDLEADER	Bruce Barthol
A TRUMPET PLAYER	Glenn Appell
A TV DIRECTOR	Audrey Smith
A TV ANNOUNCER	Bruce Barthol
A TV CAMERAPERSON	Paty Silver
A TV PRODUCER	Audrey Smith
LIBRARIAN	Paty Silver

© 1983 by San Francisco Mime Troupe.
CAUTION: All rights strictly reserved. Professionals and amateurs are hereby warned that *Factperson, Factwino Meets the Moral Majority*, and *Factwino vs. Armageddonman* are subject to a royalty. They are protected under the copyright laws of all countries covered by the International Copyright Convention. Permission in writing must be secured before any kind of performance is given. All inquiries should be addressed to the San Francisco Mime Troupe, 855 Treat Street, San Francisco, CA 94110.

Script by Joan Holden, Andrea Snow, Bruce Barthol
Directed by Sharon Lockwood
Musical director, Bruce Barthol
Songs by Andrea Snow *and* Bruce Barthol
Backdrop by Spain
Costumes by Paty Silver *and* Wilma Bonet
Band: Glenn Appell, Bruce Barthol, *and* Barry Levitan

NOTE

Factperson was written to be performed by a cast of ten, including three musicians and a stage manager.

All three plays were performed on a bare stage with a large wooden prop box serving as an adaptable set piece. There was a window in the painted backdrop.

Factperson
San Francisco Mime Troupe

SCENE ONE

A diner. Counter at side, window to kitchen.

COOK: *(Through window.)* Rita. Reeeta. Where is that new girl? *(Enters, sets counter and wipes it.)* What do I hire a waitress for? I knew she'd be late. *(Checks watch.)* Well, she's not late yet. But she's gonna be late. 10:29:58. 10:29:59. 10:30!
RITA: *(Bursts in.)* I made it!
COOK: You're late! *(Shows watch.)*
RITA: Five seconds? But there was an accident—an old man collapsed on the bus.
COOK: What else is new? Change.
RITA: *(Changing coat for apron.)* I wanted to give him artificial respiration—but all I could remember was tourniquets.
FRANK: Just practice first aid on these counters. I gotta revive last week's liver. (Exits.)
RITA: *(Scouring.)* Oh, it was terrible. A person should know these things. I'm gonna take a first aid course. I'll go down and sign up at the Y...
BAG LADY: *(Enters.)* Excuse me, honey, I'm a little down on my luck—you think you could let me have a cup of coffee?
RITA: Sure. *(Pours.)* You know, you look familiar. Wait a minute, weren't you on that bus?
CUSTOMER #1: *(Enters with newspaper.)* I'll take the Special. *(Unfolds paper, reads.)*
RITA: *(To window.)* Special!
COOK: *(Off.)* Special!
RITA: What's the Special?
COOK: *(Appears in window.)* Don't ask. Howard, how are ya?
CUSTOMER #1: Frank, with these headlines? "Prices Soar for Seventeenth Consecutive Quarter."
COOK: And you know who started it, don't you?
CUSTOMER #1: Doesn't everybody?
RITA: I don't. Who?
CUSTOMER #1: It's the damn communist Iranians.

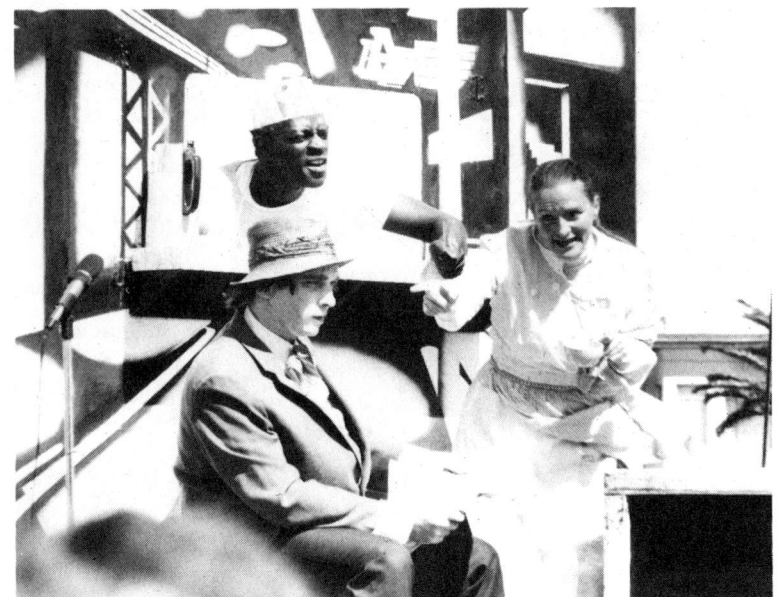

RITA: Wait a minute. Are you sure they're communist?
CUSTOMER #2: Where's my coffee?
COOK: Rita, a Special's with coffee! *(She gets it.)* You got it all wrong, Howard. The Iranians didn't start this inflation. It goes further back.
CUSTOMER #1: The damn communist Arabs.
RITA: Didn't the war in Vietnam have...
COOK: Farther than that even. You remember when they raised the coffee prices? Who started this inflation? It's the god damn Brazilians. *(Exits window.)*
RITA: Hey, wait a minute Frank. Are *they* Communists?
CUSTOMER #2: *(Enters.)* Gimme a frank with fries and a coffee.
RITA: *(Giving him coffee meant for* #1.*)* Uh—hot dog with!
COOK: Hot dog.
CUSTOMER #1: Here's a good one: "37 Illegal Aliens Lost in Desert!"
CUSTOMER #2: That's 37 Americans that won't lose their jobs.
RITA: But don't they do the really bad jobs?
BAG LADY: Honey, you need one more cup of coffee.
RITA: *(Pouring coffee.)* I mean, who'd pick the peaches?
MUSICIAN: *(Offstage.)* Over here! I'll take a coffee!
COOK: Special up! *(Produces it.)*
2ND MUSICIAN: I'll take that Special. (RITA *gives it to him.*)

CUSTOMER #1: Hey, where's my Special? Where's my coffee?

COOK: Rita, a Special's with coffee!

RITA: *(Pours coffee.)* Unemployment. Illegal aliens. Brazilian coffee. It's so confusing. *(Starts to give coffee to* BAG LADY.*)*

BAG LADY: Put it over there. *(*RITA *spills coffee on* CUSTOMER #1.*)*

CUSTOMER #1: Hey!

RITA: *(Wipes him off, sees headline.)* "Chrysler Lays Off 40,000 Workers" 40,000!

CUSTOMER #2: What do you expect, with all these government regulations?

COOK: *(Off.)* Hot dog up!

RITA: *(Giving hot dog to* CUSTOMER #2.*)* Didn't the government just give them a billion dollars?

CUSTOMER #2: What's this? I ordered a frank.

RITA: Right, a frankfurter.

CUSTOMER #2: Frank*burger*, beanbrain!

RITA: Franks, beans, and brains! Maybe it was only a million dollars...

2ND MUSICIAN: Miss, where's my coffee?

CUSTOMER #1: Where's my Special?

BAG LADY: I'll eat that hot dog.

RITA: OK. *(Gives it to her.)*

COOK: *(Appears.)* Frank's brains.

CUSTOMER #1: Where's my Special?

COOK: Where's his Special?

RITA: Over there..

2ND MUSICIAN: A Special's with coffee! *(*RITA *gives* CUSTOMER #1 *the brains and heads for band with the coffee.)*

CUSTOMER #1: What's this? I ordered a Special!

COOK: And they want the ERA.

RITA: Yes!

CUSTOMER #2: Frank, we're missing Milton Friedman on television.

RITA: Milton *Friedman?* You mean that Stone Age economist with the column in Newsweek? I think everything he says is all BULLSHIT! *(A shocked silence.* COOK *enters.)*

COOK: For example?

RITA: For example?...For example, when he talks about free enterprise...I mean, it's just not that way...he leaves a lot out...there's things he doesn't mention...I mean...

COOK: Uh-huh. Out.

RITA: *Out?*

COOK: Out. You can't wait tables, you got no respect for a great mind, and I can't stand a woman who talks dirty.

RITA: But...

COOK *hits window and it becomes TV screen.* MILTON FRIEDMAN *appears, mouthing silently.* RITA *takes coat and exits.* BAG LADY *follows.* COOK *and* CUSTOMERS *listen respectfully to:*

PHOTO: MICHAEL E. BRY

MILTON FRIEDMAN: ...Therefore, to save our economy and our freedom, we must abolish welfare and the minimum wage, phase out social security, stop regulating business, start regulating unions, and subsidize private schoools. *(Program ends.)*
CUSTOMER #1: It's too late for my special—but that was a lot of food for thought. *(Exits.)*
CUSTOMER #2: Frank, what'll it be?
COOK: Also Ran in the third.
CUSTOMER #2: *(Shaking his head.)* Whatever you say, Frank. *(Exits.)*
COOK: That Milton Friedman's a smart man. And think about it—that's the man that's gonna advise the man that's gonna be the next President. *(Exits.)*

Factperson

SCENE TWO

Alley outside the diner.

RITA: *(Enters disconsolate, sings* SOMEDAY.*)*

> I wish I was smarter
> That I had the facts.
> My head turns to Jello,
> My intellect cracks
>
> When I am confronted
> With stupid remarks
> I can't refute them—
> I'm lost in the dark.
>
> I can't argue back
> With jerks like my boss.
> I know he's all wrong!
> Oh, my brain is my cross.
>
> And now look at me:
> I'm out of a job,
> An unemployed waitress
> Whose mind is a blob.
>
> Someday, I'll make them eat their words,
> Someday, I'll rise above the nerds.
> Someday, I'll soar among the birds, up high

BAG LADY *enters upstage.*

> I'll be as smart as Socrates,
> My brain no longer cottage cheese,
> That's me who argues in a squeeze with ease

BAG LADY: *(Joins in.)*

> And when the world's in sad confusion
> That's the time for an infusion
> Of the facts and not illusion, so-o-o-o:

BOTH *sing in counterpoint:*

RITA:	BAG LADY:
Someday, I'll learn some history	Maybe today, you'll get your facts straight
Someday, I'll fight hypocrisy	Maybe today, you'll know the answers

Last line in unison:
RITA: Someday, the sun will shine on me, they'll see—someday.
BAG LADY: Someday, the sun will shine on you, they'll see—someday. *(Music ends.)*

RITA: Who *are* you?
BAG LADY: I am the Spirit of Information. I run Data Headquarters at the big library out there.
RITA: You mean the Main Branch?
SPIRIT: You might call it that. Listen honey, I'm on my lunch break—I get one every century—and your hot dog today was a big disappointment, believe me. Anyway, I only have time enough to grant one wish to one very deserving person. What do you want to know?
RITA: You mean me?
SPIRIT: Rita, it's high time you improved your self-image. I'm here to grant your dearest wish: what do you want to know?
RITA: I want to know every fact there is!
SPIRIT: *(Zaps her.)* Done!
RITA: I don't feel any different.
SPIRIT: What time is it in Ulan Bator?
RITA: 3:45 am, Greenwich Mean Time.
SPIRIT: *(Checks watch.)* Correct!
RITA: What a lucky guess.
SPIRIT: I'll be going. Oh—one more thing: I am the Spirit of Information, not Knowledge or Truth. That sort of thing's up to you. Yours is a power to help others. You misuse it, you lose it. Know what I mean?
RITA: Yes...No.*(Music comes up.)* Wait!

SPIRIT *exits, exchanging zap sign with entranced* RITA.

RITA: Oh, oh—acid flashback! I better be careful or I could space out for good! Down to earth now: right back on the street. Good thing I forgot to cancel my Unemployment appointment.*(Exits.)*

SCENE THREE

The Unemployment Office.

INTERVIEWER: *(Enters in no hurry, makes preparations, calls.)* All 1 pm appointments come to Window P, please.
UNEMPLOYMENT VICTIM #1: *(Enters.)* Miss, I have a 1 pm appointment—and it's now 3:45.

UNEMPLOYMENT VICTIM #2: *(Enters, followed by* RITA.*)* Window C, Window G, Window P—my book says Window A.
RITA: But there isn't any. *(They line up.)*
UNEMPLOYMENT VICTIM #3: *(A crazed man, enters at end of line.)* Your appointment at 1?
RITA: It was.
VICTIM #3: Good. *(Pushes ahead.)* You at 1?
VICTIM #2: You could say.
VICTIM #3: Good. *(Pushes ahead.)* You one too?
VICTIM #1: *(A gay man.)* I beg your pardon? Oh. Yeah.
VICTIM #3: Good. *(Pushes ahead.)*
INTERVIEWER: Does everyone here have a 1 pm appointment?
VICTIM #3: I have an 11 *am* appointment.
INTERVIEWER: If you do not have a 1 pm appointment, please step to the rear of the line.
VICTIM #3: Uh-uh. Not me. I'm wise to that now. I stepped to the rear of every line in the alphabet. The first time, I was early. I been here since ten.
VICTIM #1: Never be early.
INTERVIEWER: This is the 1 o'clock line.
VICTIM #3: I pay taxes!
VICTIM #2: You used to.
VICTIM #3: *(To* INTERVIEWER.*)* My taxes probably put you through college. Now gimme my money!
IMMIGRANT: *(Enters, goes to head of line.)* Excuse me, is this the line for give me a job?
VICTIM #3: A job, huh? Sure, take a job—take all the jobs!
IMMIGRANT: Many thank yous. *(All react with hostility.)* I would like some information.
INTERVIEWER: This is not the information window.
IMMIGRANT: It is the only window open.
INTERVIEWER: It's closed. *(Loudly.)* It is now 4 pm. Please return at 8 am tomorrow.
VICTIM #3: Tomorrow? *(All groan and moan.)* I need money today!
INTERVIEWER: Your check will be mailed when you've completed your interview.
VICTIM #3: Mailed??
VICTIM #1: Look out.
RITA: It's the new system—actually it's a lot easier— *(*INTERVIEWER *puts up "Closed" sign.* VICTIM #3 *knocks it over.)*
VICTIM #3: *(Grabs* IMMIGRANT *with one hand,* INTERVIEWER *with the other.)* I'm an American! *(Fumbles in coat.)* Politicians and

government people robbing us blind—foreigners coming here grabbing up all our jobs—

VICTIM #1: I hate to say it, but he's got a point.

VICTIM #3: *(Pulling gun.)* I don't know who to blow away first.

RITA: *(Rips off her coat. Fanfare. She is* FACTPERSON!*)* How about Raleigh Warner, Jr.?

VICTIM #3: Who the hell is Raleigh Warner, Jr.?

FACTPERSON: Chairman of the board of Mobil Oil Corporation. His salary was one million dollars last year.

VICTIM #3: Where is this guy? I'll blow him away, too.

FACTPERSON: No good, pal, unless you could get rid of all of them. *(Takes gun.)* Because it's those people, and their investment decisions, that cause unemployment—not immigrants. *(Holds* IMMIGRANT*'s hand.)* Where she comes from the average wage is 8¢ an hour. *(Disbelieving response.* IMMIGRANT *nods.)* And government workers aren't taking your money, either. This woman hasn't had a raise in four years.

INTERVIEWER: That's a fact.

Factperson

FACTPERSON: And her work load has doubled.
INTERVIEWER: Twice!
VICTIM #3: What I said before, everybody, forget it—I must have got carried away.
VICTIM #1: Ahh, we all have days like that. *(All shake hands.)*
VICTIM #2: Don't worry about a thing, fella.
VICTIM #3: Tell you what, let me buy everybody a drink. *(VICTIMS #1, #2, IMMIGRANT accept.)* You got $5?
VICTIM #1: Sure. *(VICTIMS #1, #2, IMMIGRANT exeunt.)*
FACTPERSON: If you want to know where your tax money's going, check out the defense budget. *(Gives him gun back.)*
VICTIM #3: And I'm gonna read up on this Raleigh Warner, Jr. *(Exits.)*
RITA: *(Coming down.)* Whoa...
INTERVIEWER: *(Comes out from behind counter.)* Thanks! Where did you learn all those facts?
RITA: I don't know!
INTERVIEWER: That's a really cute cape.
RITA: Cape? *(Discovers it.)* Oh, my God...
INTERVIEWER: *(Reads name on back.)* "Factperson"—is that you?
RITA: "Fatperson?" Oh, no! I just lost fifteen pounds!
INTERVIEWER: "Factperson"—F-A-C-T. You just go around giving people the facts they need?
RITA: I guess so...I think I'll take that drink. *(Gets her coat.)*
INTERVIEWER: Wait—can I come with you? Have you got a little more time to talk? I'd like to get some facts about toxic wastes...*(Follows* RITA *off.)*

SCENE FOUR

The Post Office

Sign appears: Factperson, now understanding her mission, seeks to put her newfound powers to good use.

Sign changes to: Draft Registration Today. *Two* YOUTHS *enter.*

JIMMY: Wait a minute, Rock. I'm too young to die. Let's come back tomorrow.
ROCK: Aw, man, they're gonna get your ass anyway. At least this way, we got a choice. Check out this brochure I got from the recruiting office. We could be artillerymen, man! *(Reads.)* "Range and direction: set. Crew: step back. Fire! The earth

shakes. Thunder rolls from the muzzle of the gun. The shell screams toward the target—direct hit! You hear the..."

JIMMY: Screams of your own men you just blew the shit out of. Cool it, man. We got to think this over. Let's go get fucked up.

ROCK: Ri-i-ight.

ULTRALEFTIST: *(Enters with megaphone.) You brothers being fucked up by the draft?*

JIMMY: Us?

ROCK: I only got a sister.

ULTRALEFTIST: *Conscription is the latest tool in the bosses' arsenal to ensnare workers in the ruthless coils of their war machine.*

ROCK: Where you from, man?

ULTRALEFTIST: Milwaukee. *Smash the draft! Workers of the US and USSR must unite to overthrow superpower HEgemon—heGEmony—ha-choo!*

JIMMY: This vato's from Disneyland.

ULTRALEFTIST: *Strike the death blow to fascist America!*

YOUTHS *grab him.* RITA *enters to mail letter.*

ROCK: Death blow to America?

ULTRALEFTIST: Yeah!

ROCK: That's my country you're talking about. You think you could get away with this in Russia?

ULTRALEFTIST: That's my point...

JIMMY: Hey man, I'm an American.

ULTRALEFTIST: Brothers, refuse to sacrifice yourselves on the altar of corporate profit!

ROCK: I'm gonna sacrifice myself for the hostages, man. America got to get some respect. Well, Jimmy—what's it going to be? *(JIMMY hesitates.)*

ULTRALEFTIST: Don't do it!

JIMMY: Let's sign up.

RITA: This is a job for Factperson! *(Fanfare. She transforms.)*

FACTPERSON: You boys are ready to fight for your country?

ROCK: Damn right—otherwise the Russians are going to take over the whole world!

FACTPERSON: *(Hits center window, map appears.)* Here's the scary map Time Magazine shows us to prove that.

JIMMY: See all that red, man?

ROCK: I saw that in Scholastic Magazine!

FACTPERSON: But here's a map they never show you. *(Map changes.)*

ROCK: What's all that purple? *(Points to China, India, etc.)*

Factperson

FACTPERSON: Places the Soviet camp has *lost* since the late 1950s—representing one third of the world's population.
ULTRALEFTIST: But Soviet social imperialism is still the number one threat!
FACTPERSON: In fact, the main conflict in the world today is between the developed countries, east or west, and third world countries—*(using map)*—that want independence.
JIMMY: Then how come they always say the Russians are coming?
FACTPERSON: Ah HA! *(Map changes.)* American banks and corporations have billions invested in the areas colored green.
ROCK: Hey, they got it covered!
FACTPERSON: And their best-paying investments are in the third world. Now in the 1980s, more and more third world people will try to take back their own countries.
JIMMY: Hey, man—it's already happening. Nicaragua, El Salvador...
FACTPERSON: And our government will use "the Communist threat" as an excuse for military intervention.
ROCK: Ahh, come on.
FACTPERSON: All right—if you do go to war, where to you think they'll send you?
ROCK: Hell, baby—to defend our oil: Iran, Saudi Arabia...
FACTPERSON: Or to prop up police states in Central America.
JIMMY: *(To* ROCK.*)* You trying to get my booty to sign up?

Third youth enters.

JIMMY: What's happening, Sly?
SLY: Gimme some. *(Slap hands and horseplay all around.)* I was just on my way in here to sign my death warrant, man.
JIMMY: Shit man, before you do that, let's take a walk down to my crib, wax my ride, and have a little talk.
SLY: Say what?
ROCK: Say, are you hip to overseas investment?
SLY: Overwhere?
JIMMY: Police states in Centroamerica?
SLY: What you cats talking about?
JIMMY *and* ROCK: We talking about not signing up.
SLY: Hmm. *(They wait.)* I could get to that *(*YOUTHS *exeunt trading zap sign with* FACTPERSON.*)*
ULTRALEFTIST: Gee—you really know how to connect.
FACTPERSON: It's not me—it's the facts. *(Starts putting coat on.)*
MRS. GALLO: *(Enters with big stack of letters.)* Rita, honey!
RITA: Oh, hi Mrs. Gallo. *(To* ULTRALEFTIST.*)* It's my landlady. *(Hurries into coat.)*

MRS. GALLO: I see you got a new outfit.
RITA: Well...
MRS. GALLO: Nice, a young girl should wear the bright colors. But whattaya doing here, I thought you had a new job?
ULTRALEFTIST: She's got a really important job.
MRS. GALLO: Oh yeah? Itsa pay good?
RITA: Oh—Uh—it's very rewarding. Oh, Mrs. Gallo, what's all the letters? Sending out your Christmas cards early or something?
MRS. GALLO: These? Oh, no—all thesea eviction noices.
RITA: Eviction notices?
MRS. GALLO: It's so sad. So many people can't make it today. But I trust you, Rita. Your rent is one month behind, but you are my favorite tenant. *(Whispers.)* I see you got a new boyfriend.
RITA: What, him?
MRS. GALLO: He makes good money?
RITA: Oh, actually...
MRS. GALLO: Oh, you don't have to explain nothing. Don't worry. I was young myself once. Arrivederci, you two. *(Exits.)*
RITA: Arrivederci.
ULTRALEFTIST: *Down with petit-bourgeois landlord reaction! (Chases* MRS. GALLO *with megaphone.)*
RITA: *(Stops him.)* Facts!
ULTRALEFTIST: *(After a split-second hesitation.)* Proposition 13 benefits real estate speculators!
RITA: Cut the megaphone!
ULTRALEFTIST: *(Follows* MRS. GALLO *off.)* Ma'am, do you know how many millions in tax savings went to the biggest landlords as a direct result of...
RITA: I think I'm getting good at this. I know I should be out looking for a job—but there's so much work for Factperson! I've only been doing the easy stuff—schools, welfare offices, bus stops—maybe I'm ready to move into more hostile territory. *(Exits with purpose.)*

SCENE FIVE

A hall north of Market Street. Enter GEORGE *and* EDNA, *furtively.*

EDNA: I don't feel right here, George—please!
GEORGE: I thought it over, Edna. I had to come.
EDNA: So you came. Now let's go before somebody sees us.
GEORGE: There is nothing to be ashamed of.

EDNA: Then how come you're so nervous?
GEORGE: It's a big step. But there's lots of people taking it with us.
TEACHER: *(Also enters furtively.)* You folks here for the same reason I am?
EDNA: We're not *really* here—I mean we haven't decided...
GEORGE: *You* haven't. I've made up my mind—to something big.
EDNA: What does that mean?
RITA: *(Enters.)* Is this "Democrats for Reagan?"
GEORGE: Damn right! *(TEACHER and EDNA nod sheepishly.)*
TEACHER: Are you one of the regulars?
RITA: I saw a poster. I'm checking it out. *(She does.)*
TEACHER: I can understand how your husband feels.
EDNA: We lost our gas station—he's been very depressed. Then he started reading that economist—what's his name? The one who wants to close public schools?
TEACHER: Milton Friedman.
RITA: Milton Friedman?

PHOTO: MICHAEL E. BRY

CHAIRWOMAN: *(Enters.)* Welcome, everybody, to our get-acquainted meeting. I'm thrilled to see so many new faces. If Ronald Reagan were with us tonight, I know he'd be thrilled, too, to see so many Americans willing to stand up and be counted against the Soviet Menace—*(All but* RITA *agree,* EDNA *perfunctorily.)*—Big Government—*(Same reactions.)*—the union shop...*(*TEACHER *agrees.)*
GEORGE: Wait a minute...
CHAIRWOMAN: And the Equal Rights Amendment.
EDNA: I'm leaving. *(Starts off.)*
CHAIRWOMAN: How many of us are worried about—street crime?
EDNA: Maybe I better wait for George.
CHAIRWOMAN: Unemployment?
TEACHER: I'm an unemployed teacher.
CHAIRWOMAN: How many of us are suffering from inflation?
RITA: You mean hot air?
EDNA, GEORGE, TEACHER: I am! It never stops! Me!
CHAIRWOMAN: How many of us have stopped to realize that if this country keeps on bowing to the Russians, we could end our days in the United States of Soviet America?
TEACHER: Oh, my God!
EDNA: Oh, George!
GEORGE: It's all right, honey—I'm here.
RITA: Hogwash!
CHAIRWOMAN: *(Ignoring her.)* Ronald Reagan is the only candidate pledged to double our defense budget, abolish unemployment, and slash the taxes of every American, rich and poor, across the board.
TEACHER: That gets my vote.
EDNA: It sounds as if he can do something.
GEORGE: He's going to put things back the way they're supposed to be.
CHAIRWOMAN: Now, we all know that old myth that calls the Republicans the party of big business—then why is the Reagan campaign being financed mainly by the contributions of little people, like you? So before we settle down to lick envelopes, I'd like to ask all of us to get out our checkbooks...
GEORGE: I'm putting in cash.
EDNA: George...
TEACHER: I lost my job, so I can't give too much. The best I can do is—$75.
GEORGE: I'll beat that.
EDNA: George!

GEORGE: You got to sacrifice for what you believe in. I hereby contribute—$768!
EDNA: Oh, no! Our life savings!

Fanfare. RITA *sheds her coat.*

FACTPERSON: That wouldn't buy two wing nuts for an M-1.
GEORGE: An M-what?
TEACHER: It's Factperson! I've heard about her! She has the facts!
FACTPERSON: An M-1—a supertank the Defense Department spent 8 billion dollars on—so overweight, when they tried it out, it got lost in the mud.
TEACHER: $8 billion?
EDNA: Numbers that big don't mean much.
FACTPERSON: Try a comparison. Cost overruns in the Defense Department for one single year would finance all our public schools for a decade.
CHAIRWOMAN: That spending creates jobs!
FACTPERSON: Defense spending creates fewer jobs per billion dollars than any other form of government spending—but, it creates bigger profits.
GEORGE: What do I care how they spend the money, as long as I get my tax cut?
FACTPERSON: What was your gross income last year?
GEORGE: Don't get personal.
EDNA: Seven thousand.
FACTPERSON: Let's see—that puts you in line for a tax cut of—$75.
GEORGE: *(Disappointed but brave.)* That's $75 I can use.
FACTPERSON: Now if you made $200,000, like our chairperson's husband...
CHAIRWOMAN: Really! This is outrageous! You're just boring everyone with your facts and statistics!
EDNA: I'm not bored.
FACTPERSON: Your tax saving from the Reagan program would be $12,000.
EDNA: Twelve thousand! That's more than we *make*!
CHAIRWOMAN: It's getting late, so if we'll just hand in our pledges... *(Makes for* GEORGE's *contribution.)*
GEORGE: Get your hands off my money, you Gucci bag! Me and my wife are going to take a vacation.
EDNA: Oh, George—after 25 years!
GEORGE *and* EDNA: Thanks, Factperson! *(Exit, with zap signs.)*
EDNA: I like that...

TEACHER: I could still vote for Carter, on account of the Supreme Court, but...or should I vote for Barry Commoner?
FACTPERSON: Do you know what Eugene Debs said when he ran for President? "It's better to vote for what you want, and not get it, than vote for what you don't want, and get it."
TEACHER: How about Nobody for President? All this heavy thinking's hard work—I could really go for a hamburger, what do you think?
FACTPERSON: Great idea! I haven't eaten all...
TEACHER: Thanks, Factperson! *(Exits with zap sign.)*
FACTPERSON: I should have asked the old lady for all the facts, plus a salary. *(Picks up coat and exits.)*

SCENE SIX

A bar in an outlying steeltown.

Sign: The Dire Necessities of Everyday Life Force RITA to Detour from Her Chosen Path.

Enter CONNIE, *the bar owner;* JUDY, *the barmaid;* CHUCK *and* RAMON, STEELWORKERS; BANDLEADER *and* TRUMPET PLAYER.

BANDLEADER: *(Sings.)*

> Welcome to Steeltown
> Welcome to Steeltown
> Welcome to Steeltown, USA
> They're gonna shut the mill down
> They're gonna shut the mill down
> They're gonna shut down Steeltown USA.

Cheerless applause.

BANDLEADER: Well, hey, we want to welcome you now to the last set of the night at Connie's Corner Club. Hey, it's been more than groovy playing here for the last fifteen years for twenty bucks a night. But who's complaining? It's been steady and we want you always to remember that I am Mark Antony and this is the Nihilist. Remember when it was the Nihilis*ts*? Well, hey we had to cut costs—we laid off the guitar player. No good. We're not making it. Connie's not making it. Nobody's making it. You making it, Judy?

JUDY: Nah.
BANDLEADER: It's too heavy.
JUDY: Hit it, guys. *(Sings.)*

> I seem to have a knack
> For picking the wrong locale.
> My first job was at MacDonald's on the Love Canal.
>
> Then I moved to Pennsylvania,
> Got a job on a catering truck.
> I worked at Three Mile Island till the damn thing almost blew up.
>
> My story's not unusual,
> I know I'm not the only one;
> There must be something we should do,
> Something should be done. *(Repeat.)*

CONNIE: *Takes mike.)*
> You know you're not the only one;
> My story's just as sad,
> Put all my hopes into this place, everything I had.
>
> The small guy just can't make it,
> **There's nothing I can do**
> Except to cut my losses,
> Shut the place down and move.

Hands mike to CHUCK, *who starts to sing but can't. Band leaves, offended.*

CHUCK: It's not you guys—I'm too depressed to sing. This scene's too depressing to be a musical. I used to think a steel mill was beautiful—big noise, big heat, big machines. Now all I see's a big slag heap.
JUDY: I don't get it—how come everything in this country's dying? Guess there's nothing I can do but clean out my locker. *(Exits.)*
RAMON: That's it.
CONNIE: What?
RAMON: There's nothing you can do!
CONNIE: Thanks.
RAMON: And there's nothing I can do...But a whole town can do something.
CHUCK: It could take Kool-aid.
RAMON: We could take over the plant. *(They stare at him.)* We could run it.

CONNIE: His mind snapped.
RAMON: Look, this town knows how to make steel, right? *(They allow this is so.)* Steel's important—steel's needed, right?
CHUCK: So?
RAMON: So we could do all right. Right?
CHUCK *and* CONNIE: Wrong!
CHUCK: The experts can't make that plant pay.
RITA: *(Enters.)* Pretty far to go to look for a job—this depression's getting depressing. Hi—are you looking for an experienced waitress?
CONNIE: You came to the wrong place, honey—I'm closing down.
RITA: Oh, no.
CONNIE: This whole town's closing down—cause the union didn't know when to stop.
CHUCK: Now wait a minute...
CONNIE: They kept on grabbing a bigger and bigger piece of the pie—pretty soon, the company couldn't make any profit.
RAMON: Bullshit?
CONNIE: What's bullshit?
CHUCK: What you said about the union. She's got two beers to sell—so she's against unions. The union only asked for a living wage. But foreign steel's cheaper.
CONNIE: On account of the wages.
CHUCK: On account of do-gooders, environmentalists, people that don't care about the working man—that force the companies to spend so much on regulations, they got no capital left to modernize production! Right, Ramon?
RAMON: Bullshit.
CHUCK: What's bullshit.
RAMON: What you're all saying! What the company's saying! What they say on TV! It's all bullshit!
CONNIE: Isn't it terrible? You see that when plants close—mental breakdowns, wife-beating, suicide...
RAMON: What about US Steel's stock, huh? You want to bet they're still paying dividends?
RITA: You're right about that one.
RAMON: Yeah?
RITA: They have capital, but they don't reinvest it in steel. They're putting it in chemicals, minerals, shipping.
CONNIE: Whatever makes money.
RITA: They even bought a shopping center.
CHUCK: That's sick.

CONNIE: What're they supposed to do? Business is business. They gotta put their money where it makes the most profit.

RITA: What if it's overseas?

CONNIE: Now that's different.

RITA: In ten years, American business has multiplied its overseas investment ten times—and a big hunk of that was in foreign steel.

CHUCK: Well—no jobs around here, huh? I better keep moving.

RAMON: Hey Connie, give her a beer.

RITA: Thanks.

RAMON: You're the person I need. Someone who has their facts down, right?

RITA: Oh, no...I...

TV crew bursts in: DIRECTOR, ANNOUNCER, PHOTOGRAPHER.

DIRECTOR: Joe! Let's get some light in here! You people—move over there. No, over here, yeah, we want to see some live action, we want some depression. Let's get some slump in those shoulders. Put some base on the black guy, I can't see him. OK now, look natural—you're on national TV.

CONNIE: National! I gotta say hello to my daughter in Pittsburgh! Hi, honey...

DIRECTOR: OK—5, 4, 3, 2, 1—you're on.

ANNOUNCER: Good evening, America. Unemployment and the specter of depression stalk Steeltown, California this evening. At Connie's Corner Club, pathetic and depressed former steelworkers face grim futures as burdens on the taxpayer. We'll examine their plight on tonight's live edition of *Free to Lose.*

CHUCK: Live!

ANNOUNCER: With revered, best-selling economist, Milton Friedman.

RITA: Milton Friedman!

CONNIE: In my bar!

CHUCK: He'll explain the whole thing.

MILTON FRIEDMAN: *(Enters.)* Unemployed steelworkers. A pitiful sight? *(Workers bristle.)* No—an inspiring picture of the vitality of our economic system. *(Workers slump.)* Only in a free, or capitalist society, are competitive forces led by an invisible hand to restore a healthy balance to a free market.

CONNIE: Healthy for who?

RITA: For the one hundred giant corporations that own half of this country's assets. Free market? When four companies produce all the cars? Eight companies produce three-quarters of the steel? Come on, Milton—who are you kidding?

MILTON FRIEDMAN: *(Aside.)* Who the hell's this?

Fanfare. RITA *rips off her coat.*

CHUCK: It looks like...
CONNIE: It can't be!
RAMON: It is!

ALL THREE: Factperson!
CONNIE: In my bar!
FACTPERSON: I couldn't resist. *(They make a fuss over her.)*
MILTON FRIEDMAN: She's got facts—get her out of here. It says in my contract...
DIRECTOR: There's a story here, Milton—stay in it!
FACTPERSON: That invisible hand you like to talk about, Milton, is the free hand monopolies have to fix prices, transfer capital, and withhold investment. In a free market, when demand slumps, businesses suffer.
CONNIE: You ain't kidding.
FACTPERSON: But in the three recessions this country has suffered since 1970, corporate profits have risen even faster than unemployment.
CHUCK, CONNIE, RAMON: You're kidding.
MILTON FRIEDMAN: *(Crowding* FACTPERSON *off camera.)* This "Factperson" must be pretty short of facts, if she blames monopolies for recession and depression. These crises result from government interference with free and voluntary forces of the market.
FACTPERSON: *(Crowds him.)* In the mid-19th Century, government was still pretty laid back.
MILTON FRIEDMAN: *(Crowds her.)* And our nation enjoyed its greatest period of economic growth.
FACTPERSON: Yet, since the 1850s, the United States has suffered recession or depression on an average of *once in four years.*
RAMON: 1979, 1974, 1970...
FACTPERSON: The fact is, crisis is built into capitalism. It just doesn't work.
ANNOUNCER: *(At a signal from* DIRECTOR.*)* This concludes tonight's segment of *Free to Lose.*
MILTON FRIEDMAN: Let me go! I'm just getting hot. Constant change! Dynamism! Transformation! Growth! Hallmarks of a free society. In an unfree, or socialist system, the government would have kept that inefficient mill running, just to keep these workers employed.
CHUCK: No shit?
MILTON FRIEDMAN: Or assigned them to other jobs...
RAMON: You gotta be kidding.
MILTON FRIEDMAN: Regardless of whether those jobs produced profit. But American workers are free to choose.
CHUCK: What?
MILTON FRIEDMAN: Well—they can go back to school.
RAMON: Back?

MILTON FRIEDMAN: They can use their initiative. They can start a business.

CONNIE: How about keeping one open?

RAMON: Yeah! *(Buttonholes* CONNIE, CHUCK.*)*

ANNOUNCER: This lively episode of *Free to Lose* has been brought to you by big oil, big steel, and the Chubby Group of insurance companies. Join Milton Friedman next week for a visit to: Paradise of Freedom, South Korea.

DIRECTOR: Cut! *(Hustles crew off.)*

MILTON FRIEDMAN: How'd I do? How'd I do?

DIRECTOR: You were great, Milton—great. *(Exeunt.)*

CHUCK: What the hell—we got nothing to lose.

CONNIE: OK, say we take over the plant—you can't run a business without capital.

RAMON: Hey, Factperson—where can we get some loans?

FACTPERSON: *(Finishing beer.)* Well, working people, through their pension plans, now own 25% of all corporate stock... *(Puts coat on.)*

CHUCK: Let's go down to the local.

RAMON: Come on!

CONNIE; I'm gonna see the Mayor, the Chamber of Commerce—I'm even gonna visit our Congressm...Congressperson.

RITA: Wait! You think now you might need a waitress?

JUDY: *(Enters with suitcases, still in tears.)* Did I miss something? I just couldn't stop crying.

CONNIE: Gee, Factperson—maybe if business picks up...Judy, get behind that bar—I'm staying open!

JUDY: All right!

ALL: Thanks, Factperson! *(Exeunt* CONNIE, CHUCK, *and* RAMON, *giving zap sign.)*

RITA: It could work—worker-run industries are making it in different places: there's the South Bend Lathe company in Indiana...Republic Hose in Youngstown, Ohio... *(Phone rings.)*

JUDY: *(Answers.)* Connie...It's for you.

RITA: Me?

JUDY: She says she's your landlady.

RITA: She must have seen me on TV. I bet she was thrilled. Hi, Mrs. Gallo...You did? Well, thanks. Huh? No, no, no. I'm here looking for a job. No. What? No. I know my rent is two months overdue. What? Just a second. You can't do that to me. Wait a minute..."Communist?!" *(A loud "click," then* RITA *hangs up.)*

JUDY: Aw, honey, don't worry about it—you've probably been kicked out of better places. Have a seat and have a beer.

TV PRODUCER: *(Enters.)* Where is she? I've got to find her. *(Checks out* JUDY.*)* You're not her. Oh, don't tell me she left. I had to hire a

helicopter to get here. Where is Factperson?
JUDY: You must mean her. She don't look so fat to me.
RITA: That's FACTperson, FACTPERSON, F-A-C-T!
PRODUCER: That's the voice. *(Checks* RITA *out.)* And I guess that's the face.
RITA: OK. If you're a bill collector, just take me. I'll go quietly.
PRODUCER: Wild sense of humor. Baby, you were fantastic. I am Rhoda Corroda, Channel 15, and I want to put you on TV.
JUDY: TV!
RITA: That's funny. I was just on TV.
PRODUCER: The kid's great! Let me see, now. Year's contract, weekly spot—I can offer you five thousand dollars.
RITA: What a minute: I made six thousand last year. And that's not including tips.
PRODUCER: *Wild* sense of humor. Five thousand dollars a *week.*
RITA: Five thou... *(Faints.)*
JUDY: *(Catches her.)* Honey, honey, look... Hey, lady, how about me. I got a great act. I can sing...
PRODUCER: No time, no time. I got to take the kid to Sassoon. *(Drags* RITA *off.)*
JUDY: You know, some people get all the breaks. *(Exits.)*

SCENE SEVEN

A TV studio. Enter PRODUCER, ANNOUNCER.

ANNOUNCER: It's a coup for you, Rhoda. I hear the sponsors love her.
PRODUCER: They're talking prime time but she doesn't love the sponsors. I thought computers would be perfect—you know, memory banks? "Hewlett Packard made the pineapple bombs they used in Vietnam." "Look, I'll get you baby food. Nestle's." "They're killing infants in Africa." The arguments we had, I thought she'd blow the show.
ANNOUNCER: It'll pass. Would you believe I was like that once?
PRODUCER: Come on!
ANNOUNCER: The kid's doing great. Check her out on the monitor. *(Exits.)*

PRODUCER *opens center window.* FACTPERSON *appears with frozen smile.*

FACTPERSON: And now, a question from a viewer in Modesto. *(Reads.)* "What was Erik Estrada's name before it was Erik, and is it true his marriage is on the rocks?" Enrique, and I don't like to comment on his marriage, but at this moment he is on the beach

with Chris Reeves in Acapulco. Next. *(Reads.)* "Dear Factperson: Disinfectant doesn't get my bathroom bowl white enough. If I switch to bleach, will I get the same germ-killing action?" I always brush with Crest. And last...*(Reads.)* Oh, my God. *(Bravely.)* "Please, Factperson: how big should my penis be? Tiny." Well, Tiny, the average erect penis varies from 4½ to 8½ inches—I can't take any more of this!
ANNOUNCER: *(Breaks in.)* What do *you* want to know? Send your burning questions care of this channel, and be with us next week for *It's a Fact,* starring TV's thrilling new discovery, Factperson: F-A-C-T.

PRODUCER *shuts window.* FACTPERSON *enters disconsolate.*

PRODUCER: Fabulous, baby—fabulous.
RITA: I just can't believe these are the things people want to know.
PRODUCER: Oh, we got some heavy questions, but we had to can them.
FACTPERSON: You *what?*
PRODUCER: Look, people watch TV to blank out, not to hear a lot of depressing facts. And the sponsors certainly wouldn't...
FACTPERSON: Screw the sponsors! I only took this show to give people information they *need.*
PRODUCER: Sure, honey. Here's your check. (FACTPERSON *opens it slowly.*) Look, maybe next week we can get into some more serious stuff—how about nature study? Of course we gotta stay away from ecology...*(Exits.)*
FACTPERSON: *(Stares at her check.)* $5,000 on one piece of paper...I'm going to get something I've always wanted—an apartment on Telegraph Hill! (MAID *enters, mopping.*) And some real copper cooking pans..and a hair dryer...
MAID: Excuse me, miss.
FACTPERSON: Oh, sure, hi...
MAID: I saw your show. It was very interesting.
FACTPERSON: Thanks...and a silk blouse for my mother, and...
MAID: Do you really know every fact there is?
FACTPERSON: Just ask me.
MAID: I need to call my daughter in Louisiana. Do you know what time it is in Bogalusa?
RITA: *(Long pause.)*...That's funny...Ask me another one.
MAID: What was the combined defense budget for 1979?
RITA: ...What's this?...I can't...oh, no! It's you!
SPIRIT: You knew it, you blew it. Know what I mean?
RITA: Yes—but *no*! I didn't think—people need me! Please—give me another chance!
SPIRIT: From now on, Rita, you're on your own. *(Exits.)*

RITA *exits heartbroken.*

EPILOGUE

A library check-out desk.

LIBRARIAN: *(Sets desk, calls backstage.)* The stacks are closing! This library is no longer open evenings. Please check out your books. We close in five minutes.

WOMAN: *(Screams offstage.)* Get out of here, you pervert!

FLASHER *enters, flashing* LIBRARIAN.

LIBRARIAN: I've seen it, thank you. *(FLASHER exits.)*
RITA *enters with enormous pile of books.*

LIBRARIAN: Well, my best customer. So many different subjects—you know you *can't* learn every fact there is.

RITA: I gotta try.

LIBRARIAN: Do you mind if I check out the other people first. *(RITA steps aside.* EDNA *enters, checks out book.)* "The Military-Industrial Complex." How'd you get interested in that?

EDNA: I like to know where my tax dollar's going. Good night *(Exits, giving zap sign.)*

ROCK: *enters with book.*

LIBRARIAN: That's the thickest one yet.

ROCK: "Patterns of Underdevelopment." Dig it, they do it on purpose. See you next week, sister. *(Exits giving zap sign.)*

VICTIM #3: *(Enters, now calm.)* Excuse me, ma'am—I know it's late, and you've had a hard day, but I've been trying to find this book for two weeks. "The Public be Damned," by Raleigh Warner Junior.

LIBRARIAN: That book must have been stolen—you're the third person that's asked for it recently. Come back tomorrow and I'll show you the biographies of some other disgusting millionaires.

VICTIM #3: I'd like that. Thank you—and have a nice evening. *(Exits giving zap sign.)*

LIBRARIAN: So heartening, to know that people really want information.

RITA: Yeah! Listen—I won't take all these now—it seems like other people have a lot of fields covered. I think I want to know—history.

LIBRARIAN: Start with Herodotous. And the Chinese historians. Come on—I shouldn't do this after hours, but—let me show you some wonderful books. Now the Romans are marvelous...*(Exeunt, to stacks.)*

Factwino Meets the Moral Majority was first presented on July 25, 1981, in Mission Dolores Park, San Francisco, with the following cast (including later substitutions):

A LIBRARIAN	Paty Silver/Sharon Lockwood/Melody James
GEORGIANNA, a single mother	Wilma Bonet
Two BOOK BURNERS	Bruce Barthol, Esteban Oropeza
The SPIRIT OF INFORMATION	Audrey Smith
SLEEPY, a street person	Dan Chumley/Chuck Solomon
BUDDY, also a street person	Joaquin Aranda
SEDRO F. WOOLEY, his longtime companion	Shabaka
A FUNDAMENTALIST	Esteban Oropeza
A NURSE	Brian Freeman
DELA, a young woman in trouble	Audrey Smith
JIMMY, her boyfriend, the cause of her trouble	Dan Chumley
RIGHT-TO-LIFER	Paty Silver/Sharon Lockwood/Melody James
EDNA, a convert	Wilma Bonet
GEORGE, her husband	Dan Chumley
REV. BEN KINCHLOW	Audrey Smith
Members of the Moral Majority	Paty Silver, Brian Freeman, Esteban Oropeza
ROBOT, a smart machine	Wilma Bonet
ARMAGEDDONMAN	Dan Chumley, Bruce Barthol
DICK, a bar owner	Bruce Barthol
BARNEY, a hedonist	Brian Freeman
CLYDE, an activist	Esteban Oropeza
Some working MUSICIANS	Glenn Appell, Bruce Barthol, Stephen Herrick, Craig Knudsen, Paty Silver/Sharon Lockwood/Melody James
JERRY FALWELL	Dan Chumley
A TV CREW	Paty Silver/Sharon Lockwood/Melody James, Stephen Herrick

Script by Joan Holden *with* Brian Freeman, Tede Matthews, Peter Solomon, *and* Henry Piccioto
Directed by Sharon Lockwood
Musical director, Bruce Barthol
Songs by Bruce Barthol
Costumes by Paty Silver, Wilma Bonet, *and* Nora Long
Band: Glenn Appell, Bruce Barthol, Al Guzrian, Stephen Herrick, Craig Knudsen, *and* Muziki (Duane Roberson)

Note: A cast of eleven played all roles.

Factwino Meets the Moral Majority

San Francisco Mime Troupe

A sign appears from behind the curtain: A year has passed since the SPIRIT OF INFORMATION visited our planet to save a nation threatened by a rising tide of ERROR.

The sign changes to: The SPIRIT chose a champion and endowed her with the power of knowing EVERY FACT THERE IS. But FACTPERSON misused her gift—and lost it. The rest is history.

The sign changes again to: After the Budget Cuts...

SCENE ONE

LIBRARIAN: *(Enters, sets box as counter, calls to stacks.)* Please check out your books. Library hours have been shortened. Closing time is now 1 pm.
GEORGIANNA: *(Enters.)* Can you recommend a book...where it talks about...on abortion?
LIBRARIAN: We're closing. Come back tom...go on in. Sex Education, shelf B12. I'd look at *Our Bodies, Ourselves.* *(GEORGIANNA hurries off.)* And we've also got Pope John's Encyclicals.

MAN *enters with large stack of books.*

LIBRARIAN: Oh, my best customer—This is your third visit today. How do you read so many books so fast?
MAN: Uhhh...Evelyn Woods.
LIBRARIAN: Wait a minute—it says here you've got 2,200 books overdue.
MAN: Must be some mistake.

SECOND WEIRDO *enters with large stacks of books.* LIBRARIAN *pulls slips and stamps furiously.*

LIBRARIAN: With all the cutbacks and layoffs, there's no way to keep up with the paperwork. The *Joy of Sex*—tell me about it—*The Origin of Species?*—Picasso's *Nudes*—they're wonderful, aren't

they?—*Women Loving Women*—hmmm—*(Ends with paper flying everywhere.)* I'm not really complaining—I'm so glad people still want to read.

MAN: We'll be back next week to check out history. *(Exits.)*

GEORGIANNA: *(Enters with a book.)* If this is supposed to be a joke, it's not funny.

LIBRARIAN: The Bible?

GEORGIANNA: That's the only book on the whole shelf. It's also the only book under Science. I *have* a Bible—and it hasn't helped me. Right now I need information! *(Exits.)*
LIBRARIAN: All those books gone—the Bible—oh no! I didn't think it could happen here! Who's going to save knowledge? Help! Oh, who am I calling for? Nobody works here anymore but me.
OLD LADY: *(Enters with book.)* Excuse me, honey, I was putting in a little overtime on the top floor when I heard a voice calling for help.
LIBRARIAN: Intelligence is in terrible danger! It's the Moral Majority—they're clearing out every book they don't like. Pretty soon there'll be nothing left on the shelf. It seems as though ignorance has been on the march ever since Factperson left.
OLD LADY: Factperson? Who's he?
LIBRARIAN: She. I keep her picture. She knew everything. But the best part was, she made people want to know—just the opposite of the Moral Majority. Then she disappeared—dropped out, I guess, like so many people.
OLD LADY: I fired her.
LIBRARIAN: What?
OLD LADY: She broke the contract.
LIBRARIAN: Contract? Hey—you said you were on overtime.
OLD LADY: It's a rough century.
LIBRARIAN: Cen...and we don't have a top floor! Wait a minute—who are you?
OLD LADY: I am the Spirit of Information. I run General Reference at the Big Library out there.
LIBRARIAN: You mean...the Main Branch?
SPIRIT: That's right.
LIBRARIAN: Then you *do* exist—just like they taught us in Library School. Thank God you've come—I was beginning to despair.
SPIRIT: Despair is the enemy of light.
LIBRARIAN: I'll be brave—if you'll stay with us now.
SPIRIT: Stay on one insignificant planet?
LIBRARIAN: Of course you can't—then bring Factperson back.
SPIRIT: She knew it, she blew it.
LIBRARIAN: But we really need someone like that—someone who can inspire people, make people think.
SPIRIT: I guess I got my work cut out. Hold the fort, honey. Help is on the way. *(Exeunt.)*

Sign: Where Will the Spirit Find Another Lover of Truth?

SCENE TWO

Wino Park on Sixth Street, that evening. SLEEPY, *a silent wino, enters, stretches out.*

Offstage, hymn singing turns to argument, which grows louder. SEDRO *and* BUDDY *are kicked on stage.*

SEDRO: Yeah? Yeah, you holy all right—you *full* of holes. You talk about saving people, ignorant as you is, you couldn't even save your ass from a hemorrhoid!

BUDDY: How come you can't just keep your mouth shut and eat? That's the third rescue mission we been kicked out of this week. I didn't even get to finish my jello.

SEDRO: Try to pose a few philosophical questions—what you gonna do with people that's only read one book? "The Bible—the only true word of God." What about the *Koran,* man? What about the *Bhagavad-Gita?*

BUDDY: What about some Ripple?

SEDRO: Good idea. Nobody fucks with my mind but me *(Bottle is empty.)*

SPIRIT *enters with flashlight, tired and discouraged. Sees winos and shakes her head. Sits.*

BUDDY: Come on, partner, we gotta fix you up. You get too sober, you start thinking about Cleveland.

SEDRO: I don't wanna think about that.

FUNDAMENTALIST: *(Enters.)* Could I ask you gentlemen a few questions? I'm a college student. We're conducting a nationwide poll.

BUDDY: Welcome to the university of the streets. My friend here, Sedro F. Wooley, knows everything. *(*SPIRIT *gets interested.)* How much you want to pay?

SEDRO: Shame on you, man here is looking for information.

BUDDY: You tell 'im, Sedro. I'm gonna go look for some change. *(Exits.)*

SEDRO: A poll, huh? This the first time I been consulted. What is it you want to know?

FUNDAMENTALIST: Do you believe in the atheistic theory of evolution that denies God and reduces man to the level of an ape?

SEDRO: Where you say you go to college?

FUNDAMENTALIST: Reliable Bible Institute in Throwback, Virginia. Our school protects us from the confusing ideas that throw many youth today into doubt.

Factwino Meets the Moral Majority

PHOTO: RON BLANCHETTE

SEDRO: Did you know your arm is made the same as a salamander's?

FUNDAMENTALIST: It is?

SEDRO: When you were in your mama's belly, you had gills like a fish.

FUNDAMENTALIST: What would that mean?

SEDRO: Meditate for a moment on the fact that your blood has precisely the same mineral composition as sea water.

FUNDAMENTALIST: Salty?

SEDRO: Right. I don't *believe* in evolution...

FUNDAMENTALIST: Oh, good. *(Marks it down.)* "No."

SEDRO: Because it's only a theory. But I accept it, 'cause it's the best theory we got. Now...

FUNDAMENTALIST: Next question: Do you believe that licensed and practicing homosexuals have a right to preach perversion in our public schools?

SEDRO: Look here: I don't believe anybody has a right to impose their trip on anybody.

FUNDAMENTALIST: "No" again! Brother, this poll is going to prove that a majority of Americans think just like we do.

SEDRO: We who?

FUNDAMENTALIST: All of us who are joining Jerry Falwell's Christian Crusade.

SEDRO: Jerry *Fal*well? That mealy-mouthed preacher who invented the medieval-minded Moral Majority? Man want to make ignorance the national religion?

FUNDAMENTALIST: He's already converted most of the Congress. And this summer, Brother Jerry's bringing his Crusade here, to the heart of Sodom.
SEDRO: San Francisco?
FUNDAMENTALIST: You can help him clean up your city. Report any public figure you know to be an atheist, communist, feminist, homosexual, or secular humanist. *(Ready with pencil.)*
SEDRO: You talking to a secular humanist, junior. Tradition of Epicurus, Erasmus, Thomas Paine, and Mark Twain.
FUNDAMENTALIST: Who?
SEDRO: Get out of my face.
FUNDAMENTALIST: That's all right, brother—Jesus loves you, whether you like it or not.
SPIRIT: *(Steps between the two.)* You better run, son. I just saw Jesus on Fifth and Market!
FUNDAMENTALIST: He's come to join our crusade! Or could it be the end of the world? *(Exits.)*

SEDRO: *(Sings.)*
    Jesus, they're using your name again,
    To sanctify their means and ends,
    The Inquisition is here again,
    And they're doing it in your name.

    Books and witches to the flames,
    Bless the missiles, bombs, and planes,
    The armies of night are drawing near,
    The armies of the night are drawing near.

    I'd stand and fight but not alone,
    People just don't want to know.
    I'll ease my pain and ease my mind
    And lose it all in rotgut wine.

SPIRIT: *(Approaches.)* Excuse me, mister. I been sitting here worrying... how much is the defense budget for 1981?
SEDRO: $700 million a *day*. Say, did you see my buddy? He's a little guy, about...
SPIRIT: I got to call my daughter in Tanzania. Do you know what time it is in Dar-es-Salaam?
SEDRO: Twelve hours later than it is here. *(Aside.)* Woman's crazy. *(To Spirit.)* Be seeing you.
SPIRIT: Seems like you already know every fact there is.

SEDRO: *(Sings.)*   What good is knowledge or the facts?
SPIRIT: *(Sings.)*   If you know then you must act.
    The armies of the night are drawing near.
    People have got to hear the warning.
SEDRO: People don't want to know.
SPIRIT: You can see the storm clouds forming.
SEDRO: I've seen it all before.
SPIRIT: The armies of the night are drawing near.
SPIRIT *and* SEDRO: The armies of the night are drawing near.
    The armies of the night are drawing near.

SEDRO: If you was my fairy godmother, I'd only ask for one wish.
SPIRIT: Shoot.
SEDRO: Give me a way to make people think.
SPIRIT: *(Zaps him.)* You got it.
SEDRO: What was that?
SPIRIT: You know your mission.
SEDRO: I do?
SPIRIT: You know it's dangerous.
SEDRO: It is?
SPIRIT: You've got the power. But remember: if you booze it, you lose it. You know what I mean? *(Exits.)*
SEDRO: Shit! "If you booze it, you lose it." Women always want to get in somebody's business. *(Calls offstage.)* Buddy! I need a drink. *(Exits.)*

Sign: When will FACTWINO discover his power?

SCENE THREE

NURSE *enters, sets scene.*

Sign: Early the next morning, at a South of Market Clinic.

NURSE: Please have a seat and wait for your name to be called. *(Exits.)*

DELA *and* JIMMY *enter.*

JIMMY: See you later, baby. Give me a call when it's over.
DELA: You mean you ain't gonna stay?
JIMMY: Hey, baby, this is women's business, know what I mean?
DELA: Yeah...you mean you don't want to deal with it.
JIMMY: Hey, who fixed it up so you could stay at my sister's house? Who got you here at five o'clock this morning?
DELA: Who got me here period? "Oh, Dela, baby, I can't stand it. Ooh, it hurts so bad. Prove you love me. I'm a *man,* Dela! I need you!" And then, "Nothing ain't gonna happen if you wash with lemon juice."
JIMMY: It ain't my fault, my brother said it would work. Anyway, Dela, I don't like what you're doing.
DELA: Me!
JIMMY: It ain't nothing but murder, baby. And it's on your conscience because I told you I would support my child.
DELA: Off of stolen TVs? (GEORGIANNA *enters.*) You can't support your habit!
JIMMY: Be cool, Dela, there's people here. Call me when you got a smile for me. *(Exits.)*
DELA: I don't even like him.
GEORGIANNA: Is this your first...? I mean are you...? Uh...
DELA: Uh huh.
GEORGIANNA: *(Suddenly noticing.)* How old are you?
DELA: I'm sixteen. My father'd kick my natural ass if he found out.
GEORGIANNA: My parents are back in Iowa. They haven't spoken to me since I got divorced. My brother's here somewhere...but how could I tell *him?*
RIGHT-TO-LIFER: *(Enters.)* Good morning. Have you girls thought about your choice?
GEORGIANNA: Have I *thought* about it? I haven't slept in two weeks!
RIGHT-TO-LIFER: Will you be able to sleep tonight?
DELA: Who are you?
RIGHT-TO-LIFER: I'm a counselor.
GEORGIANNA: Thank God! Help me decide!

RIGHT-TO-LIFER: Decide to kill your innocent baby?
DELA: It's not a baby yet. I want to finish school!
RIGHT-TO-LIFER: You wouldn't be in this mess if we had prayer in schools instead of sex education.
GEORGIANNA: My baby's three. This is an accident.
RIGHT-TO-LIFER: You had your fun but you don't want to pay for it.
DELA: Who had fun?
GEORGIANNA: Please. I just got a job. I get up at 5:30 every day with Miranda. 7:30, I drop her off. We don't get home till 6:00. I bring home two hundred dollars; fifty goes to the sitter. How could I double that? How could I take care of two, when I barely got time to love one? I'd have to go back on welfare.
RIGHT-TO-LIFER: Which is it going to be? This? *(Shows picture.)*
DELA: Aw-ww-w.
GEORGIANNA: What a cute baby!
RIGHT-TO-LIFER: Or *this? (Shows second picture.)*
DELA: Yuk! Don't make me look at that!
GEORGIANNA: Oh, no! I can't stand it!

All freeze as BUDDY *and* SEDRO *enter.*

BUDDY: I knew it was around here someplace. Worked the street all night, made forty-seven cents. This place pays twenty dollars. You even get a glass of orange juice.
SEDRO: Hold it, partner. Something tells me this ain't the blood bank.
DELA: I can't do it! I guess this means I gotta marry Jimmy. Maybe it won't be so bad. At least we'll always have a TV.
GEORGIANNA: Thank you. Now I know what I'm going to do.
RIGHT-TO-LIFER: Quit your job, raise your two babies, and pray some nice man will marry you in spite of your past.
GEORGIANNA: No...go back to the sitter's, pick up Miranda, and throw both of us off the Golden Gate Bridge!
DELA: No!
RIGHT-TO-LIFER: See why we need an anti-abortion amendment? If there were a law against it, you wouldn't have to choose.

SEDRO *rips off his coat. He is* FACTWINO. *He zaps her.*

RIGHT-TO-LIFER: And neither would a twelve-year-old girl who'd been raped. Senators and congressmen would make the choice for her.

SEDRO *is astonished.*

GEORGIANNA *and* DELA: Wait a minute.
RIGHT-TO-LIFER: Of course there'll always be the illegal options...backstreet butchers, coat hangers. Can laws stop abortion or just make it dangerous?
GEORGIANNA: Whatever got you thinking like that?
RIGHT-TO-LIFER: I don't know...my brain started buzzing, and suddenly everything seems so complicated.

FACTWINO *stares, amazed.*

GEORGIANNA *and* DELA: Really. *(Three women sit, confer excitedly.)*
RIGHT-TO-LIFER: How many so-called "Right-to-Life" congressmen voted for all those deadly nuclear weapons?
NURSE: *(Enters.)* Dela Jimenez? (DELA *stands.*) Child, you got in under the wire. The Moral Majority is trying to get a new law passed...if it goes through, we'd have had to notify your parents.
DELA: Whoa! I want to be a mother...in about fifteen years.
RIGHT-TO-LIFER: You're making the right choice. (DELA *goes inside.*) Well, it is her right to choose.
NURSE: Georgianna Strumpf?
GEORGIANNA: Do I have a right to my life with Miranda?
RIGHT-TO-LIFER: Aren't your lives human lives? (GEORGIANNA *goes in.*) What about the right to a *decent* life?
NURSE: Uh, if you're here for counseling (RIGHT-TO-LIFER *discovers* SEDRO *and* BUDDY.), that starts at 10:00, after VD. *(Exits.)*

BUDDY: Sedro...
FACTWINO: You know, it's a funny thing about abortion laws...there wasn't any until the late nineteenth century. Not even in the Catholic Church.
RIGHT-TO-LIFER: Really?
BUDDY: Sedro!
FACTWINO: And another funny thing: those laws were passed in reaction to a worldwide women's rights movement.
RIGHT-TO-LIFER: Women's rights? Maybe I'll go to that rally this afternoon and agitate for the ERA. Hmmm.
FACTWINO: What rally's that?
RIGHT-TO-LIFER: The big one...the kick-off rally for the Christian Crusade.
BUDDY: Say, lady, you got fifty cents?
RIGHT-TO-LIFER: Certainly. *(Gives him money.)* Take my advice though, you wouldn't want to go in those clothes. *(Exits.)*
FACTWINO: *What?*
BUDDY: What are you staring at? You the one that looks ridiculous. Like those shorts, though. *(Reads the back of cape.)* "Factperson?" You got to advertise it?
FACTWINO: Holy shit.
BUDDY: Dancing around, messing in women's business...you embarrassing. Anyway, we got ninety-seven cents. Let's go buy some wine.
FACTWINO: Come on! I really need a...*(Stops.)* Buddy, I can't drink!
BUDDY: What's wrong, Sedro? What's gotten into you?
FACTWINO: The power!...Wait—did she say something about a rally? *(Exeunt.)*

SCENE FOUR

Sign: Later, on the steps of City Hall.

GEORGE *and* EDNA *enter.*

GEORGE: Edna, there ain't nothing here but bums and fountains. I'm going back to the camper.
EDNA: You'll do no such thing, George. We're going to do what we promised.
GEORGE: What *you* promised. I'm not going to parade *my*self in any born-again ballyhoo. You know, you're not the same person, Edna, since you started watching all those evangelists on TV.
EDNA: I've seen the light, George. I've found out what's wrong with America.

GEORGE: You didn't even look at America. We been in thirty-five cities and fourteen national parks, and all you want to do is sit in the RV and wait for the "700 Club."

EDNA: All right, George. You won't do this for the Lord. And you won't do it for me. But maybe, just maybe, you'll do it for the children.

GEORGE: The children! Our kids are quitters, Edna. I wouldn't give either of 'em the time of day.

EDNA: You never did give 'em much time.

GEORGE: Oh, yeah? Who bought all Georgianna's Rainbow Girl dresses?

EDNA: Because you never let me get a job!

GEORGE: Who worked two jobs and still took Clyde to Pop Warner's Football League?

EDNA: He hated football!

GEORGE: Because you mothered him half to death!

EDNA: Stop it, George. There's people watching.

Music off-stage.

GEORGE: Oh, shit.

EDNA: Feel the spirit, George! Go with it!

REVEREND *and* FUNDAMENTALISTS *march on-stage singing* THE ARMY OF THE RIGHTEOUS:

> We're the armies of the righteous
> We're marching with the Lord
> We're the armies of the righteous
> We're marching off to war.
>
> If you disagree with us
> It's not just that you're wrong
> But you'll burn in Hell forever
> While we sing celestial songs.
>
> We're the armies of the righteous
> We're marching with the Lord
> We're the armies of the righteous
> We're marching off to war.

REVEREND: Thank you, thank you. Welcome to the kick-off rally for our great Save the Family Crusade. *(Cheers.)* Brother Jerry can't be with us just yet, he's *(Ad libs from headline of the day.)* But we're here to talk about love. We love! We love old people, that's

Factwino Meets the Moral Majority

why we want Social Security cut, so more old folks can move in with their children. We love the home, home the way the Lord intended it. That's why we want Mom in the kitchen, not standing in line at a unisex toilet.

CHORUS: Amen!

REVEREND: We love!

CHORUS: Love!

REVEREND: We are filled with love!

CHORUS: We're full of it!

REVEREND: We're here today, friends, in the very bowels of Gomorrah by the Bay. We are here to declare war on the enemies of love. Our forces will be felt in every classroom, every Planned Parenthood center, every pervert resort. We are going to root out those strangers, those foreign elements, those alien ideas that are eating the bud of family life like the medfly. Family life...

EDNA: Go on, George.

GEORGE: You do it.

EDNA: But George, I'm a woman.

GEORGE: I'll lend you my hat. *(EDNA pushes GEORGE.)* Uh, well, uh, uh...

REVEREND: Come forward, friend. Tell your story.

GEORGE: *(Takes out photo.)* This is a picture of our family. Our children. We gave them everything. Georgianna left first; she married right out of high school.

EDNA: It was an all-white wedding.

GEORGE: They came out West someplace...then she up and left the guy, six months after she married him. Like to broke her mother's heart. Naturally, I had to disown her. This is my boy, Clyde. I pinned all my hopes on him...then he quit college halfway through! Said he'd rather die than live in Iowa!

BUDDY *and* FACTWINO *enter; others freeze.*

BUDDY: Is this one of them anti-nukular rallies? We won't get a penny out of them.

FACTWINO: No, these people are pros. Pro-horseshit, I believe. Mmm, I have work to do.

REVEREND: Now *why* did such misfortune come to your home?

GEORGE: That's what I don't understand.

EDNA: Our family was destroyed by atheistic, communistic school-teachers!

REVEREND: Now you're talking.

EDNA: By immoral TV programs.

REVEREND: I hear you.
EDNA: By government interference!
REVEREND: Tell it!
EDNA: And lured away by the false glitter of hot tubs and narcotics. (FACTWINO *can't stand it. He zaps her.*) Wait a minute...Do you think the economy might have something to do with it?
ALL: *What?*
EDNA: I mean, the family farm, like we grew up on, that's gone...and the factory jobs are all drying up...new jobs, they're for women, I guess 'cause we're cheaper—could these things be affecting the family?
REVEREND: No way.
GEORGE: Yeah—what kind of future would Clyde have in Iowa?
EDNA: Where were you supposed to find time for the kids? I mean, how many families can make it on one paycheck?
FACTWINO: Not many. Only seventeen percent of US households have a mama who stays home while papa goes off to work.
GEORGE: Who's the weirdo in the outfit?
EDNA: This is San Francisco, George. (*To* FACTWINO.) What do you think, mister—is immorality destroying the economy or is it the other way around?

FACTWINO: Well, I know a very smart man once wrote, "Every age, every state of economic development invents the ideology it requires..." *(Aside.)* Was that Marx or Lenin?
GEORGE: What kind of economy requires a Moral Majority?
FACTWINO: Good question! You know who said that children, church, and kitchen were the only legitimate concerns of women?
GEORGE: Jerry Falwell!
FACTWINO: Adolf Hitler.
GEORGE: Whoa. It's all coming together, you know what I mean? Edna, if we ever hear from our kids, we got a lot of things to talk about.
EDNA: What do you mean *if*? Let's get busy and find 'em.
GEORGE: How're we going to do that? They could be any place.
EDNA: You know what it says in the Bible, George.
GEORGE: That again?
EDNA: "Seek and ye shall find."
EDNA and GEORGE: *(To* FACTWINO.*)* Thanks, mister. *(Exeunt.)*
REVEREND: Wait a minute! Brother, you are possessed by Satan.
   (FACTWINO *zaps him.* REVEREND *begins singing* "THE ZAP RAP.")
     Am I really knocking at Heaven's door
     When I serve the rich and milk the poor?

FACTWINO: Well, devil's sure to toast your ass
If you keep working for the ruling class.

CHORUS: Hey! What is this? *(FACTWINO zaps them.)*
We've been told by Brother Jerry
Questions are unnecessary

FACTWINO: If you don't ask questions, and afraid to doubt
Your head shrinks, and your mind strikes out.

CHORUS: That's right!
FACTWINO: That's right!
CHORUS: That's right!
FACTWINO: That's right!

Everybody knows now's the time
To turn on the lights for the hopeless blind.
Use your mind
Use your eyes
Don't listen to that mindless jive.
Be free!

CHORUS: Free!

FACTWINO: And drop your chains.
Get smart.

CHORUS: Smart!

FACTWINO: And grow some brains.
Be free!

CHORUS *exits, clapping and rapping.*

BUDDY: You had 'em all softened up. We could have scored, man.
FACTWINO: Buddy, we scored. But that was just the preliminary bout. I'm looking for the main event. Where's Falwell?
BUDDY: You know, you smell funny.
FACTWINO: What do you mean? I haven't had a drop in over twenty-four hours.
BUDDY: That's what I mean.
FACTWINO: But while I wait on him to show, we can hit some politicians' press conferences...school board meetings...
BUDDY: How 'bout hitting the bottle?
FACTWINO: Can't do it, Buddy. Some radio stations...
BUDDY: "Factperson" can't have any fun?

FACTWINO: You don't understand, Buddy. You see, I'm a man with a mission.
BUDDY: I understand you ain't got time for your old Buddy. Now are you going to come with me and score some wine?
FACTWINO: Guess this is where we part company, partner. Because if I booze it, I lose it.
BUDDY: Well, you just lost me. *(Exits.)*
FACTWINO: Wait—he just don't understand. I've got to fix Falwell—I got to fix him. And then, I got to figure out how he fits in. *(Exits.)*

Sign: A big order for our teetotalling titan—bigger than he knows.

SCENE FIVE

ROBOT *enters, sets scene.*

Sign: In a Secret Shelter Underneath the Potomac...

ARMAGEDDONMAN *enters. He has two heads, whom we shall call* BUSINESS *and* WAR.

BUSINESS: Earth and her inhabitants, surrender your riches to me!
WAR: Let humanity cower in fright, puny insects before my boundless power. I command the most lethal war machine in history. See this button? With this button *(Reaches for it.)* I can destroy the whole world.
BUSINESS: *(Stopping him.)* Not yet—I'm not done with it.
WAR: Okay, Okay. But I am invincible.
BUSINESS: It helps to have a friend in the White House.

ROBOT *enters with drinks.*

WAR: To the president!
BUSINESS: To the people who make it all possible!
WAR: You mean the fifty percent who don't vote?
BUSINESS: I mean our shock troops, our little soldiers of God, who fight our battles at election time. If they didn't exist, we'd have to invent them.
WAR: Ah, yes: to the Moral Majority! *(They both laugh, drink, and then sing* ARMAGEDDONMAN.*)*

> There is less but we want more
> So we take it from the poor
> You can't stop us, no one can
> Call us Armageddonman.

PHOTO: MICHAEL E. BRY

In the water, in the air
Our poison's everywhere
You can't stand us, no one can
Because we're Armageddonman.

Karl Marx predicted our demise
But it's on crises that we thrive
Find a new market or a war will do
We'll see our historic mission through

Even though our race is almost run
When we are through, you'll all be done
What we don't use up, we'll blow away
On that Armageddon Day.

Round the world we're number one
We'll win the war that can't be won
You won't survive, no one can
Thanks to Armageddonman.
Thanks to Armageddonman.
Thanks to Armageddonman.

BUSINESS: Enough partying. There's a planet to suck dry. *(Computer alarm.)* What the...
ROBOT: Danger Detection System Early Warning Emergency Alarm.
BUSINESS *and* WAR: It's the Danger Detection System Early Warning Emergency Alarm.
WAR: Armageddon is here! *(Reaches for the doomsday button.)*
BUSINESS: Don't do it! *(To* ROBOT.*)* Request more information.
ROBOT: Danger Detection System Report. Place: San Francisco. Nature of emergency: major setback for New Right.
WAR: Why can't it ever be the Russians!
BUSINESS: *(To* ROBOT.*)* More information!
ROBOT: Factperson II turns Moral Majority demonstration into pro-choice, pro-ERA parade.
WAR: Let's nuke the bastard.
BUSINESS: Who is this Factperson?
ROBOT: Described as elderly Negro in comic-book outfit, possessed of mysterious ability to make people think.
BUSINESS: *Think!* Shit.
WAR: Let's kill him.
BUSINESS: No. Give 'em something to think *about*. *(To* ROBOT.*)* Get hold of Jerry. We'll set this Factperson's facts straight.
WAR: Then we'll kill him. *(Exeunt.)*

SCENE SIX

SLEEPY *enters, sets scene, reclines.*

Sign: Unaware he is the object of a sinister search, FACTWINO continues to pile triumph on triumph, giving no thought to SECURITY—

Sign: or to the BUDDY he has left behind. Soon, on Sixth Street...

BUDDY *enters tanked and tearful and shakes sleeping wino.*

BUDDY: How many years? How many cold nights I found him a newspaper? How many foggy mornings I made us a fire? Now he tosses me away like an empty bottle. Let's drink to friendship. *(Bottle is empty.)*
ROBOT: *(Enters.)* Good evening.
BUDDY: Good e... *(Aside.)* Jesus Christ! *(To* ROBOT.*)* Say—you got a quarter?
ROBOT: Here is five dollars.
BUDDY: Five dollars! Whoo! Hey, you're beautiful! *(Leaving.)*
ROBOT: Let's talk.
BUDDY: Uh, I'd like that—but I gotta get something at the store.
ROBOT: I have wine. (SLEEPY *wakes up as* ROBOT *produces bottle.)* Let's have a party.
BUDDY: Hmmm. "Chateau Rothschild 1976." You ever taste Annie Green Springs? *(Drinks, chokes.)* No offense, I like sweet wine. (SLEEPY *has bottle, chug-a-lugs.)* Hey! She give it to me! *(Grabs bottle back.* SLEEPY *goes back to sleep.* BUDDY *drinks throughout the following.)*
ROBOT: Where is your friend, Factperson?
BUDDY: I don't have a friend! The son of a bitch.
ROBOT: Why has he abandoned you?
BUDDY: I don't want to talk about it. You know what he told me?
ROBOT: What did he tell you?
BUDDY: You know, you're all right. At first I thought you was kinda hard looking.
ROBOT: What did he tell you?
BUDDY: The worst part is, I understand him. You know why? 'Cause I'm the only one that knows about Cleveland.
ROBOT: Cleveland? Recording—beep.
BUDDY: Let it *all* hang out! He keeps it secret. You see, he was The Rapper.

ROBOT: The Rapper? Beep.
BUDDY: On the radio. On a rhythm and blues station in Cleveland. In the '50s. He used to rap the facts...till they called him a communist.
ROBOT: Communist? Oh, boy. Beep.
BUDDY: Turned up to work one day, they'd put a preacher on in his time-slot. I bet you think that's why he started drinking.
ROBOT: Started drinking? Beep.
BUDDY: Nope. It was because nobody out there said nothing. Total silence.
ROBOT: Total silence. Beep beep.
BUDDY: Not now! Ever since he got that new outfit, he's a big shot.
ROBOT: What did he tell you?
BUDDY: Huh?
ROBOT: What did he tell you?
BUDDY: Oh, yeah. Those words that cut me like a knife. "We gotta part company, partner—because if I booze it, I lose it." *(Sobs.)*
ROBOT: "If I booze it, I lose it." Beep.
BUDDY: Aw-ww-w.
ROBOT: Can you keep a secret?
BUDDY: Like a sphinx, lady. My lips are sealed.
ROBOT: Do not tell Factperson that Jerry Falwell will invade Castro Street just after sundown tomorrow night.
BUDDY: Tomorrow night? Castro Street?
ROBOT: Do not tell Factperson. The party is over. *(Exits.)*
BUDDY: Serve him right if I didn't tell him. Yeah, but when he hears how I got the secret out of her, he's gonna learn to appreciate me. *(Shakes* SLEEPY *.)* Hey, sleepy! Wake up! We gotta find Sedro!
SLEEPY: Where's Sedro? *(Exeunt.)*

SCENE SEVEN

Sign: Deep in the Heart of the Castro.

DICK *enters the Target Bar and calls off-stage.*

DICK: Hey, Bill. Did you pick up the tickets for the "Oblivion Express" dance?...*(Voice answers* "yes.") Good! *(Checks cash.)* This one's stamped "Gay Money." Isn't that cute? My former stigma is now my meal ticket. If they could see me now...*(Checks further.)* We're out of amyl nitrate! *(Exits.)*
BARNEY: *(Enters in a huff.)* Bartender! That butch burnout of a bouncer asked me for three pieces of picture ID! I mean, really. He told me

it was getting too dark in the jungle. I can be insulted on the street for free. Hey—let's have some music. *(Punk band enters.)* I just want to forget. Pretend it never happened.

BANDLEADER: *(As music vamps.)* We just want to let you know that you're right on target at Dick's Target Club. That's right, yeah. I'm Mark Antony and these are the Nihilists. *(Ad libs: introduces band members. They begin singing* BECAUSE YOU'RE STUPID.*)*

These fearful times make willing slaves
Who seek their freedom in their chains.
Reagan's election was no surprise:
You voted for Nixon twice.
Why? Because you're stupid.
Stupid, stupid, stupid, stupid.

Blame it on the black folks
Blame it on the Jews,
Blame it on anyone not like you.
You can blame it on the reds,
Blame it on the greens,
But you never put the blame on the
    man who pulls the strings.
You must be stupid.
Stupid, stupid, stupid, stupid.

TV preachers quote the Lord,
Say, "Beat your plowshares into swords.
Live your life the Christian way,
Send your money and you'll be saved."
Why? Because you're stupid.
Stupid, stupid, stupid, stupid.
Stupid, stupid, STUPID!

BARNEY: I *must* be stupid to spend half my paycheck in this polyester paradise. Something tells me this is not the place I'm going to meet Prince Charming. Bartender! Bartender! Hey, can a lady get a drink or is this the YMCA?

DICK: *(Enters.)* Relax, Barney. You're here, the music's hot, and the night is young.

BARNEY: Yeah, and I'm not getting any younger. Give me one of your Martian Mai Tai's. I need to calm down. (DICK *makes drink while* BARNEY *checks out poster.)* Hmmm, "Oblivion Express," next Friday, hottest disco party of the season—fifteen dollars.

DICK: You coming?

BARNEY: What else is there to do on a Friday night in Babylon-by-the-Bay? *(Jeers and screams from backstage.)* The wolves are at the door.

DICK: No sweat, the Hulk will take care of them. *(*CLYDE *enters, dazed, leaflets in hand.)* Look what the ill winds blew our way.

CLYDE: Contradictions! I tried to leaflet these dispossessed youth and they started queer-baiting me. I didn't even tell them I was gay.

BARNEY: Pulleeze, honey...Hey, don't I know you from someplace?

CLYDE: I don't know—I meet a lot of people through my organizing. Here's a leaflet for the anti-Moral Majority rally next Friday. With the New Right trying to deny us our basic human rights, it's time we build coalitions and *fight back!*

DICK: Jeesus...

BARNEY: I'm not into politics anymore. That night I'll be shaking my booty at the "Oblivion Express." Honey, I'm gay, not glum.

CLYDE: Jerry Falwell and his gospel squad even hate disco.

BARNEY: Well, they should start a punk band.

DICK: Hey, buddy, take your rap somewhere else. People come here to forget their troubles.

BARNEY: Wanna dance?

CLYDE: I usually need a few drinks before I can...

BARNEY: Dick, give this man a double.

DICK: Here, this should soothe the savage beast.

BARNEY: Now darling, pretend I'm an exotic cabaret chanteuse, à la Dietrich. It's Berlin in the late '30s.

CLYDE: And we're making out in the back of a Nazi paddy wagon with pink triangles on our concentration camp drag...
BARNEY: That was then—in Germany. We are in San Francisco. I fled Florida to be free! Stop trying to bring me down. Want a qualude?
CLYDE: We *did* meet before—in Miami, during Anita's Holy War. I had flown down to help the forces.
BARNEY: And I was in the field office, answering phones, while the men were off in the front lines.
CLYDE: One moonlit night we went walking on the beach by the Fontainbleau.
BARNEY: Then we went to your sleazy hotel room.
CLYDE: This is getting embarrassing.
BARNEY: *Then,* when the election was over, you winged it back to Frisco—I was just another forgettable layover in the jet-set world of political intrigue.
CLYDE: I had to get back to my anti-Bakke organizing work. They were cutting back childcare—district elections were...
BARNEY: See why I get bored with politics?

Shouting match outside. TV REPORTER *and* CAMERAPERSON *burst in.*

REPORTER: Wide shot. Pick up the fruit salad. *(Into mike.)* This is Dana Datsun and your Eyewitness News team at the Target Bar On San Francisco's Castro Street, where Romeo and Julian are about to be hit with a *big* surprise.
DICK: *(Enters.)* What's all the—TV cameras? *(Heads for* BARNEY.*)* Barney, would you get out of sight?
BARNEY: *(Preening.)* I am out of sight.
REPORTER: Who are you, sir?
DICK: I'm the owner. What you see tonight, it's not really typical. Usually we have dart games, football pools—
CLYDE: What you see is a parasite that preys on this community and...
REPORTER: Speak into the mike sir—you're on national TV.
CLYDE: Good! Because somebody's got to stand up and say...national? But—uh, Mom and Dad, if you're watching in Iowa...I'm sorry you had to find out like this. I always meant to write but—I didn't know how to—oh, this is terrible—this is going to kill Dad.
REPORTER: Glimpse of a family tragedy there. A bizarre scene on Castro-Street tonight as—*(More shouting offstage.)* Here he comes, the mighty mullah of the Moral Majority—*(*FALWELL *enters.)* the Reverend Jerry Falwell.

CLYDE: Jerry Falwell! I don't care about the cameras, I have a few words to...

FALWELL: Let us pray. I want every head bowed and every eye closed. Oh, Heavenly Father, bless all those Christians out there who are sickened in their very souls by the filth they see on their TV screens tonight.

BARNEY: *(Waves.)* Hi, there!

FALWELL: These—can I call them men?—are the enemy within that is delivering this country straight into the hands of the communists.

DICK: I'm a Republican!

FALWELL: Lord, a growing number of fundamentalists are demanding the death penalty for homosexuals.

CLYDE: You heard him.

FALWELL: But I—in the spirit of Christian forgiveness—call only for an end to all so-called gay rights. Amen, amen.

DICK, CLYDE, BARNEY *start to protest.*

REPORTER: These men don't like that message! Tell us, Reverend, why did you choose a gay bar as the site of your first personal appearance in San Francisco?

FALWELL: Well, Ms. Datsun, tonight I'm going to be wrestling with Satan. And I want to meet him on his home ground.

SEDRO: *(Enters.)* Jerry Falwell?

FALWELL: Speak of the devil.

SEDRO: *(Sings.)* Ring the bells, I have arrived
Going to blast away all Falwell's jive.
Say hey, boom-di-ay
I'm back with facts, going to save the day.

DICK: It sounds like...

BARNEY: It can't be!

CLYDE: It is!

SEDRO: It had to be a barroom.

DICK, BARNEY, CLYDE: Factperson II!

REPORTER: Remember, you saw it here on Eyewitness News.

FACTWINO: You got your cameras cranking? *(To* FALWELL.*)* I am gonna make you think. (FALWELL *shakes his head "no."*) I hereby challenge Jerry Falwell to a hands-down, no-holds-barred debate—on any topic he sees fit to choose.

REPORTER: This could be the confrontation of the century. Factperson II is unbeaten! He's made opponents from every walk of life eat their words as soon as they utter an error! Will Falwell risk it?

FALWELL: I accept. *(Gays cheer.)* On one condition.

PHOTO: MICHAEL E. BRY

FACTWINO: I am going to allow him a handicap. Because this man has not used his mind, has not asked himself a single question in twenty-five years. Well, name your game, Falwell, and warm up your brain—you are in for an experience. Okay, one condition. What is it?

FALWELL: One problem with being a preacher, everybody thinks you're a prude. I don't like that. Let me buy you a drink.

FACTWINO: Huh?

FALWELL: Bartender. (DICK *is glad to comply.*)

FACTWINO: Thanks—I never drink when I'm working. State your proposition.

FALWELL: You haven't worked in twenty-five years.

FACTWINO: Stop—stop stalling, Falwell. Say something stupid so I can make you refute it.

FALWELL: What was it they used to call you back in Cleveland—The Rapper?

FACTWINO: Come out with it, Falwell—any of that shit you spout every day!

FALWELL: Soon as you empty that glass. Bottoms up—right boys? Surely Fact*wino's* power can't be so fragile that a little booze would cause him to lose it?

REPORTER: Fact*wino?* The pavement philosopher is certainly losing his *equanimity.*

FACTWINO: You been spying on me!

FALWELL: I'm a pastor, brother, I know human nature. I know your very deepest fear.
FACTWINO: No one knows that!
FALWELL: You're afraid nobody will care what you say. Nobody cares about a communist. When they shut you up, like they did before, nothing will be heard but—total silence.
FACTWINO: No! *(Raises glass to lips. Freezes.)*

SPIRIT OF INFORMATION *enters.*

SPIRIT: I don't hold with entrapment. Mr. Falwell?
FALWELL: Huh?
SPIRIT: I was goin' down Castro Street collecting beer cans and peoples said you was in here, and, suh, I be watching your show every Sunday but seem like I always be missing things, so I sure would like for you to splain me what's this here sexual humorism you talks so much about on TV.
FALWELL: Sexual—secular humanism is an atheistic, amoral philosophy that destroys the American family and the great Christian principles on which our founding fathers built this great nation. Now—
SPIRIT: I was hoping you'd say that. *(Exits.)*

FACTWINO *bangs the glass down. Thunder crashes. Lightning flashes. He zaps* FALWELL.

FALWELL: Since our founding fathers were founding a Christian country, why didn't they just come out and say so in the Constitution? Now I know that one or two of them were unbelievers—Jefferson...Franklin...Madison...
FACTWINO: And George Washington, who said—and I quote—"The government of the United States is not in any sense founded on the Christian religion."
FALWELL: Well, there may be some problems with the Constitution. Okay. Some of our friends in Congress are getting ready to rewrite it. But the *true* building block of this country is the Christian family: Dad, Mom, and the kids, in the order God meant. *(Zap.)* Of course, when the country was founded, it was more like Grandpa and Grandma, two uncles, three aunts, six children, and the hired man.
FACTWINO: You talking 'bout white folks now.
FALWELL: The family has evolved...no...
DICK, BARNEY, CLYDE: *Evolved?*
FALWELL: I mean the family's changing and...could I have a glass of water?

REPORTER: Falwell is feeling the strain now.
FALWELL: But one thing never changes! The inerrant, unalterable Word of God: the Holy Bible! *(Zap.* FALWELL *crying.)* Then how come it contradicts itself three times inside the first two chapters? Because the text evolved—no! Because men wrote down different parts at different times and naturally there were—no! If there are errors, there are no absolutes! No absolutes, no morality! What's to stop me from fornicating that fruit there?!
BARNEY: No way!
FALWELL: What's to stop me from whipping out a machine gun and cutting down the whole Osmond family as they kneel in prayer? *(Mimes machine-gunning.)* Ack-ack-ack-ack-ack-ack—
FACTWINO: Better give that boy a bourbon. (DICK *does,* FALWELL *belts it.)*
REPORTER: Well, champ, in another minute you'd have had us thinking that atheism is as American as apple pie.
FACTWINO: Better for you, too—it don't contain any sugar. See I believe that the human heart and the human mind keep us moral.
REPORTER: What do you call that religion?
FACTWINO: Secular humanism. (FALWELL *is raving.)*
REPORTER: *(To camera.)* Miss Muggins? *(They take* FALWELL *out.)*
BARNEY: What a man! That's the end of the Moral Majority.
FACTWINO: After them, what? I need to think. I need a drink.
DICK, BARNEY, CLYDE: No!
FACTWINO: I need to get out of here! *(Exits.)*
BARNEY: Let's have some music! Let's boogie!
CLYDE: It's a little soon to celebrate. There's millions of them out there. You oughta meet the jerk my sister married. You oughta meet my *parents!*

Music: EDNA *enters.*

EDNA: Oh, I hope he's still here—where's my son?
CLYDE: Mom?!
EDNA: Clyde! After five long years! *(They embrace.)*
CLYDE: I'm sorry, Mom. I don't know how to explain...
EDNA: You don't have to, dear—we saw you on TV.
CLYDE: *We?* You mean Dad's here?
EDNA: He's parking the RV. Have you seen your sister?
CLYDE: She's here? Is that why you came to California?
EDNA: It's a long story, but we like it here. We want to stay. Oh, I'm sure your father's lost—all those people on the street look alike— I'm going to go stand on the corner, and you stay right here in case I miss him. Oh, we'll all be together again—*(Exits.)*

BARNEY: I wish *my* mom were like that.
CLYDE: Something's turned her around! Wait'll you meet my dad.

Music; GEORGE *enters.*

GEORGE: Clyde?
CLYDE: Yes, Father? *(Cringes.)*
GEORGE: Son—you don't know what it meant to me to hear you say right on TV how much you care about your old Dad. Now if only your sister were...

Music; GEORGIANNA *enters.*

GEORGIANNA: Excuse me, I'm looking for my brother—the TV showed him here, he...
GEORGE: Georgianna!
GEORGIANNA: Daddy!
CLYDE: Georgie!
GEORGIANNA: Clyde! *(All embrace.)* You mean you ran away because you were a little...?
CLYDE: A lot.
GEORGIANNA: And Daddy—you mean you don't mind?
GEORGE: Funny thing—a lot of things changed in my mind since I met this old colored guy in a funny-looking suit.
CLYDE, GEORGIANNA: You, too?
GEORGE: Where's my grandchild?
GEORGIANNA: At the sitter's.
GEORGE: I want to see her!
GEORGIANNA: Where's Mom?
CLYDE: She's out looking for Dad! We better look for her. But wait—there's someone I'd like you both to meet. This is Barney. *(All shake hands.)*
GEORGE: He's tall, isn't he?
BARNEY: *(Indicating leaflets.)* Aren't you forgetting these?
GEORGE: Anti-Moral Majority? *(*CLYDE *cringes.)* After we find your mother, we can all pass 'em out. These people are giving Christians a bad name.
DICK: Hey, and after the rally, everybody make it back to the Target for the big Fight Facism Benefit Boogie.
GEORGE: *(To* BARNEY.*)* May I have the first dance? *(Exeunt.)*

EPILOGUE

Sign: Some weeks later, on Sixth Street.

Enter SLEEPY; *he sleeps. Enter* BUDDY *with fruit juice and newspaper.*

BUDDY: Hey, Sleepy—wake up! I just scored yesterday's New York *Times!* Here, have a hit of this carrot juice. *(*SLEEPY *shudders.* BUDDY *reads.)* "Economy Slows—Signs of Recession." I saw it coming. "1000 Jobseekers Riot in New York." You think there could be a connection? Whoo— "Moral Majority in Fast Fade!" Did you hear that? "Moral Majority chapters nationwide are dissolving in the wake of the much-publicized mental breakdown of their one-time leader, Jerry Falwell! Falwell, arrested recently in Las Vegas while clad in a leopardskin jumpsuit, had only this to say, 'Where's Bo Derek?' " All right, Factwino!

SEDRO *enters with huge stack of books.*

BUDDY: Hey, Sedro—you gotta see this!
SEDRO: Why you think I been to the library?
BUDDY: Don't you understand, partner? You won! You done knocked out the Moral Majority!
SEDRO: I *understand* that somebody or something wanted the Moral Majority to keep folks' minds off the real problem. Now I got to figure out how they going to move next. Let's see here: we got George Orwell, *1984;* Fanon, *The Wrteched of the Earth;* this one, *The Use of Military Power in History* by Engels—now we're getting warm...

ROBOT *enters.*

ROBOT: Factwino?
BUDDY: *(Shielding* SEDRO.*)* He ain't here! *(To* SEDRO.*)* That's her! That's the one tricked the secrets out of me!
ROBOT: If you see him, tell him: tripling the defense budget is the only way to save our economy.
BUDDY: No!

SEDRO *can't help it—he becomes* FACTWINO. *He zaps the* ROBOT. *But the zap doesn't take. Three times he zaps; three times the zap bounces off.*

ROBOT: Your power only works on human intelligence. *(Zaps him.* FACTWINO *is paralyzed.)*

FACTWINO: What th...
ROBOT: Lasers.
BUDDY: No! You can't...*(She stops him with a zap.)*
FACTWINO: Buddy!
ROBOT: Microwave partial lobotomy. Now you will meet Armageddonman.
FACTWINO: Arma—who?
ROBOT: You'll find out. Come. *(He must obey.)*
FACTWINO: Buddy! Sleepy! You out there! Somebody say something!
ROBOT: Hahahahaha. *(Exits.)*
BUDDY: *(Wakes slowly.)* Hey, wasn't there somebody else here before? Seems like I—whose overcoat? What's all these books? Oh, well—come on, Sleepy. Let's go sell this stuff and buy us some wine. *(At this,* SLEEPY *wakes. Exeunt. Signs appear.)*

Is This the End?

Will FACTWINO be forgotten?

What happens when the SPIRIT meets ARMAGEDDONMAN?

Watch This Space.

Factwino vs. Armageddonman was first presented on July 9, 1982, in Civic Center Plaza, San Francisco, with the following cast (including later substitutions):

A LIBRARIAN	Sharon Lockwood
A DESPERATE MAN	Esteban Oropeza
BUDDY, a street person	Joaquin Aranda
FACTWINO, aka SEDRO F. WOOLEY, another street person	Shabaka
A PUNK	Dan Chumley
An AFFLUENT LADY	Wilma Bonet
A highschool GIRL	Wilma Bonet
A FACTIVIST	Esteban Oropeza
An ULTRALEFTIST	Dan Chumley
A SINGLE MOM	Audrey Smith/Brian Freeman/ Marie Acosta-Colón
ROBOT, a smart machine	Wilma Bonet
The SPIRIT OF INFORMATION	Audrey Smith/ Brian Freeman/Marie Acosta-Colón
ARMAGEDDONMAN	Dan Chumley, Joaquin Aranda
SLEEPY, a street person	Esteban Oropeza/Dan Chumley
A PRIEST	Craig Knudsen

Script by Joan Holden, Robert Alexander, *and* Henri Picciotto
Directed by Brian Freeman
Choreography by Sharon Lockwood
Music and Lyrics by Bruce Barthol, Glenn Appell,
except "Blow This Mother Up" by Shabaka
Music Director, Glenn Appell
Costumes by Wilma Bonet, Sharon Lockwood, *and* Nora Long
Backdrop by Spain
Band: Glenn Appell, Muziki (Duane Roberson), Craig Knudsen, David Rokeach, Mary Burnley, *and* Glenn Veale

Factwino vs. Armageddonman
San Francisco Mime Troupe

Signs open the show:

The *Spirit of Information* has intervened *twice* to save a great nation from *error*...

Each time by endowing a *lover of truth* with a *superpower of clarification.*

The first, *Factperson,* misused her power to know *every fact there is.*

Ignorance triumphed at the polls, and *Fundamentalists* declared war on Knowledge.

The *Spirit* armed *Sedro Wooley.* a pavement philosopher, with the amazing ability to *Make People Think.*

As *Factwino,* he mopped the floor with the *Moral Majority*—only to be kidnapped by the main enemy, *Armageddonman.*

One *Witness* saw our hero's disappearance—but his *memory* has been *erased.*

Months later, as the *Defense Budget Doubles,* a lonely *Servant of Knowledge* suffers a *Crisis of Faith.*

SCENE ONE

The Library

LIBRARIAN: *(Enters with huge stack of books, announces.)* Please make your final selections: the library will close in fifteen minutes. Remember, we're no longer open weekends. *(Works.)*

DESPERATE MAN: *(Enters from stacks.)* Hey! You call this a library? I've got fourteen books on this list, and you don't have any of them!

LIBRARIAN: I'm sorry, sir—it's these cutbacks. I try to track down missing books, but I'm all alone here now, and there's no money for new acquisitions—but if you tell me what you're looking for, I might be able to help.

DESPERATE MAN: I have to know what's going to happen to the economy. *(Shows newspaper, "Stock Market Rising Thru Ceiling, Small Businesses Crash Thru Floor.")*
LIBRARIAN: A lot of people are asking that. I'm afraid the experts disagree. It seems there are so many questions...
DESPERATE MAN: I need answers! Whatever happened to that old wino who knew it all?
LIBRARIAN: Factwino. I wish I knew.
DESPERATE MAN: He probably knew so much, it made him blow his brains out.
LIBRARIAN: Wait...*(MAN exits.)* Day after day—failing people—not meeting their needs! I ask myself—why keep this place open? Because to close it would be like turning out the lights. *(Takes purse out, gobbles vitamins.)* I'm tired, that's all that's wrong with me. I ought to stop coming in at 6 to catch up on the indexing, and start catching up on my sleep...*(Nods out.)*

BUDDY *enters stealthily from stacks, concealing books.*

VISION OF SEDRO: *(Enters.)* Hold it, Buddy.
BUDDY: Who—who's that?
VISION: Don't you remember?
BUDDY: Remember who?
VISION: Put the books down, Buddy.
BUDDY: But I ain't had a drink since breakfast!
VISION: Put 'em down *(BUDDY obeys.)* Help me, Buddy.
BUDDY: Who are you?
VISION: Remember!
BUDDY: Why can't I remember?
VISION: Remember! *(Exits.)*
BUDDY: I can't remember nothing—except I'm thirsty. *(To sleeping* LIBRARIAN.*)* Say lady, I just had a mystical experience. You got fifty cents? *(Sees her purse, takes it.)*

LIBRARIAN *wakes with bloodcurling scream.* BUDDY *exits with purse.*

PUNK: *(Enters.)* Whoa—who got mugged?
LIBRARIAN: I had a nightmare. The same one—I keep having it over and over!
PUNK: I get them all the time too. What's yours about?
LIBRARIAN: I don't know. I never remember. I wake up screaming and my memory's black—I just have this desperate feeling of loss.
PUNK: I wish I didn't remember my dreams. They're always about the same thing—the end of the world. *(Exits to stacks.)*

LIBRARIAN: So many young people without hope...*(Resumes work.)* I don't know if I could go on, if I hadn't promised the Spirit of Information I would never fall into despair.

AFFLUENT LADY: *(Enters, slams book down on counter.)* Excuse me, miss—Have you read this book?

LIBRARIAN: *(Glances at book, recoils.)* No, and I'm not going to! I know more than I want to know about *that!*

LADY: Do you know that a nuclear war is bound to damage the ozone layer?

LIBRARIAN: *(Politely.)* Very interesting. *(Seeing* PUNK *enter from stacks, with video tapes.)* Excuse me.

LADY: Enough ultraviolet light would enter to blind us!

PUNK: Do like me, lady—always wear sunglasses. *(Gives* LIBRARIAN *tapes.)*

LADY: Animals can't wear glasses—they'd be blind too. And insects —*bees!*

PUNK: Blind bees. Gag me with a fork.

LIBRARIAN: Here's your videos—*Tron, Blade Runner, Death Race 2000.*

LADY: Young man, you ought to read this *book—The Fate of the Earth.*

PUNK: Hey, reading's depressing. At least in science fiction films there's still a future.

LIBRARIAN: Wait...

PUNK: What for?

LIBRARIAN: ...I don't know. *(PUNK goes.)*

LADY: I think I am going to commit a desperate act. *(Exits.)*

LIBRARIAN: *(Desperate, sings.)*
>Things are not just getting bad
>That's been true for years.
>But what I notice day by day is
>Things are getting weird.
>I wake up in the morning,
>My mind is full of dread:
>Remnants of forgotten dreams—
>Afraid to leave my bed.
>What can I do?
>
>Once I knew a hero who showed up just in time
>To save the day.
>He brought light to the shadows,
>He made the bad guys go away.
>He stood for truth and justice,
>But most of all, he stood for me.
>He can lead us out of this insanity.

I'm afraid to read the papers,
I can't stand to watch TV.
Desperate people, crimes and war
Are all I ever see.
People just don't want to read
It's video instead.
Boys and girls with Pacman minds
And earphones on their heads.
I can't believe the world is quite
As crazy as it seems.
Why can't I remember all those
Terrifying dreams?
What can I do?

Once I knew a hero
Who showed up just in time to save the day.
He brought light to the shadows,

He made the bad guys go away.
But heroes are like fairy tales,
They vanish when the clock strikes twelve.
Leaving no one but ourselves.
Who will lead the way?

He'll come back—I know he will—I hope. *(Puts coat on, finds purse missing.)* Oh, no—somebody's stolen my purse! *(Exits.)*

SCENE TWO

Sign: Other *Followers of Factwino* carry on the *Fight.* Nearby...

A street.

High School GIRL *enters with radio blasting, calls to friends, waves, etc.*

FACTIVIST: *(Enters.)* Excuse me, Miss—excuse me! *(Whistles. She switches radio off.)* I'm a member of the Gay Latino Factivists and—*(She switches radio on.)* It's a coalition formed in honor of Factwino. We give people information that helps them think. We're out today giving people in the community the real facts about nuclear war.
GIRL: We're going to win. My boyfriend told me.
FACTIVIST: Win or lose, *mi hija,* San Francisco would be the first place that got hit.
GIRL: *(Switches radio off.)* Saint Ignatius High School too? *(Or ad libs name of local building.)*
FACTIVIST: The blast would flatten every building in the city!
GIRL: *Que gacho.*
FACTIVIST: Downtown would broil at 1500 degrees!
GIRL: That's hot. How come nobody ever told me that?
FACTIVIST: Because the government doesn't want people to know.
GIRL: That's cold.
FACTIVIST: But we're gonna show 'em we know what's happening and we ain't gonna stand for it!
GIRL: *Orale.*
FACTIVIST: *(Handing her a leaflet.)* Bring all your homeboys to this big rally on Saturday.
GIRL: Tomorrow?
FACTIVIST: Twelve o'clock.
GIRL: I'll still be sleeping. Because if we're all gonna die, I'm gonna give it up to Edwin—tonight! *(Exits.)*

FACTIVIST: At least now she has the facts. *(ULTRALEFTIST enters.)* Ah—this one ought to be easier. Hey brother—coming to the rally tomorrow?
ULTRALEFTIST: *(Takes leaflet, reads.)* "Stop the MX, Stop the Cruise Missile, Stop the Neutron Bomb." What about women?
FACTIVIST: What?
ULTRALEFTIST: I'm a feminist male. And don't you want to stop gay oppression?
FACTIVIST: Sure, but—
ULTRALEFTIST: I'm straight.
FACTIVIST: I would never have guessed.
ULTRALEFTIST: You don't raise one single anti-imperialist slogan. "Freeze the Arms Race—Fund Human Needs"—there's nothing here the average Democrat couldn't agree to!
FACTIVIST: Because if the United States deploys these new weapons, the Russians will put their missiles on hair-trigger alert, and the clock hands will move closer to midnight. Are you coming to the rally, Butch?
ULTRALEFTIST: The name's Timmy! I'm coming—but I'm bringing my own leaflets. *(Seeing* SINGLE MOTHER *enter.)* Right on, sister, right on!
SINGLE MOM: *(Ignoring him.)* Hey, is that a Factwino tank top? That is *bad!* Factwino—I pinned all my hopes on him.
FACTIVIST: Why not start a Factivist chapter in your neighborhood? You can read all about it on the back of this leaflet.
SINGLE MOM: A rally, huh? You want to hear a story? I lost my welfare when I got a job at Social Services—now I lost my job 'cause they're cutting back welfare. Can't get Medi-Cal cause my unemployment's too high—can't stay on unemployment cause my job was too short. Then, my boyfriend moves in with me to save on his rent—and now my ex-husband wants to take away my child.
FACTIVIST: I can see how the arms race might seem a little abstract.
SINGLE MOM: It did, till one day my daughter says, "Mama—you're lucky, Mama: you had a baby." I said, "You got *time* to get *that* lucky." She says, "Uh-uh, Mama—I won't live long enough to have babies. Cause there's gonna be a war, and us children now, we're gonna be the last children in the world." *(Holds up leaflet.)* A rally? I'll be there! *(Exits.)*

LIBRARIAN *enters.*

FACTIVIST: Good evening! Gee—you look like you had a hard day.
LIBRARIAN: Average, really—somebody stole my purse.
FACTIVIST: If you want to restore your faith in humanity, come to our giant rally tomorrow.
LIBRARIAN: What happened, did the 49'ers win? *(Or local joke.)*
FACTIVIST: No—we're gonna have some great speakers! We're aiming to turn out 100,000 people tomorrow to protest the arms race and stop nuclear war.
LIBRARIAN: *(Hands leaflet back.)* I can't come—I'm very busy tomorrow. I'm a public servant. I have to find missing books.
FACTIVIST: Ma'am, do you know that in the world right now, there are 50,000 nuclear warheads that could be launched in eight minutes?
LIBRARIAN: Excuse me—I think I see my bus.
FACTIVIST: There's no bus coming.
LIBRARIAN: I guess I'll take Bart. *(Starts off.)* Oh, no—I don't have the fare!
FACTIVIST: Here. *(Gives it to her.)* And take one of these to read on the train. *(Tries to give her a leaflet.)*
LIBRARIAN: No, thank you. I'm sorry. Look—I'm trying to hold on to my sanity right now—and the way I do it is, I don't think about THAT. *(Exits.)*
FACTIVIST: Sometimes it seems as if people just don't want to know. *(Sighs.)* This is a job for Factwino! (Exits.)

SCENE THREE

Sign: Meanwhile, in a *Secret Stronghold* deep under the desert...

ROBOT *marches* FACTWINO *on and subjects him to electronic tortures.*

FACTWINO: I'm gonna get you one day, you Mitsubishi motherf... Not so much for what you doin' to me, but for what you done to my little Buddy. Hitting him with laser beams, knocking out his memory—
ROBOT: Poor Factwino. *(Gets bottle.)* Have a drink.
FACTWINO: No way! That's against my contract: if I booze it, I lose it. Why don't you tell your master Armageddonman that he can torment my body, he can torture my mind—making me read *Readers Digest,* watch them TV reruns—but he will never make me destroy my power. People need me! People believe in me! My mind is strong because it's stored with the masterpieces from the

past... Shakespeare, Ralph Ellison, Malcolm X: "I went to Mecca and saw Muslims of every color..."
ROBOT: News time.
FACTWINO: "News?" Those fascist fantasies y'all make up to mess with me?
ROBOT: "Moscow Massacres 9 Million in Mideast."
FACTWINO: That's crap.
ROBOT: "Salvadorean Rebels Surrender."
FACTWINO: Bullshit!
ROBOT: "US Economy in Upswing."
FACTWINO: Getting way out now.
ROBOT: "Factwino Forgotten."
FACTWINO: That's a lie!... You got any more on that?
ROBOT: "Nationwide Polls Reveal: Public Silent on Fate of Former Hero Factwino. 97% Respond They Do Not Wish to Think."
FACTWINO: Shut up! Get out of here!... My very deepest fear...
ROBOT: *Total silence. (Exits.)*

FACTWINO: If it ain't true, how come nobody ain't saved me? How come Buddy don't return my psychic signals? How come I ain't heard from *her*—that crazy magic lady with the glasses, the one that gave me the power? *(Sings.)*

> They don't know me anymore,
> I stand alone, just like before;
> My Buddy's gone, my spirit too.
> The pact I made I kept in full:
> No compromise, no drinking booze—
> Dare to struggle, dare to lose.

SPIRIT OF INFORMATION *(Enters and sings.)*

> Listen, son: now's not the time
> To turn your back or turn to wine;
> You lit a spark that now is blazing
> And the battle outside now is raging.

FACTWINO: You didn't forget me! You're here! And you know how to get out of here! Battle's raging, huh? Well, what are we waiting for?
SPIRIT: There is no way out unless you defeat Armageddonman.
FACTWINO: Unless *I* defeat him? You mean you ain't gonna help me?
SPIRIT: I'm disqualified. I made a bad mistake once.
FACTWINO: Mistake? I thought you were like the Goddess of Truth.
SPIRIT: Not exactly. I am the Spirit of Information. I run General Reference at that big library out there.
FACTWINO: The *Main* Branch?
SPIRIT: You have all the powers that are mine to give. Now you got to use them to stop Armageddonman. *(Sings.)*

> It's the breath of life they want to smother
> So fight for life, for the earth, your mother.
> Fight for your sisters and your brothers,
> If you lose this fight there won't be another.

FACTWINO: "Won't be another?" Wait a minute—who or what *is* Armageddonman?
SPIRIT: I thought you'd never ask. He's somebody you've known a long time.
FACTWINO: I have?
SPIRIT: You always used to bad-rap him.
FACTWINO: I did?

SPIRIT: One time, you called him, "The Double-Headed Dealer of Doom."
FACTWINO: That was on the radio, back in Cleveland.
SPIRIT: '56. Right before they took you off the air.
FACTWINO: But that was just a figure of speech—a mere metaphor for...you don't mean...?
SPIRIT: I do.
FACTWINO: Holy shit.
SPIRIT: Summon your power. If any man can defeat Armageddonman, you can. Bye.
FACTWINO: You said "if."
SPIRIT: If you don't, this branch may close—permanently. *(Gives him the zap sign.)* You know what I mean? *(Exits.)*
FACTWINO: A titanic task—but it's humanity's only hope! I—Sedro F. Wooley—have got to stop Armageddonman by making him think! My magic zap—*(Practices.)*—it's a long time since I done used it. To activate it against Armageddonman, first I got to get him to utter an error.
ROBOT: *(Enters.)* The time has come. Now you will meet Armageddonman.
FACTWINO: *(As she marches him off.)* Power of intelligence, be with me now *(Exeunt.)*

SCENE FOUR

Sign: Upstairs, at the *Nerve Center of the Empire*

ARMAGEDDONMAN *enters, two-headed as before.*

BUSINESS: Blind microbes, fumbling through your pitiful endeavors, you know not who is the master that you serve.
WAR: State, party, nation—merely painted curtains.
BOTH: Unseen, *we* rule! *(They sing.)*

BOOM, BOOM, BOOM

> It's we who are the masters,
> You're just puppets in our play,
> And though you may not like it
> We will never let it change;
> And if you would resist us
> Or force us from the stage,
> We have a grand finale
> That will end the whole damn play.

Boom, boom, boom,
You know we're gonna do it.
Boom, boom, boom,
You're all gonna fry.
Boom, boom, boom,
You know we're gonna do it;
And when we do it to ya'
You'll just die.

The slaves are getting restless,
We can hear them cry for peace;
And though the weather's sunny
They are talking of a freeze.
We'll use them and confuse them,
We'll bring them to their knees,
And we'll decide the question,
To be or not to be.

Boom, boom, boom, *(Repeat chorus.)*

WAR: But I don't like this peace movement.
BUSINESS: You have no imagination. This comical convulsion of the conscious is the opportunity we've waited months for. It's our chance for perfect revenge—on *him*.
WAR: The man who guessed our secret—then mocked us? *(They growl.)*
BUSINESS: The man *they* love—*(Indicates audience.)*—while *we* must hide in shadow. What if that man were to betray the peace movement?
WAR: Delicious! Love this guy. *(Calls.)* Bring in the prisoner!

ROBOT *marches* FACTWINO *on.*

ARMAGEDDONMAN: Surprise.
FACTWINO: The twin titans of terror, business and war. Just as pretty as I've always pictured you.
BUSINESS: Welcome to the Nerve Center of the Empire. Your beautiful android jailer is the central brain of a worldwide system of military computers...
WAR: That can unleash Armageddon the moment I push that button. We get what we want. Does the roar of the crowd seem distant, Sedro? They're silent, and you're helpless.
FACTWINO: I know that now. I see it's useless to resist you. Have pity on me, please—get me a drink!
WAR: *(To* ROBOT.*)* Riunite—on ice.
BUSINESS: Nice! *(*ROBOT *brings drink.)*
FACTWINO: But my hands are tied.
WAR: Lift those laser bonds. *(*ROBOT *obeys.)*

FACTWINO: *(Secretly practices a few zaps, then lifts glass to lips as* ARMAGEDDONMAN *watches breathlessly.)* I know I'm about to destroy my power—but I'd rather do that than have *you use it.*
BUSINESS: *(Stops his hand.)* Wait—did you say "use it?"
WAR: How?
FACTWINO: You could have forced me to *make people think your thoughts.*
WAR: Huh?
BUSINESS: That's brilliant! The champion of truth conveys *our* message.
FACTWINO: Oh, no! I've said too much!
WAR: You dug your own grave!
FACTWINO: Please don't make me do this—please, I beg you! But I see it's hopeless. Okay. I give up. What's your message?

BUSINESS: Make them think *this*: all the world's a stage for one great conflict. America defends world peace and freedom...
WAR: Against relentless Communist agression.

   FACTWINO, *with a mighty effort, hurls his strongest zap.* ARMAGEDDONMAN *staggers, hit in both heads.*

WAR: Let's put ourselves in the Russians' shoes. Suppose we'd been invaded twice, lost twenty million people in a war, and faced an enemy with A-bombs?
BUSINESS: All the world's a stage, but when it's bare—who will have won?
WAR: Wow—this is really an experience.
BOTH: Our brain—it's buzzing!
BUSINESS: Factwino—give us a hug! *(All hug.)* Maybe there's something to this "planet consciousness!"
FACTWINO: All right!
WAR: Maybe there's something better out there!

FACTWINO: There is!
BUSINESS: So what?
FACTWINO: Huh?
WAR: Who cares?
FACTWINO: But I made you think!
BUSINESS: Amazing, isn't it? But you overlooked one small detail. Your power compels thought from human intelligence—but for thought to make a difference, it must touch human *feelings*.
FACTWINO: And you don't have them.
BOTH: That is the secret of our power.
WAR: Now have a drink—old man. *(ROBOT enters with bottle of ripple hooked up to intravenous feeding device.)*
FACTWINO: *(Trying to distract them)* Look—a Russian missile!
BOTH: Where?
FACTWINO: There! *(Tries to make a run, but there is no escape.* FACTWINO *hammers on the fourth wall.)* Oh, no!
BUSINESS: If my calculations are correct, once the alcohol enters his bloodstream, it will destroy his will—and place his power at our command.
FACTWINO: You'll have to kill me first. *(ROBOT zaps his arm open.)* Oh-h-h—

ROBOT *marches him off as* ARMAGEDDONMAN *exits laughing.*

Sign: Will *Factwino* be forced to serve *Falsehood?*

SCENE FIVE

Sign: A Small Park on Sixth Street

A silent wino, SLEEPY, *enters and sleeps.* ROBOT *enters in dark glasses, with leaflets. She wakes* SLEEPY *to give him one. He looks, babbles excitedly, passes out again.* ROBOT *exits.*

LIBRARIAN: *(Enters, with books.)* What a day—in four hours I've recovered three books. Let's see now—345 6th Street. That's funny —343's over there—347's over there—not again! What sort of depraved, degenerate person would give the library an address that doesn't exist? *(Sits, exhausted.)* That nightmare woke me up again last night—but that sunshine feels nice...*(Leans back, oblivious to sleeping wino, and falls asleep.)*
BUDDY: *(Enters with bottle and purse.)* Hey, Sleepy—who's your girl-friend? Here, have a hit of this. (SLEEPY *does.*) Some weird stuff in this purse—I couldn't sell any of it. Three packs of Kleenex—

whole alphabet of vitamin pills—police whistle—Mace—and this picture of a raggedy looking old black guy in a Superman suit. He signed it, too. "Factwino." FactWINO. I like that!
VISION OF SEDRO: *(Enters.)* Buddy! You got to help me!
BUDDY: Help who?
SEDRO: Me, remember? *(He is dragged off.)* Help! Remember!
BUDDY: Remember who? Wait! I don't remember! I can't remember...

LIBRARIAN *wakes up screaming.* BUDDY *and* SLEEPY *jump, picture falls.*

BUDDY: Oh, shit! *(Stashes purse.)*
LIBRARIAN: Oh! Where...what?...*(Sees winos.)* Eek!
BUDDY: What's the matter, lady—what's wrong?
LIBRARIAN: I don't know!
BUDDY: Here, have some wine—good for the shakes.
LIBRARIAN: No! Oh, God—I can't take this much longer, being tortured by something I can't even remember! I'm sorry if I made a scene—I'll go now.
BUDDY: Can't remember? Don't go, lady! Wait! I got the same thing wrong with me!
LIBRARIAN: Really?
BUDDY: This voice tells me "Remember"—but I can't. Then it goes, and I feel like I lost my best friend.
LIBRARIAN: I feel as if I've lost everything.
BUDDY: I feel as if I'm supposed to do something.
LIBRARIAN: But you don't know what it is.
BUDDY: Here. *(Passes bottle.)* Makes it easier. (LIBRARIAN *takes hanky from pocket, wipes bottle, drinks.)* I ain't told nobody else.
LIBRARIAN: They wouldn't understand. *(Drinks.)*
BUDDY: Sometimes I wonder why I even go on living. Habit, I guess. You got fifty cents?
LIBRARIAN: I don't have anything—somebody stole my purse. (BUDDY *cringes. She drinks.)* Hey, is either of you gentlemen Mr. Sedro F. Wooley?
BUDDY: Sedro F. Wooley...seems like I ought to know that name.
LIBRARIAN: He's supposed to live at this address. 'S'funny—a perfect record for fifteen years, then one day he checks out books and never returns them.
BUDDY: Maybe he died.
LIBRARIAN: Maybe he was kidnapped—by aliens! Hey—what's my picture of Factwino doing here? *(Kisses it.)*
BUDDY: You in love with that guy?

LIBRARIAN: You'd love him too. *(Hands bottle back. It's empty.)* He makes sense out of this madness. He brings clarity out of confusion. Factwino is the only hope this world has left! Where is he now?

SLEEPY *struggles up, babbling. He hands her leaflet, subsides.*

LIBRARIAN: *(Reads.)* "Rally Against Nuclear War"—no thank you. I don't want it. I'm not going. Wait—the other side—what's this? Oh! Oh! He hasn't deserted us!
BUDDY: Huh?
LIBRARIAN: Come on!
BUDDY: Wait. You almost forgot your purse. *(Hands it to her. Exeunt.)*

SCENE SIX

Sign: Soon, on the steps of City Hall

FACTIVIST *leads crowd on carrying anti-nuke signs and chanting:* No more nukes! No more nukes! No more nukes!
FACTIVIST: Sexual minorities say—
CROWD: No more nukes!
AFFLUENT LADY: Seniors for a future say—
CROWD: No more nukes!
PRIEST: Concerned clergy say a pray for—
CROWD: No more nukes!
SINGLE MOM: Parents who want grandchildren say—
CROWD: No more nukes!
BAND: *(Crosses dressed in hayseed clothes.)* Humboldt County Growers say—
CROWD: No more nukes!
PUNK: People who don't give a fuck say, "Nuke the whales!"
CROWD: No more nukes!
PUNK: Where's the music?
CROWD: No more nukes! No more nukes! *(Cheers.)*
AFFLUENT LAD' *(Takes speaker's platform.)* My friends—*(Quiets them.)* I am a lifelong Republican. *(Cries of disbelief.)* I always believed that whatever my country did, was right. *(Cries of derision.)* Now I see all you beautiful people and my heart freezes, my breath sticks in my throat as I think that all of us could just disappear in an instant. The pride of our leaders could cancel, in that instant, the present, the future, and even the past. We've got to stop them friends. Humanity must put an end to this madness!

All except PUNK *cheer, chant.* PUNK *scoffs.* FACTWINO *theme is heard. All listen.*

FACTIVIST: It sounds like—
LADY: It can't be!
LIBRARIAN: *(Rushes on, with* BUDDY.*)* It is!

FACTWINO *enters, resplendent in James Brown-type new superhero suit.*

ALL *but* BUDDY: Factwino!

All except BUDDY *dance and clap as* FACTWINO *takes the stage.* PUNK *has joined the crowd.*

FACTWINO: Well alright! Let's have a big hand for the band. *(Crowd applauds.)* The Nihilists, everybody! Ain't they bad? I want to thank all you beautiful people for the support you done given me.
BUDDY: You got fifty cents?
FACTWINO: Suppose I were to tell you that I have a dream. *(Crowd applauds.)* That I foresee a day when man will live in harmony with the planet, with nature, in a world made up of truly united nations; a world without superpowers; a world without nuclear weapons. *(Crowd applauds.)* Where men and women of every race, every creed, every color, live togeother, love together, like ebony and ivory, living in perfect harmony—I have a dream! *(Crowd applauds.)* And I have traveled around the world trying to share my dream. I've been to Russia, I've been to China; I have met with all the leaders and I am convinced that world peace...will never happen, and I'm just a fool with a dream.
CROWD: What?
FACTWINO: We could rally from here to eternity and it wouldn't mean a thing, because the Russians will never disarm.
CROWD: *(Among themselves.)* Oh, no! He can't be saying that! *(Etc.)*
FACTWINO: They are on a coldhearted, relentless, godless, expanionist TRIP—and they're going to enslave the whole world if we don't stop 'em.

CROWD *is confused.*

FACTWINO: Why do you think the Russians started the arms race? They proved they didn't want peace the day they broke the Salt II treaty!
PRIEST: *(In crowd.)* He's right.

Everybody argues with his or her neighbor.

LIBRARIAN: *(To* BUDDY.*)* The US Senate refused to ratify the Salt II treaty!

BUDDY: I know that voice—and yet it don't sound right.

LIBRARIAN: Factwino's got all his facts wrong. Maybe I should get up there and—no, everybody would just think I'm weird.

BUDDY: Go ahead! Be a man!

SINGLE MOM: Look, I don't know what to think about the Russians—I just know I got a little girl, and I want to see her grow up! *(*FACTWINO *unzaps her. She staggers.)* So I better get on home and take care of her, instead of messing in white people's business.

FACTIVIST: *What?*

SINGLE MOM: If they want to blow themselves up, let 'em. Black people got more important problems right here in the Fillmore. *(Exits.)*

PRIEST: But there won't *be* a Fillmore after the fallout! *(*FACTWINO *unzaps him.)* Good. I never did like that neighborhood anyway—all those welfare cheats. I'm going to get myself a nice parish in Pacific Heights. *(Exits.)*

AFFLUENT LADY: Shame on him. A priest's supposed to love poor people. *(*FACTWINO *unzaps her.)* He's right. They could all have jobs. Making bombs. Out of my way, rifraff! *(Exits.)*

FACTIVIST: Wait! *(But she exits.)* What are you doing, Factwino? You're turning people off! You're destroying the movement!

(FACTWINO *winds up to unzap him.*) What's going to happen now? (*He flees.*)
FACTWINO: (*Sings.*)

BLOW THIS MOTHER UP

Would you like to be face-to-face
With your own destiny?
From the big bang it all began,
Another bang will set us all free.

All good things must come to an end
The Earth is no exception.
It's destiny!
Think about the ending: a spoil-less war
A war to put an end to them all.

One world, one bomb, one destiny,
Democratize destruction. (*Repeat.*)
The end of war, solution to pollution,
Let's blow this mother up. (*Repeat.*)

First the light to blind your eyes,
Concrete burns, men vaporize.
Then the winds, four hundred per hour.
Let's all take a radioactive shower. (*Sings.*)

Extinction is the death of death,
What a better way to go.
Ground zero is where you should go,
Don't miss the party when it all blows.

One world, one bomb, one destiny,
Democratize destruction (*Repeat.*)
The end of war, solution to pollution,
Let's blow this mother up. (*Repeat five times.*)

LIBRARIAN: (*As song ends, screams.*) It's my nightmare!

BUDDY, *on the verge of recognition, approaches* FACTWINO. FACTWINO *does not respond. He stands as if hypnotized.* ROBOT *enters, yanks* FACTWINO *off.*

BUDDY: That sound—that lady—Sedro! I remember! I'm coming, Sedro—wait for me! (*Follows.*)

LIBRARIAN: Buddy! Don't leave me!
PUNK: Let him go, lady. Look at it this way. Everybody *dies*—that's old, that's boring. But we are going to live to see the day when *everybody* dies. The ultimate experience—in my lifetime! No future—now! *(Exits.)*
LIBRARIAN: What's left?
SPIRIT OF INFORMATION: *(Enters.)* What's right?
LIBRARIAN: You are—right on time, just like you always are. Factwino's failed us...Somebody's got to save the world—send us another superhero of clarification, quick!
SPIRIT: I already struck out twice on that idea. One more time and it would be the ball game.
LIBRARIAN: *I* know—the responsibility's too much for one person. Why not make everybody supersmart? That's it—everybody needs to know everything!
SPIRIT: Then how come you trying so hard *not* to know? Uh-uh. Giving out too much information is how I made this mess in the first place.
LIBRARIAN: You?
SPIRIT: I wanted you all to understand everything. I revealed to you the deepest secret of nature—and ended up arming Armageddon.
LIBRARIAN: You meant to do right.
SPIRIT: But it went wrong. That's tragedy. This is where I bow out.
LIBRARIAN: What are we going to do?
SPIRIT: That's the question. Tell you what—I'll check back first thing in the next Millennium. I just hope somebody's home. *(Exeunt.)*

SCENE SEVEN

Sign: As News of *Factwino's Defection* Spreads, Infecting Thousands with *Despair*...

Sign: The *Nerve Center* Celebrates.

FACTWINO *is marched on by the* ROBOT, *followed by* ARMAGEDDONMAN. ROBOT *zaps* FACTWINO, *throwing him on floor.*

BUSINESS: Ah—the sweet nectar of revenge!
WAR: The champion of truth—look at him! *(Both laugh.)* The world is our hostage.
BUSINESS: And the ransom is handsome: the wealth of five continents. All ours!
WAR: Soon, I will show my faces to the world. *(The heads kiss.)*
BUSINESS: Thanks to you, Factwino, people will forget their fears. In one orgasmic moment, they will fall to their knees and worship Armageddonman.

FACTWINO: That will never happen! I won't let it happen!
BOTH: You? *(They laugh.)*
WAR: Soon, a giant spaceship will leave this miserable planet.
BUSINESS: Carrying me, myself, and our beautiful android.
WAR: As we take off, this finger will push that button...
BUSINESS: And Earth will become the blind kingdom of death. The very destruction of the planet will unleash enough energy to fuel our ship for eons...
FACTWINO: You're insane!
BOTH: What?
BUSINESS: You, Sedro F. Wooley, will be on that ship. You, a black man, a credit to your race, will be the last relic of human civilization—humanity's gift to the universe. This is your true mission, Mr. Wooley. Forget the past! *(ARMAGEDDONMAN and ROBOT exit, leaving bottle.)*
FACTWINO: Was it for this that cell first joined cell in the elemental soup of the original ocean? That a few fish found feet and dragged themselves onto dry land? We're talking about the end of knowledge—the end of the human race—the end of planet Earth. I was one of the first to warn of this danger, and now I'm the one that's helping bring it about. I'm a traitor. Once, Factwino...today, just a plain old fucking wino. Forget the past! *(Raises bottle to lips.)*
BUDDY: *(Rushes on.)* Sedro! Stop! You booze it, you lose it!

FACTWINO: What?
BUDDY: It's me, Buddy—remember?
FACTWINO: Buddy! How in the name of humanism did you get in here?
BUDDY: I followed you and that silver lady from that rally.
FACTWINO: Aw, Buddy—you saw that? *(Raises bottle.)*
BUDDY: Give it to me. *(Takes bottle.)* We went into this Bart tunnel I'd never seen before—then we took this supersonic subway ride where all the stops were states— Nevada, Utah, Colorado...it went so fast, it made my face go like this!
FACTWINO: You risked death, Buddy—for me?
BUDDY: Friends is friends.
ROBOT: *(Enters with computers beeping.)* Emergency!...Emergency! ...Intruder has penetrated Central Command...Disrupter positively identified...Buddy.

Battle royal between FACTWINO *and* BUDDY *and the* ROBOT.

FACTWINO: *(Seeing* ROBOT *about to zap* BUDDY.*)* Your mama was an adding machine.

ROBOT *sends* BUDDY *sprawling and is about to zap* FACTWINO. BUDDY *takes bottle out for a quick nip, sees* FACTWINO *in danger, and in the nick of time, pours wine into the* ROBOT. *It goes haywire.*

BUDDY: *(Unscrewing various parts.)* That's for kidnapping my partner—and *that's* for frying my brains. *(*ROBOT *is still.)*
FACTWINO: You disabled the android! Buddy, you's a hero!
BUDDY: This place gets me ascared. Let's get out of here.
FACTWINO: This way! *(*BUDDY *exits.* FACTWINO *follows, but stops as he hears:)*
ROBOT: Warning...Disconnect immediately from defense computer network...malfunction may spread to all military circuits...Disconnect immediately...Disconnect immediately...
FACTWINO: *(Calls.)* Go on, Buddy—I'm right behind you—don't turn around until you gets outside! Now's my chance. I been studying this machine for the last nine months—let's hope I done learned something. *(Fiddles with the* ROBOT.*)* Load capitve control subroutine...scramble registers...output to all processing units...OK, tinface: I think I got you where I want you.
ROBOT: Air Force computers: inoperative...Navy computers: inoperative... Ku Klux Klan computers: inoperative.

ARMAGEDDONMAN *enters.*

BUSINESS: No!
WAR: Stop that!
FACTWINO: Looks like you ain't much good without your high-tech toy.
BUSINESS: Come to Daddy, baby.
ROBOT: Not tonight: I have a headache...Not tonight: I have a headache... *(Exits.)*
WAR: Blistering bombers! This'll take hours to fix.
BUSINESS: You'll pay for this, Factwino!
FACTWINO: Not today: I got a date—with fresh air, sunshine, and my Buddy! *(Exits.)*
ARMAGEDDONMAN: *(Both heads.)* We'll meet again, Factwino—and when we do...
WAR: What?
BUSINESS: I'll think of something. *(They exit arguing.)*

SCENE EIGHT

The library.

Sign: Some Time Later

LIBRARIAN *enters and works.* FACTIVIST *enters with large stack of books.*

LIBRARIAN: *(Recognizing him.)* Hi! Say, we're holding a class here you might be interested in.
FACTIVIST: Yes. But first, I'd like to donate these books, to help people learn the truth about nuclear war.
LIBRARIAN: Bibles?
FACTIVIST: The Lord is coming soon with a cleansing fire. The skies shall turn black and the seas shall run red. Repent, or be consumed in His flame.
LIBRARIAN: Burnout. *(Checks watch.)* Oh, dear—it's almost time. *(Works faster.)*

When LIBRARIAN'S *back is turned,* AFFLUENT LADY *enters from stacks, stealing as many books as she can carry.*

LIBRARIAN: Just a minute, madam—where are you going with those books? *(Takes them from her.) With Enough shovels—Protest and Survive—Eight Minutes to Midnight*—if you want to read antinuclear literature, you're welcome to check it out like everybody else.
LADY: I don't want to read these books—I want to burn them. Especially

that one! *(Grabs at it.)*
LIBRARIAN: *(Holds on.)* The Fate of the Earth?
LADY: *(Tugging.)* Communists are putting these books in our libraries, to poison our minds and sap the fighting spirit of our youth. *(She spins off book into* PUNK, *who enters from stacks with walkman and tapes.)*
PUNK: I want to check out this tape.
LIBRARIAN: "One World, One Bomb, One Destiny" by Factwino.
PUNK: Only out a week and already it's hit the top of the charts.
SINGLE MOM: *(Enters.)* Hey, is this where they're having that survival class?
LIBRARIAN: I'm glad you could join us...
SINGLE MOM: Join you? I just came to see you honkies squirm. See, me and my daughter don't need no survival class, cause the melanin in our skin will make us radiation-proof. When it's all over, we going to take over. Glow, baby, glow.

FACTIVIST *enters from stacks as class begins.*

LIBRARIAN: Your public library offers this class to familiarize citizens with our government's plan for our nuclear survival. Let's begin with a review of the basics. When the eight minute warning is sounded, change to tennis shoes or hiking boots, don your sunglasses, and pack...?
FACTIVIST: Your Bible.
LADY: Your revolver.
PUNK: Ludes! *(Puts on headset and plays tape.* SINGLE MOM *laughs hysterically.)*

BUDDY *and* SEDRO *enter.*

BUDDY: Listen at that bullshit! Hey, Sedro—it's the perfect chance to find out if you still got the power.
SEDRO: I was full of booze, Buddy!
BUDDY: But you never took a drink! Come on partner, get in there and make these people think.
SEDRO: Buddy, I don't know if I can still do it.
BUDDY: *(Looking in disbelief at the* LIBRARIAN *as he pushes* SEDRO *forward.)* Tsk—I would never have expected that from her. *(They watch.)*
LIBRARIAN: On this map prepared by our Federal Emergency Management Agency, authorized evacuation routes from San Francisco are shown in red. *(Points to the three roads and two bridges.)* Should any of the routes be blocked for any reason, take

an emergency escape route, shown in yellow. *(Arrows pointing into ocean.)* But we all know the best protection is—
SINGLE MOM, FACTIVIST, LADY: A strong defense.

Fanfare. SEDRO *rips off his coat. He is still* FACTWINO. *He winds up, but before he can zap.*

LIBRARIAN: Bullshit! *(Throws map down.)*
CROWD: Huh?
LIBRARIAN: Are you all going to wait until your nightmare comes true before you wake up and face what you know? *(Crosses to* PUNK, *pulls earphones off. Sings.)*

> If you could see the earth,
> From far above the sky
> You'd see a shining globe
> Whose colors tell of life,
> A miracle of history,
> Or circumstance or mystery,
> With a living air and land and sea:
> Our only home and destiny.

People look at each other.

> And what if in the instant
> Of the blinking of an eye,
> You looked upon the earth again
> And saw that it had died:
> No animals or birds or trees
> Only poisoned air to breathe,
> Deadly rains and lifeless seas—
> It's the end of history.

> Would you ask, "Who let this happen?"
> Would you think it was insane?
> No one stopped the murder
> Of a planet and a race.
> Is this to be our legacy,
> An epitaph no one will read:
> "They would not save their history,
> Their children, their eternity."

An uneasy silence.

SINGLE MOM: *(Breaks it.)* Suppose me and Aisha did make it up to

Yreka—some cracker'd blow our heads off the minute we stuck our nose in the shelter. *(To* FACTIVIST.*)* You got any of those fact things on you?

FACTIVIST: I'm all out.

AFFLUENT LADY: *(Grabs anit-nuke books.)* Here—read these! *(Passes them out.)*

FACTIVIST: Yeah! Hey—how about forming a Former Factwino Groupies Affinity Group?

CROWD *exits, buzzing, as* BUDDY *stamps their books.* PUNK *is left, reading* The Fate of the Earth. *Feels* LIBRARIAN *watching.*

PUNK: "A miracle of history?"...I want to see what comes after punk. *(Exits reading.)*

BUDDY: Hey, you were awesome, lady. No—you were humungous!

LIBRARIAN: Buddy! *(They embrace.)*

BUDDY: Hey, there's somebody here I want you to meet. You ain't gonna believe this, but this is...

SEDRO: Sedro F. Wooley.

LIBRARIAN: Sedro F. Wooley...Hey! You owe me three books.

SEDRO: *(Presents them.)* Took a little time to round them up. Tell me—do you do this kind of thing often?

LIBRARIAN: I try to do something every day. Listen, if you'll excuse me, I've got a real mess in the stacks...

BUDDY: Say, lady—I never did get your name.

LIBRARIAN: Hope. *(She gives the zap sign.* SEDRO *returns it. She exits.)*

SEDRO: Well, Buddy—I think I'm going to delay Factwino's entrance just a little bit longer. Give the new talent a chance to work out. Because see, we all going up against Armageddonman. And *everybody* got to find their power. *(Exeunt.)*

Comics on the Stage
Henri Picciotto

Modern children—of all ages, as the saying goes—still need heroes and fairy tales. Even though many of us have been robbed of the myths of antiquity and of those of our tribal ancestors, we still seek those truths of the human condition which are not accessible to our rational selves. And the search still takes us back to gods and demons, dragons and heroes. Dorothy's and her companions' tribulations in the land of Oz, and Superman's fight for "truth and justice" are two examples of modern myths which have become totally embedded in our culture.

While it is the movies that guaranteed that Baum's "American fairy tale" entered our world, it is comic books that established Superman's niche in our consciousness. Comic books and the cinema are 20th Century media which have cross-fertilized each other: Suprman flies on film and TV, and R2-D2 computes in comic book frames. Dorothy has crossed the line to theater and regularly graces the elementary school auditorium stage throughout the land. **Supermen** has not. How many arms were broken when little boys with improvised capes tried to fly from building tops? The conventions of the superhero genre are strict, and their extravagant demands in the special effects department have tended to preclude its appearance on the stage—until the San Francisco Mime Troupe tackled it in 1980 with *Factperson*.

To the Mime Troupe, the comic book genre offered big, colorful characters, of the type the company excels at portraying. The superhero format allowed them to tackle the many issues of the Reagan campaign in a series of episodes. The Troupe's aesthetic requires a combination of three factors: realistic social and political analysis from a left-wing perspective; traditional theatrical structure; and modern popular cultural forms such as vaudeville, musical comedy, science fiction, or the detective story. As a long time fan, I had seen the Mime Troupe show real love for these various genres over the years. When I saw *Factperson*, though, I felt that the Troupe's grasp of the comic book world was only partial. Such basic elements of the genre as the "secret identity" and the "super-villain" went untapped. Rita changed in and out of her Factperson outfit

---

Henri Picciotto teaches mathematics at San Francisco's Urban School, was a co-author of the *Factwino* plays, and is a member of Ant Theater.

casually—there was no secret. Her arch-enemy was Milton Friedman, the right-wing economist, a colorful person on the political scene but a rather boring choice for a comic book villian!

Moreover the innovations brought into the field by Marvel Comics in the '60s (let alone anything that may have happened since) went unheeded. These include, especially, an increased complexity in the superhero's personal life. While Clark Kent's biggest problems had tended to be trivial, Peter Parker (Spiderman's alter ego), has had to face major social crises: how to respond to the draft during the Vietnam war; how to take care of an old, sick Aunt May, with very little money; and so on. While Rita, the heroine of *Factperson,* was an interesting character, she had no friends or acquaintances, and it was hard to get interested in her life. Her job and rent problems provided a rather thin story line.

I raised these criticisms in a review of *Factperson,* and in conversations with Joan Holden, the Mime Troupe's head writer. She asked me to collaborate on the script to a sequel to *Factperson.* Since one of my fondest fantasies had been to work with the Mime Troupe, I was elated.

Before writing *Factwino Meets the Moral Majority* we read some of Stan Lee's classic Marvel comics from the '60s, as well as some of his comments on the genre. His views on plot: "To us, the story's the thing."[1] Hence the increasingly thicker plots of the *Factwino* plays. On style: "I'm every bit as concerned with the way something sounds to the ear when reading it as I am with the meaning itself."[2] Hence the alliteration-laden text panels and wisecracks in the *Factwino* plays. Stan Lee's tongue-in-cheek style is also characterized by an unusual self-consciousness. The writer is often very evident. This is very much echoed by the Mime Troupe's Brechtian approach, in which the audience is periodically reminded of the actor while they watch the character.

On villains: "You've got to admit they're colorful. You've got to admit they're interesting. You've got to admit they wear the craziest costumes, and sport the wildest way-out names. And, most of all, you've got to admit our heroes need them..."[3] Hence Armaggedonman, the two-headed, cold-hearted, representative of Evil (or is it the military-industrial complex?)–and Armageddonman's android (the Smart Machine), another genuine touch of pop science-fiction. These creatures allowed the Mime Troupe actors to use their fine physical comedy performance skills. The sight of two actors in one suit as Armageddonman, dancing, hopping, turning as one, was one of the more breath-taking feats I have ever seen on any stage. And the fights between Buddy and the Robot could have been lifted straight off the page of a Marvel comic.

All these elements provide a form that is well suited to the Mime Troupe's broad comic performance style. (Comics doing comics?) But while they are important, all the trappings of the comic book genre are mainly a foil for one central feature: the superhero. Who is the hero? What are the super-powers and where do they come from? How are they used or misused? What is the hero's Achilles' heel? What is the hero's relationship to those he serves? These questions are more difficult than they seem. (When a comic book writer does not answer them well, the comic is discontinued.) The success of all three plays stems in large part from the fact that they were answered effectively by head writer Joan Holden.[4] Tackling them seriously raised the level of the plays from agit-prop to a mythical level where the political message is only part of what the play has to offer.

Conventional comic book heroes tend to be white male professionals: journalist, photographer, industrialist, millionaire, doctor, student, scientist. During the '70s comic books have featured increased numbers of black and especially female superheroes, in response to the times. But the Mime Troupe went further: with Rita, we have a working class woman heroine; and with Sedro, a black wino. These choices, combined with the "gender free" name inscribed on the superhero's cape (Factperson), are a necessary—if not original—comment on the conventions of the genre.

But the left-wing objection to the concept of a superhero cuts deeper. The argument goes that if the people trust any one "super" leader, they will become passive instead of active agents in their own cause; or that having allowed themselves to be led, they could be led for ill as well as for good. This issue is simultaneously dealt with and avoided in *Factperson*. Because she uses her powers for personal gain, Rita loses them forever! This is a rather stunning departure from the conventional invincibility of the comic book hero, and its very absurdity (from the point of view of the genre) provided the play with an exciting (and "politically correct") last scene: all those who were touched by Factperson have turned to self-education, and we see them checking out books at the library (a symbolic locale to which we return in both sequels). Thus the masses have been inspired, not supplanted, by the heroine.

But the genre fights back. Superheroes do not die that easily. As Stan Lee put it: "In the wonderful world of comics, what is past is prologue; and what is gone is never really departed."[5]

Even though Rita could never recover her powers, Factperson had to return. The continuity was provided by the Spirit of Information, a cross between goddess, fairy godmother, and bag lady. While the traditional superhero is endowed, often by accident, with various physical assets, the *Fact* heroes' powers are strictly intellectual, and granted to them by the Spirit of Information in response to the heroine's/hero's deepest wish. Rita's wish ("knowing every fact there is") is a response to her lack of education and lack of self-confidence in the face of bigotry. The Spirit transforms her into a walking encyclopedia. Of course knowledge is not enough, and she needs to exercise judgment to decide how to use it. This is where she eventually fails.

The whole concept of hero was addressed more fully in the *Factwino* plays. Factwino's power ("making people think") is at the same time greater (more magical) and more democratic (requiring more from the people he affects). His dilemma is deeper and more tragic than Rita's. To gain the power, he must renounce alcohol. However the price of heroism is actually higher. In order to carry out his mission, Sedro must leave his friend (Buddy) behind. His exalted status among the people he helps (echoed by a similar adulation from the Mime Troupe's audience) inflates his ego, as does the increasing responsibility he must bear. (While at first he is fighting Falwell's obscurantism by making people think, he is later called upon to defeat Armageddonman himself and save the planet from permanent destruction—singlehandedly.) Thus all the questions about heroism are mirrored internally in Sedro's heart and mind.

This culminates in the rally scene of *Factwino vs. Armageddonman*, where our hero's powers have been reversed and he is forced to serve his arch-enemy by making people think the wrong thoughts. While this is a standard comic book device, its use in *Factwino* is particularly poignant and stands out as the emotional peak of the trilogy. It is laden with political and personal tragedy. It is the logical apex of the hero's trajectory: as he became a servant of the people, he was forced into loneliness. As he became more and more important to the left, he became a more and more significant target for the right, and a more useful potential ally for them to buy. They cannot buy him, but they succeed in using him. Sedro must face his limitations. He is not invincible. He is a fallible human being, as we all are.

His feelings of guilt are intense, but this is not Greek tragedy. The requirements of comedy, of comic book tradition, and of the Mime Troupe's positive political outlook all dictate a happy ending. Buddy rescues Factwino and their friendship is renewed. The librarian speaks out, becoming a new crusader for truth and peace—inspired by the Spirit of Information, but not endowed with any special powers. She is Everyperson coming to the rescue. As a result, Sedro decides to use his powers with moderation.

The lessons of the trilogy are three. First, friendship and personal commitment are no less important than social-political consciousness (apolitical Buddy is the one who defeats the android to save the very friend who had abandoned him to serve "the movement"). Second, the contradiction between our need to look up to heroes and our need to act ourselves is only superficial. We need heroes precisely in order to find heroism in ourselves. To quote Ursula K. Le Guin:

> You look at the Blond Hero—really look—and he turns into a gerbil. But you look at Apollo, and he looks back at you.
>
> The poet Rilke looked at a statue of Apollo about fifty years ago, and Apollo spoke to him. "You must change your life," he said.
>
> When the genuine myth rises into consciousness, that is always its message. You must change your life.[6]

Finally, we learned the most profound lesson of magic: by the time you find the philosopher's stone, you have also learned that you may accomplish more by NOT using it (Sedro makes way for new, non-magic "talent").

The ending is consistent with comic book conventions: the villain's defeat is clearly not final. Factwino—and his script writers—finally learn the wisdom of a well-used secret identity. But the reason Rita and Sedro resonated as well as they did in the hearts of audiences was not only because they fit in a familiar cultural matrix. Armageddonman does too, but he is merely fun. Rita and Sedro we recognize, we identify with, we care about, we feel for, because they originate in a very personal place in their creators. Their dilemmas are those every American progressive has to face. The Mime Troupe has been laying out the facts and helping people think for 25 years. May they never lose their powers.

FOOTNOTES

1. *The Superhero Women,* by Stan Lee, p. 8 (Simon & Schuster, New York, 1977).
2. *The Superhero Women,* p. 106.
3. *Bring on the Villains,* by Stan Lee, p. 7 (Simone & Schuster, New York, 1976).
4. This is not to deny the importance of other contributors, including the actors and directors. See "Collaboration V: Shared Visions" by Joan Holden in *Callboard,* January 1983.
5. *The Superhero Women,* p. 210.
6. "Myth and Archetype in Science Fiction," by Ursula K. Le Guin, in *The Language of the Night,* pp. 67-68 (Berkley Books, New York, 1982).

The Dream of Kitamura
Philip Kan Gotanda

The Dream of Kitamura was first presented at the Asian American Theater Company in San Francisco on June 19, 1982, with the following cast:

PAOLO	William Ellis Hammond
ROSANJIN	Marc Hayashi
ZUMA	Amy Hill
OTSU	Diana Tanaka
SAM	Victor Wong
KARMA ONE	Emilya Cachapero
KARMA TWO	June Mesina

Directed by David Henry Hwang
Musical Director/Composer, Michael Sasaki
Choreography by Mitsuko Mitsueda
Set design by Bobby Horiuchi, Helen Plenert
Costume design by Lydia Tanji
Lighting design by Jim Schelstrate
Producers, Pam Wu, Wilbur Obata

The Dream of Kitamura was presented in Los Angeles at East West Players on March 2, 1983, with the following cast:

ROSANJIN	Jim Ishida
ZUMA	Shizuko Hoshi
OTSU	Susan Haruye Ioka
SAM	Keone Young
PAOLO	James Saito
KARMA ONE	Merv Maruyama
KARMA TWO	Shirlee Kong

Directed by Mako
Music composed and arranged by Kazu Matsui
Light and set design by Shizuko Herrera
Costume design by Shigeru Yaji
Choreography by Shizuko Hoshi
Produced by Jim Ishida, Keone Young

©1983 by Philip Kan Gotanda
CAUTION: All rights strictly reserved. Professionals and amateurs are hereby warned that *The Dream of Kitamura* is subject to a royalty. It is protected under the copyright laws of all countries covered by the International Copyright Convention. Permission in writing must be secured before any kind of performance is given. All inquiries should be addressed to the author's agent, Helen Merrill, 337 West 22nd Street, New York, NY 10011.

The Dream of Kitamura was written while the author was serving as the Rockefeller Playwright-in-Residence at the Asian American Theater Comany.

CHARACTERS

ROSANJIN: The lord. Either psychotic or prescient. Early 50s.
ZUMA: Wife of Rosanjin. Repressed. Early 50s. Movement/dance background.
OTSU: Daughter of Rosanjin and Zuma. Born soon after the crime was committed. Late teens.
SAM: Bodyguard. Salty, shrewd, survivor. Early 50s.
PAOLO: Bodyguard. Hot-blooded. Late teens.
TWO KARMIC KIDS: A kind of physicalization of the collective and individual karmas of the characters. They participate and help facilitate action on stage. They are unseen by the characters. Dance background.

SETTING

STAGE: Up center there is a throne: Large, ornate, dark, decadent. At various points on the stage there are *shoji*-like panels on runners that can be slid open and shut. They are suspended by wires at various heights and set to suggest multi-levels to the staging. The Japanese character *yume,* meaning dream, is violently splashed like an action painting in large black strokes on one of the panels. Part of the character spills onto the floor.

LIGHTING: The play takes place in shadows, pools, and shafts of light.

COSTUMES: Punked-out futuristic samurai with flourishes of cowboyism.

MUSIC

Used in much the same manner as with film, to set mood, help underscore action of scene. Instrumentation, mixture of traditional Japanese used in a western mode and contemporary electric, new wavish/electronic.

The Dream of Kitamura
Philip Kan Gotanda

PROLOGUE

Darkness. The sound of chanting: "Kitamura" *being intoned like a Buddhist sutra.*

VOICE OVER *during chanting:* Kitamura. It is a time of historical change and economic transition. Once great families of tremendous power and wealth fall into poverty and ruin, victims of the changing order. Somehow Rosanjin and Zuma have managed to maintain the life-style that their families have been accustomed to living for generations. It is a family of once great love. A crime has been committed. A robbery. A double murder. There was a witness.

The loud crack of two pieces of wooden 2"x 4" being slapped together and cut to silence. A tight spot opens on three faces, synced with the loud beat of the taiko *drum. The two* KARMIC KIDS *framing a face covered with a hideous demon mask. This is* KITAMURA. *Shakuhachi flute enters and more* taiko. *Music that is emblematic of* KITAMURA *begins. Lights come up.* KITAMURA *and* KARMIC KIDS *do movement. They hear something coming and hide. One of the* KARMIC KIDS *appears with the mask representing a* YOUNG MAN. *The* YOUNG MAN *calls,* "Otsu, Otsu." KITAMURA *who has been watching from the shadows jumps out. The* YOUNG MAN *is frightened and flees.* KITAMURA *hears someone else coming and hides again.* OTSU *appears looking for the* YOUNG MAN. *She calls his name wondering where he is:* "Pascal, Pascal." *Instead of attacking, the demon watches her from the shadows. Dim to darkness.*

ACT ONE

Darkness. PAOLO *is lit in a small pool of light down left. He is facing the audience, crouching, down on one knee, head bowed down. Suddenly he springs up, his sword drawn, staring out into the darkness.* SAM *is lit in a small pool of light down right. He is crouching in the same position as* PAOLO, *down on one knee, head bowed. Instead of springing up,* SAM *rolls over in a heap, sound asleep. We hear him snoring loudly. In the darkness we hear* ROSANJIN's *voice screaming:* "KITAMURA! KITAMURA!" *Lights come up quickly on the up stage throne area.* ROSANJIN *sleeps in the throne. He is dreaming. His voice is one of terror. His eyes are closed.* ZUMA, *his wife, rushes in from stage left. She shakes him and he awakens wild-eyed. He has the look of a man going over the edge. He clings to her and stares out into the darkness. Stage right* OTSU, *their daughter, peers in and observes but does not enter.* PAOLO *turns and observes what is going on. He runs towards the throne. He stops when* ZUMA *gives him a glaring look. He decides to back off. As he does, the lights dim on the up stage area. The scene should have a choreographed, cinematic feel to it.*

Center Stage: SAM *is still asleep, snoring loudly.* PAOLO *looks back at throne area, then disgustedly at* SAM *on the ground. Sits down on haunches and lights a match, watching the flame, thinking. Instead of blowing it out, licks fingers and grabs the match from the top burnt end, turns it over, and watches the flame burn up and out. Poof. His mind is made up.* PAOLO *moves towards* SAM.

PAOLO: I quit. *(No response from* SAM.*)* I resign! *(No response.)* I'M LEAVING!! *(*SAM *stirs. Gets up holding back.)*
SAM: Nothing more disgusting than old people that live too long. *(He faces* PAOLO, *puts his index finger to* PAOLO'*s chest.)* What's that? *(As* PAOLO *glances down,* SAM *flicks his hand up whacking his nose. Chuckling to himself.)* Attention, attention. Gotta pay attention.
PAOLO: *(Irritated.)* Sam.
SAM: *(Pounding his back, stretching like an old man.)* Yeah?
PAOLO: I'm leaving. Don't try and talk me out of it 'cause my mind's made up. I'm leaving.
SAM: *(Turns and faces* PAOLO. *Very dramatically he plugs his ears with his fingers and closes eyes.)* Alright. I'm ready.
PAOLO: What's that supposed to mean? *(*SAM *can't hear, doesn't respond.)* WHAT'S THAT... *(Stops and taps* SAM *who takes fingers out.)* What's that supposed to mean?
SAM: Once knew a man tried to stop a friend from shooting himself. Stuck his hand in there last moment and got it blown clean off, along with his friend's head. Got real depressed, no hand. Couldn't shoot his gun. Couldn't hold his chopsticks. Couldn't play with his wanger. Decided to shoot himself. Said to me, "Sam, I'm gonna shoot myself." Put the gun to his head. Coulda reached right in there and tried to stop him. Know what I did? *(*SAM *once again plugs ears with his fingers and closes eyes.)*
PAOLO: Come on, Sam. *(No response.)* SAM!! *(*SAM *takes fingers out.)* I'm leaving. I'm not committing suicide.

SAM: Kitamura. *(PAOLO doesn't respond.)* Kitamura.
PAOLO: Kitamura, so what?
SAM: He's coming.
PAOLO: I'm leaving.
SAM: He's coming fast.
PAOLO: I'm leaving fast.
SAM: Kitamura. *(Pause.)* You. Out there. Alone. At night. Riding, riding, riding. You feel the rush of the cold night air. It slaps against your face. Whips your hair side to side. A thousand stars swirl by over head. You feel free. You go faster. You feel more free. Faster. Freer. You take short gasps, drawing crisp, icy air into your lungs. Your insides burn with a cold pleasureful pain. You feel alive. So alive. Suddenly, a glimpse. What's that? A sliver of light just off to your left. You only get a fraction of a second to view its sordid beauty and...SWOOSH! Your throat is slit. Your jugular severed. You're dead. Kitamura has killed you. *(Pause.)* Out there, alone, you don't know when he could strike. It's suicide. You'd be cut to ribbons. You don't have a Chinaman's chance.
PAOLO: How many times do I have to tell you? *(Grabs* SAM *on both sides of his head.)* I'M NOT CHINESE!!

> SAM *knocks* PAOLO's *hands away and tries to poke his eyes with two fingers, Three Stooges style.* PAOLO, *in turn, blocks by putting his hand in front of his nose, Three Stooges style.* SAM *slaps* PAOLO *across the head with his free hand.* PAOLO *gets upset.*

ROSANJIN *is awakened by all the commotion. Lights come up on throne area.*

SAM: SHHH! Take it easy, take it easy. Paolo, you take yourself too seriously. I take you too seriously. Hey, you wanna die? That's your business.

ROSANJIN: Come here.

SAM: There you go, you've done it now. You got the old man up.

PAOLO: *(To* ROSANJIN.*)* Which one?

ROSANJIN: COME HERE! *(They approach the throne.)* I dreamed about him again. He's closer. He seems to be coming from the...

PAOLO: *(Interrupts.)* Did you see what he looked like?

ROSANJIN: Do not interrupt me when I'm speaking.

PAOLO: Damn it, we don't even know what he looks like. If we at least had a description or... (SAM *trying to get* PAOLO *to quiet down.)*

ROSANJIN: *(Interrupts. To* PAOLO.*)* Come here. (PAOLO *stops in mid-sentence.)* Come here. (PAOLO *hesitates, then moves closer.)* Closer. (PAOLO *moves in, their faces are very close.* ROSANJIN *suddenly slaps him hard.)* Never interrupt me when I'm speaking. (PAOLO *can barely contain his anger.* SAM *holds him back, trying to calm him.* PAOLO *has his hand on his sword.)* I dreamed about him again. He's getting very close. He may even be in the general vicinity. And he appears very powerful. Far beyond what I had originally imagined. I want around the clock protection. Someone near me at all times. Constant surveillance of the walls and grounds. Sleep in shifts. That's all. (SAM *starts to leave,* PAOLO *continues to glare at* ROSANJIN.*)* That's all! (SAM *drags* PAOLO *back to center stage.)* TEA! TEA!

ZUMA *enters with a tray carrying a pot of tea and two cups. She settles beside him and pours out two cups of tea. He reaches out and swallows the tea in one gulp. As* ZUMA *reaches out to take the other cup for herself,* ROSANJIN *snatches it away and drinks the contents. He sets the cup back on the tray, ignoring her. He is totally absorbed in himself.* ZUMA *stares at the empty cup. Lights dim on the throne area.*

SAM: Whose turn? (PAOLO *shrugs.* SAM *sticks hand out and they begin to thumb wrestle to determine. They continue talking while wrestling.)*

PAOLO: I know him.

SAM: What?

PAOLO: From somewhere. I know him from somewhere.

SAM: It's just a class thing. If you got too much money it makes you boring. All boring people look alike. *(Catches PAOLO's thumb.)* I'll take the first shift.
PAOLO: I don't like it, Sam. I don't like it one bit. We should get the hell outta here while we still can.
SAM: There you go, there you go. Taking yourself too seriously again. I'm gonna check around the grounds a bit like the old man wants us to. You keep an eye out around here. *(Starts to leave.)* Relax. Nothing's gonna happen... *(Sneaks up behind PAOLO and slashes his finger across his jugular making a cutting sound.)* ...unless you drop your guard. Attention, attention. Gotta pay attention. *(Exits, chuckling to himself.)*

OTSU *appears stage left up. Watches* PAOLO *for a moment, then approaches him from behind.*

OTSU: Where's your partner?
PAOLO: *(Whirls around, notices it's a woman.)* Who are you?
OTSU: I *asked* you a question.
PAOLO: He's looking around the grounds.
OTSU: My father hired you. He pays you to kill.
PAOLO: He pays us to defend.
OTSU: Defend? Hah! Defend what?
PAOLO: *(Motions to surroundings.)* This. You.
OTSU: Not me, not me. This is his world. Everything revolves around him. You are defending him and his world. Not me. But against what? You can't kill an illusion. Slit the throat of a dream. They're demons of his own invention. You defend him against his own mind, or didn't you know that? You aren't bodyguards, you're baby sitters.
PAOLO: Then why keep us around? Why not throw us out?
OTSU: Is not the food adequate? The pay more than adequate?
PAOLO: But if I were to believe you...
OTSU: *(Interrupts.)* You believe.
PAOLO: If I were to believe you, we serve no purpose. We merely take your money and...
OTSU: *(Interrupts.)* My *father's* money.
PAOLO: Take your father's money without rendering services. Not exactly a sound business proposition.
OTSU: No, but it keeps peace in the house. I didn't say you weren't rendering a service. I'm merely clarifying what that service really is. Besides, if I were to order you out, he would only hire someone to take your place. And he can be very mean, as you probably

The Dream of Kitamura

know. I can disagree. That's a daughter's prerogative. He allows me that luxury. I can disagree, but never disobey. *(Pause.)* Taking money for no work is like stealing. Taking food for no service is like begging. *(Turns to leave, then stops.)* Would you like your dinner served now or later? *(Exits.)*

SAM *appears.* PAOLO *continues to glare in the direction of* OTSU's *exit.*

SAM: 'Course you could be right. Who am I to say? I could be treating this thing much too lightly. I mean this could be just the tip of the iceberg we're dealing with here... *(Continues talking right through.)*
PAOLO: *(Staring after* OTSU, *quietly.)* I'm staying.
SAM: ...The fin of the shark cutting through the water, swisshhh. This could be one false move in a whole underground network of wrong moves. The shadow of some greater negativity...*(Continues.)*
PAOLO: *(Still staring, louder.)* I'm staying.
SAM: ...Some bigger darkness that is starting to emerge. Starting to split its seams and make itself so very clear.
PAOLO: I'M STAYING!!

PAOLO *glares at* SAM. SAM *looks at* PAOLO *a moment. Then facing him, slowly plugs his ears with his fingers. Dim to darkness.*

Lights up on throne area. Music/sound. This is a recollection scene played out in ROSANJIN's *mind. The two* KARMAS *lead* ROSANJIN *to center stage and set him in motion. They narrate the recollection scene while* ROSANJIN *acts it out. They also play the roles of the man and woman, utilizing masks.*

KARMA ONE: Rosanjin's dream.
KARMA TWO: Rosanjin is a young man.
KARMA ONE: He has broken into a house.
KARMA TWO: He is looking for gold and jewels.

The KARMAS *have set out a bag with jewels strewn about for* ROSANJIN *to find. While* ROSANJIN *is putting the jewels into the bag the* KARMAS *play the roles of the man and woman of the house.*

KARMA ONE: A man enters. *(Holds mask in front of face. Discovers* ROSANJIN *stealing the jewels.)* Nani mono da? Nani o yatte iru? Dorobo! Yamero! [Who are you? What are you doing? Thief! Stop!]

KARMA TWO: A woman enters. *(Holds mask.)* Anata! Kiyotsukete! Hocho moteru! [Husband! Watch out! He's got a knife!]

The MAN *attacks* ROSANJIN *who in defense stabs the* MAN. *In a stylized manner the* KARMA *floats mask to the ground.*

KARMA TWO: *(To mask.)* Anata! Anata! [Husband! Husband!] (ROSANJIN *realizes that the woman is a witness and must be killed also. He advances on her.)* Yurushite kudasai. Inochi dake o tasukete kudasai. [Please overlook me. Please spare my life.] Nani mo imasen...nani mo imasen. [I won't say anything...I won't say anything.]

ROSANJIN *stabs the woman.* KARMA TWO *floats mask to ground.* ROSANJIN *hurriedly begins to put gold and jewels into the sack. Dim to darkness.*

OTSU *is seated and* ZUMA *is behind her combing her hair. Music enters and accompanies this visual for twelve seconds. The music fades out.*

OTSU: I hate it.
ZUMA: Your father wishes it.
OTSU: Demands it. I hate having strangers lurking around the grounds.
ZUMA: They do no harm.
OTSU: They do nothing.
ZUMA: They serve their purpose. *(Pause.)* His dreams are his eyes.
OTSU: They're symptoms of his disease.
ZUMA: They reveal.
OTSU: There is no Kitamura.
ZUMA: They see for all of us.
OTSU: They see nothing. We wait for no one. He dreams the dream of all dying men.
ZUMA: I said not to speak of that in this...
OTSU: *(Interrupts.)* He dreams of death.
ZUMA: He is not dying! *(Angry pause. Combing continues.)*
OTSU: Pascal. *(No response.)* What happened to Pascal?
ZUMA: I don't know what you're talking about.
OTSU: You know very well what I'm talking about.
ZUMA: If you mean the young man you used to sneak out at night to meet, I suppose he grew tired of you. His type is not very reliable.
OTSU: I am an adult.
ZUMA: You know nothing of the real world.
OTSU: How can I? You never give me a chance.

ZUMA: We give you whatever you want.
OTSU: I want to be free.
ZUMA: Within reason.
OTSU: I want to be free to pick and choose my own friends. To go wherever I want to without having to be chaperoned, escorted, watched every second of my existence.
ZUMA: We live in dangerous times. That's part of your ignorance. You cannot see the evil in men's souls. The countryside is being overrun by thieves and murderers. Homes are broken into. People savagely killed. Family fortunes stolen into the night. *(Pause.)* We always give you what you need.
OTSU: Pascal?
ZUMA: If Rosanjin were to find out what you've been...
OTSU: I don't care what he thinks! How can you put up with it? Day in and day out bowing and scraping to his demands? His petty...
ZUMA: *(Interrupts.)* He is ill.
OTSU: That is no excuse.
ZUMA: He is ill!
OTSU: I'm not talking about him. *(Pause.)* What about you? What do you dream of?
ZUMA: I have no dreams. He dreams for both of us.
OTSU: You dream. You choose not to remember.
ZUMA: I never dream. I have no dreams. I have no dreams.

Combing continues. Music brought up slowly. Dim to darkness. Music fades out.

A candle is lit. ROSANJIN *holds it. His face is illuminated.*

ROSANJIN: I wanted to talk to you. Alone. Who told you about me?
SAM'S VOICE: No one.
ROSANJIN: You seem familiar. Do I know you?
VOICE: You hired us.
ROSANJIN: What is your name?
VOICE: No.
ROSANJIN: What is your name?
VOICE: Sam.
ROSANJIN: And the younger one?
VOICE: Paolo.
ROSANJIN: Who is he? *(No response.)* I know you.
VOICE: No.
ROSANJIN: Long ago. Another life time.
VOICE: No.

Long pause. ROSANJIN *lights* SAM's *candle.* SAM *is illuminated.*

ROSANJIN: *(While lighting the other candle he speaks.)* Watch. See. See. I like that. It excites me. There is that moment when lighting another candle when the original flame becomes very small. All its life force is being sucked up and used to give life to the other flame. And for a moment you hold your breath, not knowing if they're both going to live or die...and then POOF! They both spring back to life. But notice the original flame is slower to recover. the one that's given life seems to have lost something in the process. The one that's taken life, on the other hand, seems vital and strong. An odd outcome. Not exactly what you would expect. The life giver punished. The life taker rewarded. *(Pause.* ROSANJIN *stares at* SAM.*)* It was you, wasn't it?

SAM *looks at him. His expression reveals nothing. He blows out* ROSANJIN's *flame, turns down stage, face illuminated by the dancing light. Pauses, thinking. Then blows out his candle. Darkness.*

ZUMA *lit in a pool of light, down center right, angled slightly inward. She is seated on the ground. Music—cyclic, methodical, hypnotic. A pot of tea and two cups in front of her. She pours out two cups of tea. She pushes one cup to an area across from her as if she were serving an invisible guest. She drinks all of her own tea, sets her cup down in front of her, then looks across to the other cup. She looks both ways to see if anyone is watching. She then reaches across, takes that cup and pours its tea into her own cup, setting the now empty cup back in its original position. She picks up her cup now full with tea and is about to drink. She finds she is unable to bring herself to drink the other person's tea.* ZUMA *pours the tea back into the cup across from her and puts the empty cup down in front of her. She then takes the now full cup, pours it back into the pot, and sets it down next to the other cup in front of her. Back to original position.* ZUMA *begins the cycle of movement again. As she does, one of the* KARMAS *is lit in another pool of light up center doing the exact same movement as* ZUMA. *They are perfectly synced, the only difference being there is no tea in her pot. About half way thru the cycle a third pool of light is lit down center left with the other* KARMA *doing the same movement in sync. This one has no pot or cups and mimes everything. Now they begin to stop, start, breaking apart into different stages of the pattern. They all sync-up for the last stage of movement, ending in unison. Dim to darkness.*

PHOTO: BOB HSIANG

PAOLO *is on guard. He bends down to drink from the pond. While drinking he notices carp swimming in the water. He watches, following the movement of one of the fish. Suddenly he grabs, pulling out a flapping fish.* PAOLO *hears somebody coming, tosses the fish back, and hides. As the figure approaches he jumps out, sword raised. It is* OTSU, *carrying a small flat basket of apples and lemons to wash in the pond. She doesn't react at all.*

PAOLO: I could have killed you.
OTSU: I wish Kitamura were here. I'd feel a lot safer.
PAOLO: Don't go sneaking around like that.
OTSU: This is my house, remember? *(Starts washing fruit.)*
PAOLO: *(Decides he was a bit rough.)* May I have one?
OTSU: No.
PAOLO: Did you pick them yourself?
OTSU: As you walk by the trees drop them in your basket.
PAOLO: I'm sorry.
OTSU: For what? One apologizes for mistakes in behavior, not in birth.
PAOLO: Paolo. My name is Paolo. What is yours?
OTSU: I don't talk to strangers. *(She gets up to leave.)*
PAOLO: I'm not, you know my name now. Paolo.
OTSU: *(Stops and turns.)* Otsu.
PAOLO: Otsu? What a lovely name.
OTSU: *(Mimicking sarcastically.)* What a lovely name.
PAOLO: Your father is a man of very good taste to choose such a beautiful name.
OTSU: My mother named me and my father is a bastard.
PAOLO: Not only a lovely name but a lovely disposition, too. Tell me, where did you learn such impeccable manners?
OTSU: By playing with the servants. Here *(Tosses an apple on the ground in front of* PAOLO. *He thinks about this for a moment, then reaches down and picks it up.)* And he stoops to conquer.
PAOLO: And she would too if she didn't have something stuck up her ass. *(Takes bite of the apple.)* Hmmm. Delicious.
OTSU: *(Trying to contain anger.)* What do you say?
PAOLO: *(Speaking with mouth full.)* What?
OTSU: You say, "Thank you, Otsu."
PAOLO: *(Mouth full.)* Thank you, Otsu. *(Puts half-eaten apple back into her basket.)*
OTSU: *(As she turns to leave.)* Barbarian.
PAOLO: Bitch.
OTSU: *(Stops in tracks, returns.)* Barbarian. Is it true you kill men for the sport of it?
PAOLO: My name is Paolo.
OTSU: Barbarian, how many men have you killed?
PAOLO: None, I only kill women and babies. *(*OTSU *turns to leave.)* And a bitch now and then.
OTSU: *(Stops. Walks back and faces* PAOLO. *With extreme formality.)* Good evening.

She exits, PAOLO *staring after her.* PAOLO *is alone looking in her direction. A lone lemon rolls onto stage in front of him. As he bends down to pick it up we hear* OTSU's *voice.*

OTSU: *(Off.)* BARBARIAN!

PAOLO *is holding the lemon. Dim to darkness.*

Lights up on throne area. Recollection scene. Music/ sound. KARMAS *stand on both sides of* ROSANJIN. *Sound cue: baby crying.* ROSANJIN *is listening, looking around to see where it's coming from.*

KARMAS: *(Keep repeating over and over.)* Akanbo? Doko ni iru'n da? [A baby? Where are you?]

ROSANJIN: A baby? A baby? Where are you hiding?

ZUMA *enters. Sound cue ends,* KARMAS *stop. Lighting change. She helps him back into his throne. When he realizes that* ZUMA *is touching him, he pushes her hand away and cringes from her.* ROSANJIN *cannot stand to have* ZUMA *touch him in any way.*

ROSANJIN: There was a baby. Their child.
ZUMA: There was no baby.
ROSANJIN: I heard it.
ZUMA: You imagined it.
ROSANJIN: Crying. It was crying. It had seen me kill its mother and father.
ZUMA: You didn't kill them! Remember? Don't you remember? They were already dead when you entered the house. Someone else did it. Remember? You just took the money and left.
ROSANJIN: I must kill it. It's seen me kill. Where are you?
ZUMA: You didn't kill them. There was no baby.
ROSANJIN: And now he knows. He's coming. Kitamura. Kitamura. Kitamura.

Darkness. Sound of someone screaming. Lights come up on SAM *and* PAOLO. SAM *is lying face down spread-eagled and* PAOLO *is sitting on his butt, pulling back hard on one of his legs.* SAM *is screaming as if in great pain. A tray of empty bowls, dishes, and chopsticks sits down center. This is* SAM's *after dinner massage.*

SAM: AAHHH! AAHHH!
PAOLO: *(Stops, exhausted.)* Enough?
SAM: More, more. It feels great.

PAOLO *picks up his other leg and begins to pull. As* SAM *screams in pain,* OTSU *enters and watches.* PAOLO *immediately stops when he notices* OTSU.

OTSU: May I join you?
PAOLO: You sure you want to? The drop in altitude might kill you.
OTSU: *(To* SAM.*)* I am Otsu, the daughter of Rosanjin and Zuma.
SAM: *(Still lying on ground with* PAOLO *on top of him.)* We finally meet. He talks about you constantly. Yak, yak, yak.
OTSU: *(To* PAOLO.*)* Good evening Barbarian. *(Sits.)*
PAOLO: I'm amazed you can sit. Something must have loosened up back there.
OTSU: You mistake back bone for constipation. A common mistake for a killer of women and babies.
PAOLO: Don't forget, a bitch now and then, too.
OTSU: Taking food for no service is like begging. How was the meal, Barbarian?
SAM: *(Can't take anymore bickering. Gets up and slaps* PAOLO *on the top of the head.)* Settle down! Settle down! *(To* OTSU.*)* Don't let him rile you. You see, he always gets like this around the meal table. When he was growing up I used to put food out on the table and every time he'd reach for a bite I'd whack him with a stick. It was a little game to develop his hand-eye coordination. *(*SAM *whacks* PAOLO'*s hand with a chopstick as he reaches for a cup of tea. To* PAOLO.*)* Attention, attention. *(To* OTSU.*)* It's that memory that makes him irritable 'round the meal table. One day at dinner I pulled out the stick. Know what he did? Pulled out a club. Boy learns fast. End of game. But the memory lingers on.
PAOLO: Excuse me. The air's getting a bit stale. I think I'll check around a bit. *(Exits.)*
SAM: How old are you?
OTSU: Eighteen.
SAM: *(To himself.)* Same as Paolo.
OTSU: Why?
SAM: *(Ignoring her question.)* Absolutely no sense of humor. You probably noticed. Make an interesting case study.
OTSU: You have a rather interesting relationship with your son.
SAM: Him? My son? I got better genes in my hip-pocket. Found him. Yeah, right by the side of the road. Abandoned. Just a little baby crying away. Being the kind of man that I am, though, I decided to save his life. *(Pause.)* I left him there. Yeah, walked right on past. Saved his life.
OTSU: You left him there?

SAM: Yeah, left him there. See, Paolo—he doesn't know this—is probably illegitimate. See, that's what they do, the parents of the girl. She gives birth and they set the baby outside of the house on the road. Then they hide in the bushes. The first man comes along and picks up the baby, the whole entire family clan jumps out and stones them to death. Kill 'em both. Doesn't matter whether it's the real father or not. It's just a great excuse so they can ssave face for the family. So I saved his life. Walked right on by. Left him there.

OTSU: Yes, but he's with you. Paolo. I don't understand.

SAM: Oh yeah, that's right. Well...I lied. *(Laughs loudly to himself.)* Attention, attention. Gotta pay attention. Oh-oh, don't get mad. You're taking yourself too seriously. You're taking me too seriously. *(Pause.)* Seriously. I took him with me. I mean I couldn't leave him there. I raised him. Or, he raised me. We manage. We get by. The hours aren't good. Neither is the pay. It could be worse, though. Unfortunately, most times it is. *(Looks around at surroundings, touches the fabric of her dress.)* But then life doesn't exactly play favorites, does it.

SAM *exits, to look around.* OTSU *is about to exit when she sees* PAOLO *returning.* PAOLO *whirls around. Sees* OTSU *standing, staring at him.*

PAOLO: Don't sneak up on me like that. *(Notices she's staring at him.)* What? *(No response. Goes back to guard duty. Notices she's still staring at him.)* What?

OTSU: What? *(Still staring, hasn't moved.)*

PAOLO: *(Goes back to duty. Getting very self conscious. Can't take it anymore.)* WHAT!!!

OTSU: I'm observing.

PAOLO: You're staring.

OTSU: I never stare. It's bad manners. I observe.

PAOLO: What the hell do you want?

OTSU: What makes you think you have anything I could possibly want?

PAOLO: *(Approaches her.)* 'Cause you keep coming around here, bothering me and *(Very close.)* observing me. Why?

OTSU: I want to see what a grown-up illegitimate baby looks like. (PAOLO *just stares.* OTSU *thinks she may have gone too far.)* Sam said it... (PAOLO *starts to chuckle, then laugh.* OTSU *is confused.)* He said you were probably an illegitimate child and that I shouldn't tell you...Well, that's what he said!

PAOLO: *(Stops laughing. Serious.)* My mother and father are dead. I'm not sure. Sam never tells the same story twice. For all I know he could be my mother. You can never tell if he's lying or just making the truth sound like a lie.

OTSU: I was looking at your face. That's what I was...staring at. Sometimes, depending on the light, your face scares me. You remind me of Rosanjin. *(Pause.)* You've been watching me. Haven't you? *(No response.)* It's alright.

PAOLO: Yes.

OTSU: At first it made me furious. 'How dare he spy on me?' I thought I would play along and teach you a lesson. But then...then I began to enjoy it. The sensation of it. I began to do things in front of you. Knowing you were watching.

PAOLO: I think I knew.

OTSU: A kind of fear, it scares me. And yet I'm still in control, so it's alright.

PAOLO: At times I felt you were speaking to me. *(Pause.)* When I first met you...I really didn't...

During the course of the following sequence they find themselves being attracted to each other with an intensity exactly opposite to the words they are saying to each other. They move closer and closer.

OTSU: I think we both felt the same.

PAOLO: I mean I didn't like you.

OTSU: You were just a hired killer.

PAOLO: I didn't like anything about you.

OTSU: Something less than human.

PAOLO: I hated you.

OTSU: You were beneath contempt.

PAOLO: I wanted to kill you.

OTSU: I could have crushed you like a bug and felt absolutely no remorse.

They are very close, staring into each other's eyes.

ZUMA: *(Off.)* OTSU! OTSU!

OTSU: Zuma will be angry. *(She starts to leave, then stops. Turns to* PAOLO, *staring at his face.)* Give me your hand.

PAOLO *offers his hand, not understanding.* OTSU *takes his index finger and places the point to the center of her forehead. She begins to move it down the front of her face, over her nose, mouth, chin.* OTSU *seems curiously excited by the effect her experiment is having on her.* PAOLO *is confused but does not withdraw his hand. She stops his finger at the soft indentation at the base of her neck.*

OTSU: Meet me by the north gate. At the hour of the snake.

OTSU *exits.* PAOLO *watches her leave, then exits.*

Demon music. KITAMURA *can be seen lurking in the shadows. Dim to darkness. Music fades out.*

PAOLO *enters. He is there to meet* OTSU. *It is the hour of the snake. The murky rumblings of the demon music can be heard.*

PAOLO: Otsu? Otsu?

Suddenly KITAMURA *jumps out and attacks* PAOLO. *Loud demon music. Simultaneously,* ROSANJIN *screams hysterically. Lights bank up on* ROSANJIN.

ROSANJIN: AHHH! HE'S HERE! HE'S HERE! KITAMURA'S HERE! KITAMURA!!!...

PAOLO, *caught off guard by* KITAMURA, *retreats. Exits left.* SAM *rushes in from stage right and runs up to* ROSANJIN. SAM *stands next to* ROSANJIN *who is awake.* PAOLO *rushes in.*

ROSANJIN: *(Pointing at* PAOLO.*)* KITAMURA!!

SAM *is about to attack but sees it's* PAOLO.

PAOLO: I saw him! He's here! On the grounds!

SAM *and* PAOLO *position themselves on both sides of* ROSANJIN *who is seated on the throne anxiously staring out into the darkness. He periodically points to an area, shouting,* KITAMURA! *The whole time* SAM *and* PAOLO *have their swords drawn and are peering out into the darkness trying to protect* ROSANJIN. *At the same time,* OTSU *appears down stage left. She calls,* "Paolo? Paolo?" KITAMURA *who has been hiding in the shadows down stage appears and watches her from the shadows stage right. The demon doesn't attack her. Dim to darkness.*

ACT TWO

Darkness. ZUMA *and* OTSU *are both lit in separate pools of light.* ZUMA *is situated down and* OTSU *up stage.* ZUMA *is seated on her knees, Japanese style, and* OTSU *stands. They both face forward, staring straight ahead. There is a relationship that exists between the movement of* ZUMA's *hand and* OTSU's *monologue but it lurks beneath the surface and should only be hinted at in the scene's visual reading. They both begin and end at the same time.*

OTSU: I am naked. I am standing before a full-length mirror. My hand begins to move. I can watch everything. I pretend that my hand is not me. That the hand belongs to someone I do not know. I cannot see his face. I cannot tell if he is ugly or beautiful. He touches my forehead with his index finger and holds it there. I cannot move. He begins to press harder with the pointed finger. I watch everything. It hurts. I cannot move. He pulls back,

Slowly ZUMA's *right hand begins to rise. She notices and watches. Her hand has a life of its own independent of her. It begins to move in a graceful figure-eight motion in front of her face. She is both frightened and intrigued. It is like a beautiful poisonous snake seducing its victim.* ZUMA *watches. Suddenly the hand whips around close to her face. The hand is clenched except for the index and little fingers which jut out menacingly. She is afraid. The two fingers begin to move to-*

releasing the pressure. I think he is going to pull away but it remains pressed ever-so-slightly against my skin. It begins to move. I can feel it pass over the bridge of my nose, over my lips, my chin, the front of my neck...It stops at the soft indentation at the base of my neck. It begins to move again. Now it's passing between my breasts. It feels like the toe of a rabbit...No...like a smoothly-polished, cold acorn... No. ..like the head of a lizard...The wet tongue of an alligator...I cannot move, I watch everything. It continues...

wards her eyes. She tries to move away. They jab at her eyes. She opens her mouth to scream.

ZUMA has opened her mouth to scream just as OTSU is finishing her monologue. We hear a scream. But instead of ZUMA's voice we hear PAOLO's. This is perfectly synced so it appears that PAOLO's voice is coming out of ZUMA's mouth. Cross-fade from ZUMA and OTSU to PAOLO. He is screaming in his sleep. He is having a nightmare. SAM rushes in and wakes him. PAOLO sits up wide-eyed, breathing hard.

SAM: You haven't had a nightmare like that in a long time. Not since you were a kid.
PAOLO: Well, they're back. Ever since we got here.
SAM: Same?
PAOLO: Only more vivid. I could see the blood dripping off my sword. But the two bodies...I couldn't make out their faces. *(Getting up.)* My turn. Any sign of Kitamura?
SAM: Nothing. Not a goddamn thing. Sucker disappeared into thin air.
PAOLO: Look, I saw him. He attacked me.
SAM: Then he's gone now. We woulda smoked him out by now. This Kitamura fella has a way of coming and going that ain't exactly human. *(Bending over, hurts back.)* AHHH!

PAOLO: Here. *(Starts pounding* SAM's *lower back nervously. He's doing it all wrong.)*
SAM: Enough! Enough! You'll only break whatever still works. I'm gonna get some shut eye.

SAM lies down. PAOLO *stretches. Appears to be thinking about something. Draws sword and moves towards the sleeping* ROSANJIN. PAOLO *stares at* ROSANJIN. *His sword is drawn. It appears he may be about to strike.* ZUMA *enters and sees him.*

ZUMA: Stop!

PAOLO *and* ZUMA *look at each other for a moment.* PAOLO *lowers sword.*

PAOLO: I thought I heard something. I was checking around.
ROSANJIN: *(Waking up.)* What? What? Kitamura? Kitamura?

PAOLO *withdraws.*

ZUMA: *(Staring after* PAOLO, *to* ROSANJIN.*)* Nothing, nothing. Only a bad dream. Go back to sleep. Sleep, sleep.

ROSANJIN *goes back to sleep.* ZUMA *continues to stare after* PAOLO. *Dim to darkness.*

The lemon ceremony: OTSU *and* PAOLO *lit in a pool of light. They are seated on their knees, facing each other. In front of* OTSU *is a cutting board with an overripe lemon and a knife upon it. Upstage a bright floodlight that silhouettes the couple and shoots directly into the audience begins a very slow build from barely visible to blinding. The sound/music, a slow pulsing drone, also builds from a very low volume.* OTSU *and* PAOLO *stare into each other's eyes, unmoving. There is great fire here. Each movement, pause, glance has the quality of tension about it. Everything is delicately balanced between the fires of passion and the logic of propriety; controlled, but precariously so. At any moment things could explode into a seething heap of heavy breathing and skin. Pause. They both look down at the cutting board.* OTSU *proceeds to cut the lemon into several small slices. She picks up a slice and holds it up in front of her face.* OTSU *slowly moves the lemon slice towards* PAOLO's *mouth. As it nears* PAOLO, *he parts his lips to receive the lemon. As he starts to close his lips,* OTSU *withdraws the slice so it barely touches his inner mouth.* OTSU *sets the lemon slice on the board.* PAOLO *picks up another slice and repeats the same ritual with* OTSU, *allowing her only to barely taste the lemon*

The Dream of Kitamura

piece. He sets his slice on the board. Pause. The sound and flood light continue to grow in intensity. Simultaneously, they reach down and pick up the other's lemon slice. They bring the slices up to face level. Then, at the same time, they slowly insert the lemon pieces into each other's open mouth. Now, they begin chewing. Their faces contort. Eyes water. They moan. Gasp. They both reach out and savagely grab each other by the hair. Their heads thrust back. The light from upstage floods the audience, framing the black silhouetted profile of PAOLO and OTSU with blades of dancing light. The sound pulsates loudly. The air is thick with the pungent odor of lemons. They breathe heavily. They chew hard. Black out/cut to silence.

Darkness. Lights up on SAM *sleeping on the ground.* ZUMA *enters. Kicks him hard. He awakens.*

ZUMA: Who is Paolo?
SAM: *(Groggy.)* What? What?
ZUMA: Where does he come from? Who is he?
SAM: *(Waking up.)* Kitamura? Who? What?
ZUMA: Who is Paolo?
SAM: *(Slowly understands what's going on. Decides to play the same trick on* ZUMA *that he played on* OTSU *earlier.)* Paolo? Found him. Yeah. Right by the side of the road. Abandoned. Just a little baby crying away. Being the kind of man that I am though, I decided to save his life. *(Pause.)* I left him there. Yeah. Walked right on past.

Saved his life. (SAM *pauses, waiting for* ZUMA *to respond. She doesn't. He continues.*) See, Paolo—he doesn't know this—is probably illegitimate. See, that's what they do, the parents of the girl. She gives birth and they set the baby outside of the house on the road. Then they hide in the bushes. The first man comes along and picks up the baby, the whole family clan jumps out and stones them to death. Kill 'em both. Doesn't matter whether it's the real father or not. It's just a great excuse so they can save face for the family. Not me, though. Walked right on past. Left him there. Crying away. Bye-bye. So long... (SAM *continues to mutter, waiting for* ZUMA *to respond about the obvious.*) See you later, alligator... After while, crocodile...
ZUMA: What if it's a woman?
SAM: What?
ZUMA: The person who passes by. What if it's a woman who picks up the baby? (SAM *stares at her in disbelief.*)
SAM: (*Muttering to himself.*) Must be taking myself too seriously. I gotta start paying more attention.
ZUMA: He's not your son?
SAM: No, no, no. (*Starts to walk away.*)
ZUMA: Wait. (SAM *stops.*) Come here. (SAM *returns.*) Closer. (SAM *moves closer.* ZUMA *grabs his head with both hands and jerks it to the side. She stares intently at his ear lobes.*) Your ear lobes.
SAM: What?
ZUMA: They're large. That's a sign of wisdom. Looking at you one would never think. Rosanjin has large ear lobes, also. (*While she speaks,* SAM *takes hold of her right hand. He reads fingers.*) In his youth he was a man of great physical beauty. I felt great pride to be seen walking beside him. I was his woman.
SAM: (*Examining fingers.*) Right or left handed? (ZUMA *withdraws her right hand and offers her left.* SAM *takes hold of her index finger.*) The index finger. Called Jupiter. Reflects one's leadership qualities. The ability to control.
ZUMA: I serve. My life is one of service.
SAM: Long. Prominent. Much potential to lead.
ZUMA: I do not lead. I serve.
SAM: Your actions dictate destiny.
ZUMA: No.
SAM: If not now, then in the past.
ZUMA: No.
SAM: If not now, then in the future.

ZUMA: Rosanjin controls. Then, now, and in the future. I serve Rosanjin.
SAM: *(Moves to little finger.)* Mercury. Symbol of one's communicative skills.
ZUMA: I do not like to speak. I have nothing to say.
SAM: Firm. Good length. Much hidden potential.
ZUMA: No. *(Pause.)* Yes?
SAM: The joints are knotted. It turns outwards away from the rest of the fingers. Stunted. Alienated.
ZUMA: Rosanjin is the family tongue. He speaks for all of us. Rosanjin is my mouth. His words are mine.
SAM: *(Moves to middle finger.)* Saturn. Symbolic of one's principles. The ability to distinguish right from wrong.
ZUMA: I serve. I am not called upon to make such choices.
SAM: Look at the relative length to the other fingers. Extremely long. Extremely prominent. Very strong principles of right and wrong.
ZUMA: Right and wrong are not concerns of mine What is right is that I serve Rosanjin. What is wrong is to falter in any way in my service to him.
SAM: *(Moves to ring finger.)* Apollo. Creativity.
ZUMA: *(Interrupts.)* What about the thumb? I'm told the Chinese ignore everything else and only read the thumb.
SAM: The thumb symbolizes one's personal will. In men it also reflects the size of one's manhood.
ZUMA: Your personal will is very big.

SAM: Yes, I know.

ZUMA: What about my thumb? *(SAM looks at it. His expression changes.)* Yes?

SAM: You have the "killer's thumb."

Dim to darkness.

Darkness. A pool of light down center. SAM *walks into it, facing down. He begins to narrate a story. As he does, the two* KARMAS *appear on both sides of him, three or four steps up center from him. They hold puppets in their right hands. Black scarves are draped over them.*

SAM: A marriage. Two noble houses become one. A woman. *(Woman puppet's covering removed.)* A man. *(Man puppet's covering removed.)* She... *(Woman puppet moved forward.)* is a formal creature, fiercely proud of the great family line that she represents. The continued life of this rich and ordered universe is as important to her as life itself. He... *(Man puppet moved forward.)* is a second son, whose older brother has fallen in a great battle defending the lands. As the second son, he inherits all. Title, as well as, responsibility.

Through following narration, puppets slowly turn to face each other. Move towards each other. Embrace.

SAM: It is an arranged marriage, long pre-ordained by the politics of the ruling classes. Still, for a time, it is a harmonious union. Peace and prosperity flourish within the walls of the domain, and great love within the interiors of their hearts. However, around them, the world is crumbling. It is a time of great historical change and economic transition. Once great family lines fall into poverty and ruin, victims of the changing order. *(Puppets beginning to embrace.)* Somehow, the woman, the man, have managed to escape this fate. They continue to live in the manner that their families have been accustomed to living for generations. How is this possible while all around them topples into historical obscurity? A mysterious, if not troubling turn of events. A crime is committed.

Puppets abruptly stop in their embrace at the mention of the crime. From this point on they slowly break embrace, pulling apart while continuing to stare at each other.

SAM: A robbery. A double murder. It is never discussed. It is an unspoken secret whose truth is shared. Nine months after the crime is committed, a child is born. A daughter. The secret festers. Great love decays under the weight of its unspoken burden. There was a witness. *(Puppets both turn forward, facing straight ahead.* SAM *acts out the part of the witness, as if it was he.)* He saw the robber. He saw the murderer. The witness points his finger. (SAM *raises his hand and points down stage.)* It was...

ZUMA *and* ROSANJIN *rush out of the shadows up stage. They are upstage of* SAM *and the* KARMAS. *They stare straight ahead down stage.* SAM *stops his narration abruptly. Brings his arm down. The puppets slowly become lifeless. Their coverings are put back.* ZUMA *and* ROSANJIN *slowly turn to look at each other.*

SAM: *(Looking down stage.)* Just a little entertainment. Thought you might enjoy it. A puppet show. I'm making up the story as I go along. You know, just a little puppet show. It doesn't mean anything. Really, it doesn't mean anything.

ROSANJIN *and* ZUMA *turn to look straight ahead, then slowly withdraw up stage into the shadows.* SAM *continues to watch them, staring down stage into darkness. Dim to darkness.*

Tea party: Darkness. Lights up on ROSANJIN, ZUMA, OTSU, SAM, *and* PAOLO. *They are seated on their knees.* ROSANJIN *is up center. On his immediate left is* ZUMA. *Next to* ZUMA *is* OTSU. *On* ROSANJIN's *right are* SAM, *then* PAOLO. *They form a half circle. In front of* ZUMA *is a tray. On it is a pot of tea and five tea cups. Silence. They all look straight ahead. Faces in normal expression. Down right the two* KARMAS *face each other, leaning on swords which they whack together at the appropriate moment to keep beat. With each beat, the characters look, at the person for whom they feel the following: love, distrust, sexual desire, hate. In that order. A beat. Everyone at the same time turns their heads to look at one of the people in the half circle. Their faces freeze in absurd expressions a la Hokusai/Sharaku. A beat. Again, at the same time, they all turn their heads to look at someone else. This continues for four beats. Each time a different conformation is created. At the end of the fourth beat they are once again looking straight ahead in normal expression. This should be choreographed.* ZUMA *begins to pour tea into one cup. It is for* ROSANJIN.

ROSANJIN: *(To* OTSU.*)* Do you hate me? *(No response from* OTSU.*)*

ZUMA: Rosanjin?
ROSANJIN: Do you hate me!
OTSU: *(Quietly.)* No. *(Pause.)*
ROSANJIN: *(To* ZUMA *and* OTSU, *as if* PAOLO *and* SAM *were not there.)* What do you think of the two guards? *(No response. To* OTSU.*)* Are they handsome? Ugly? *(To* ZUMA.*)* Do they eat us out of house and home? *(To* OTSU.*)* Does he run his tongue down the nape of your neck? *(To* ZUMA.*)* Does his conversation bring you both pleasure *and* pain?
ZUMA: It was your idea to have them here in the...
ROSANJIN: *(Interrupts.)* THAT'S NOT WHAT I ASKED!! *(*PAOLO *is about to speak. To* PAOLO.*)* SHUT UP!!
OTSU: They seem to be serving their purpose.

ZUMA *serves the tea to* ROSANJIN. ROSANJIN *takes a sip of the tea. He immediatley looks up. Something is wrong with the tea.*

ROSANJIN: *(To* OTSU.*)* Serve Zuma tea. *(*OTSU *pours a cup and offers it to her. (To* ZUMA.*)* Hold out your hand. *(*ZUMA *holds out her hand. Not sure what he is doing.)* Stick your index finger out. *(*ZUMA *obeys.* OTSU *still holds the cup of very hot tea.)* Put it in.
OTSU: Rosanjin, please...
ROSANJIN: PUT IT IN!

ZUMA *and* ROSANJIN *stare at one another. She slowly sticks her finger into the hot water. She refuses to show any signs of pain. Her face is a strange mixture of pain, hatred, and fierce pride.*

ROSANJIN: TOO HOT? *(Motions for* OTSU *to pull cup away. Softly.)* Too hot? *(Pause.)* It should be exactly the same temperature as my own body. No more, no less. As the tea enters my body it should be like two old friends reuniting after a long absence. Embracing and settling down together for a quiet evening. If it's too hot it burns the tongue. If it's too cold it numbs the lips. If it's too hot there is only pain. If it's too cold there is no pleasure. *(Pause. Looks at* OTSU. *An idea comes to him. To* OTSU.*)* Stand. *(*OTSU *hesitates, not sure what he means.)* Stand. *(*OTSU *stands, still unsure what he wants.)* Turn around. *(He watches while* OTSU *turns completely around. To* ZUMA.*)* Stand. *(*ZUMA *stands and* OTSU *is about to sit. To* OTSU.*)* No, remain standing. *(An idea comes to him as he watches them both standing. He's figuring this out as he goes along, not premeditated.)* Stand back to back. *(Pause. Idea further develops in his head.)* Hold each other's hands. Hold your arms out, straight out. *(They let go of each other's hands and hold their arms out.)* No! No! Keep holding hands, keep holding hands. Straight out, your arms straight out. *(Pause, thinking.)* Now turn around. Yes, I like that. Stay back to back. Keep holding your hands. Arms straight out. Yes, I like that. Now as you're turning, when you pass by me, look straight at me and say "Rosanjin." *(Pause.)* No, make that, "Rosanjin, I love you." Yes.

They slowly turn in a circle, back to back. As they pass in front of ROSANJIN *they say,* "ROSANJIN, I love you."

ROSANJIN: Louder. *(They get louder.)* Faster. (They start to move faster.) Louder! Faster! LOUDER! FASTER!
PAOLO: STOP IT! STOP IT! *(He jumps up and stops it.* PAOLO *and* SAM *help the women to seat themselves.)*

Long pause. They all look straight ahead. The KARMAS *whack their swords, a beat. They turn to look at one of the people. Beat. They change again. They go through the same cycle as before. At the fourth beat they are facing straight ahead.*

ROSANJIN: *(To* OTSU.*)* Pour the tea. For everyone. *(*OTSU *begins to pour.)* You like the young one, don't you? Be careful of that one. He's got hot blood in him. That makes you crazy in the face of danger. He'll be the one that meets Kitamura head on. The older one is more experienced. He'll keep his cool. He'll hold back. He won't lose his head and go charging in the first opportunity, chopping at anything he sees. He'll wait. Choose his opening.

Then strike. Kitamura? Dead. *(Notices how* OTSU *is pouring the tea.)* NO! NO! *(Takes pot away from* OTSU.*)* You still don't know how to serve! *(While speaking, demonstrates the correct method of pouring tea. Pours a little in each cup, back and forth.)* What's important is the evenness of flavor. As you pour, the tea is taken from lower and lower in the pot. Consequently, the flavor is stronger. You must pour the tea so the difference in the potency in the pot does not disturb the evenness of the flavor of the tea in the cups. *(*ROSANJIN *stops in mid-pour and looks at* OTSU.*)* Do you hate me?

OTSU: No.

ROSANJIN: *(To* ZUMA.*)* Do you hate me?

ZUMA: No.

> KARMAS *whack their swords with a loud singular clack. The five characters all turn simultaneously to the front, staring straight ahead. Dim to darkness.*
>
> Lights up on OTSU *and* PAOLO.

OTSU: Tonight. By the north gate.

PAOLO: Are you sure?

OTSU: You were there. You saw.

PAOLO: I know but...

OTSU: *(Interrupts.)* You were there!

PAOLO: SSHHH! Alright.

> OTSU *is staring at* PAOLO's *face. She begins to laugh strangely.*

OTSU: I cannot tell. *(*PAOLO *stares, not following her logic.)* I cannot tell if you are ugly or beautiful.

PAOLO: *(Confused.)* What?

OTSU: *(Returns to original line of thought.)* It's agreed then. You'll meet me by the north gate. At the hour of the ox. You'll take me away from here. I want to forget.

> OTSU *and* PAOLO *embrace, then exit. Demon music enters momentarily, then fades out. Dim to darkness.*
>
> Lights up on SAM *and* PAOLO. PAOLO *has just told* SAM *that he is leaving with* OTSU. SAM *appears upset.* PAOLO *turns to leave. Suddenly we hear* ROSANJIN *scream. Lights come up quickly on throne area.*

The Dream of Kitamura

ROSANJIN: **KITAMURA! KITAMURA! KITAMURA'S HERE!**

> ROSANJIN *has just awakened from a dream.* SAM *and* PAOLO *run and position themselves on both sides of his throne with swords drawn.* ROSANJIN *keeps pointing into the darkness and shouting,* "KITAMURA!" SAM *and* PAOLO *keep turning in the direction that* ROSANJIN *points, ready to defend.* OTSU *appears down right. She is there to meet* PAOLO.

OTSU: Paolo? Paolo?

> KITAMURA/ZUMA *who has been lurking in the shadows jumps out with knife drawn.* OTSU *screams.* KITAMURA/ZUMA *realizes she has made a mistake as she wanted to kill* PAOLO.

OTSU: **KITAMURA'S HERE! KITAMURA'S HERE!**

> SAM *and Paolo hear Otsu's screams and run stage right and down to rescue her. At the same time* ZUMA *exits left and up to get away.* ZUMA *runs right into* ROSANJIN *who believes it is* KITAMURA *attacking him.* ROSANJIN *draws his sword.* KITAMURA/ZUMA *in an effort to defend herself stabs and kills* ROSANJIN. *As she stands over the fallen* ROSANJIN, PAOLO *comes running back in. Thinking that it is* KITAMURA, PAOLO *attacks and kills* ZUMA. *He stands over the two bodies, his sword in hand.* SAM *and* OTSU *rush in.* SAM *moves forward and removes the mask, revealing that it is in fact* ZUMA. OTSU *turns and stares at* PAOLO.

> OTSU *exits,* SAM *and* PAOLO *move down left.* SAM *recounts his story of the original crime to* PAOLO. *At the same time the two* KARMAS *each bring to life the bodies of* ROSANJIN *and* ZUMA. *They raise them up and at the appropriate moment set them into motion.*

SAM: It was dark. I could barely stand. I had been drinking all night at a tavern and now I was trying to make my way home. I stumbled and fell. I lay there face down in the dirt. I felt sick. I could hear a dog barking in the distance. My right shoulder ached. I struggled to my feet. I leaned against a wall in the shadows and relieved myself. I looked upward towards the sky and watched the stars. It was a beautiful night.

> SAM *pauses.* SAM *and* PAOLO *observe the story unfolding center stage. The* KARMAS *set* ZUMA *in motion.*

KARMA TWO: Zuma is a young woman.
KARMA ONE: She has broken into a house.
KARMA TWO: She is looking for gold and jewels. *(ZUMA is putting the jewels into the bag that the KARMAS have set out. The KARMAS play the roles of man and woman again.)*
KARMA ONE: A man enters. *(Holding mask in front of face. Discovers ZUMA stealing the jewels.)* Nani mono da? Nani o yatte iru? Dorobo! Yamero!
KARMA TWO: A woman enters. *(Holding mask.)* Anata! Kiyotsukete! Hocho moteru! *(The man attacks ZUMA who in defence stabs the man.)*
KARMA TWO: *(To man.)* Anata! Anata! *(ZUMA realizes that the woman is a witness and must be killed also. She advances on her.)* Yurushite kudasai. Inochi dake o tasukete kudasai. Nani mo imasen...nani mo imasen.

ZUMA stabs the woman. ZUMA turns to run, leaving the jewels behind. She freezes at the door.

SAM: I heard a noise. In the shadows up ahead I could see the figure of someone sneaking out of a window. The figure turned to look at me.

ZUMA turns to look at SAM, then exits up towards where ROSANJIN is now standing. ZUMA and ROSANJIN look at each other. SAM continues his story.

SAM: It was a thief escaping into the night. Then the idea came to me. If this thief got away with it, it must be safe. They're probably not even home. I entered by the same window. It was dark but I could make out a bag lying on the ground with gold and jewels strewn about. As I bent down to pick it up, that's when I saw the first body. I didn't move. I didn't breathe. A little ways away I saw the second body. It was a woman. She had been stabbed in the neck. A pool of blood surrounded her head like a dark red halo. I stood perfectly still. The house was absolutely quiet. *(Sound cue: A baby's crying.)* A baby. Where was it coming from? I had to quiet it down before it woke someone up. *(Finds baby and begins rocking it. The crying dies away. End sound cue. ZUMA sends ROSANJIN into the house.)* I heard something. I hid in the shadows. I could see a man entering the house.
KARMA TWO: Rosanjin is a young man.
KARMA ONE: He has broken into a house.
KARMA TWO: He is looking for gold and jewels.

ROSANJIN *enters. He sees the bag of valuables on the ground and proceeds to fill it with more of the gold and jewels. He's about to leave when he sees a body/mask. He's terrified. As he backs away from it he stumbles over the other body/mask. He's paralyzed with panic. Suddenly the baby begins to scream.* ROSANJIN *begins searching frantically for the baby to shut it up.* SAM *tries to quiet it without success. Afraid of being discovered and flustered over all the racket,* SAM *flees into the night carrying the baby with him.* ROSANJIN *continues to look as the baby's cries get fainter and fainter.* ROSANJIN *turns back to the bodies lying on the ground. He picks up the bag of valuables and exits. He approaches* ZUMA, *they face each other.* ROSANJIN *stares at* ZUMA *accusingly.*

ZUMA: What?
ROSANJIN: Nothing.
ZUMA: *(Notices blood on* ROSANJIN's *hand.)* Blood.
ROSANJIN: *(Stares at blood. Then holds out bag of gold and jewels to* ZUMA.) Gold and jewels.

As ZUMA *reaches out for it,* ROSANJIN *drops it on the floor. They stare at each other. Dim to darkness.*

EPILOGUE

Lights up on a small area down left. In a small pool of light PAOLO *is lit. He stares straight ahead. Expressionless.* OTSU *is lit in a small pool of light down right. She also stares straight ahead, expressionless. They slowly turn and move towards each other. They perform a brief dance/movement together, ending facing each other. During this* ZUMA *and* ROSANJIN *enter from up stage and observe them from the shadows.* SAM *pokes his head in from the wings and watches.* OTSU *and* PAOLO *stare at each other for a moment. Their expressions reveal nothing. They slowly move towards each other and embrace.* OTSU *is facing stage left. In a small pool of light, the demon mask and sword are lit on the floor a small distance away from her.* OTSU *stares intently at them.* OTSU *and* PAOLO *begin to darken. As they dim, a group human wail from the cast begins to build. The mask and sword grow bright.* OTSU *and* PAOLO *continue to dim. The human wail reaches a feverish pitch. The two wooden clackers are whacked together loudly. Wail abruptly stops.* OTSU *and* PAOLO *continue slow fade into darkness. Mask and sword begin slow fade into darkness.* OTSU *and* PAOLO *disappear in blackness. Then, in silence, the mask and sword are also engulfed in blackness.*

One To Grow On
a play for young people
Brian Kral

One To Grow On was first produced May 16, 1980, by the Rainbow Company Children's Theatre in Las Vegas, with the following cast:

TIMOTHY KURTZ, at 16	Joe Kucan
TIMOTHY KURTZ, at 12	Kirk J Stowers
GRANDFATHER	Charles McCrea
FIRST YOUNG MAN	Scott Davidson
SECOND YOUNG MAN	Ron E. Leach
THIRD YOUNG MAN	Danny Marre
MARGARET HARTLEY	Loy McCrea
KARL KURTZ	David R. Sankuer

Directed by Jody Johnston
Scenery by David Sankuer
Costumes by Karen McKenney
Lighting by Michael Dorough

All technical crews (light board operators, sound technicians, property crews) were made up of members of the Rainbow Company Children's Ensemble. The Rainbow Company is a theater training program for young people, sponsored by the City of Las Vegas.

"Nature never sends a great man into the planet, without confiding the secret to another soul."
                    Ralph Waldo Emerson, "Representative Men"

Time: the not-distant past, as seen from the present.

Place: a small mid-western town.

The play is divided into numbered scenes, but the action should be continuous.
Timothy may be played by either one actor, or two, representing the separate ages.

©1983 by Brian Kral.
CAUTION: All rights strictly reserved. Professionals and amateurs are hereby warned that *One To Grow On* is subject to a royalty. It is protected under the copyright laws of all countries covered by the International Copyright Convention. Permission in writing must be secured before any kind of performance is given. All inquiries should be addressed to the author, Brian Kral, 2101 Perliter, North Las Vegas, Nevada 89030.

One To Grow On
a play for young people
Brian Kral

ACT ONE

SCENE ONE

TIMOTHY KURTZ, *a young man with brown hair, wearing light blue jeans and a pajama top, enters stealthily. He carries an old BB gun and is concentrating on an unseen object on the opposite side of the stage.*

TIMOTHY: *(To himself.)* Shhh. Don't make a sound. *(He lowers himself slowly to the ground.)* Quiet, now. Or you'll scare it away. *(Lying on his stomach, he aims along the barrel at the object. Long pause. Finally he lays the gun flat and lowers his face to the ground.)* I couldn't do it. *(He gets to his feet and faces audience.)* I lay there for over fifteen minutes in the cold, wet grass, with the rusty old BB gun I'd found in the garage pressed against and bruising my shoulder, and still I couldn't do it. The worst that would've happened would be that the BB, if it fired to begin with, would've drawn a small drop of blood, and sent him hopping back to his family. But I just didn't have it in me. *(He kicks a can in the direction of the object.)* Go on. Shooo! You've got better things to do. *(He walks forward to the audience.)* That's the kind of summer it was—full of the promise of hunting and fishing, and long hikes through the woods. It was the kind of summer you find in an Ernest Hemingway book. And it was the kind of summer my grandfather would've liked as a kid, instead of having to work, which is what he did most of his life. *(There is a loud bird-call. He aims. He walks over and sits on the fence.)* Grandpa would have liked Ernest Hemingway. They were meant for each other, cut from the same cloth. They could have spent hours together, oiling their rifles and their boots, and then tracking a fox or deer through the forest. That's what my grandfather had in mind every summer I came to visit. *(Pause. He starts with renewed energy.)* I don't think many people read Hemingway today. They figure he's outdated. But I've read him. *(With an honest, deferential nod.)* He was okay. *(Standing up from the fence.)* But I couldn't have led that kind of life any more than I could have lived my grandfather's life, or he could have lived mine. Each person's different, that much I know. My grandfather and I were as different as any two people should be and still be related. And we'd have never succeeded living each other's lives. *(He smiles.)* It was all we could do just to try and *understand* them. *(He opens the gate in the fence and heads towards the house.)*

SCENE TWO

TIMOTHY *enters the kitchen, which is represented by the small kitchen table and the kitchen counter in the back. Skeletal walls meet to form one corner of the kitchen; other than that, it is suggested through props.* TIMOTHY's GRANDFATHER, *Tim Christensen, stands at the counter preparing the breakfast. He has on his work trousers but is in slippers and a t-shirt with his hair slightly askew.*

GRANDFATHER: *(Dishing up oatmeal.)* So? Did you get us a rabbit for dinner?

TIMOTHY: *(Sitting at the table.)* How'd you know it was a rabbit?

GRANDFATHER: There hasn't been a deer in that front yard for over fifteen years, not since they put the highway through. So that left it either a rabbit or a small dog.

TIMOTHY: Oh, yeah? Why would I want to shoot a dog?

GRANDFATHER: *(Setting down a bowl.)* I thought all you Indians ate puppies for breakfast.

TIMOTHY: Is that true? Where'd you hear that?

GRANDFATHER: *(Laughing.)* Don't ask me. Aren't you the local authority on Indians?

TIMOTHY: Just because I'm part Indian doesn't mean I know what *all* of them do. I can't answer for *everybody*.

GRANDFATHER: *(Setting down other bowl.)* That's true. But maybe you should look into it all the same.

TIMOTHY: *(Eating his oatmeal.)* They've got a great book on Indians down at the Ben Franklin.

GRANDFATHER: *Don't go bringing* any more books in this house. I never see you going anywhere as it is without a book sticking out of your back pocket. All that reading'll ruin your eyes.

TIMOTHY: Oh, Grandpa...

GRANDFATHER: And, besides that, you spend too much money on them.

TIMOTHY: Reading is one of the cheapest ways there is...

GRANDFATHER: You're not going to learn anything reading books! The only way you learn is to get out and do. Now, eat your breakfast before it gets cold. *(He pours milk on his oatmeal.)* You want some toast?

TIMOTHY: *(His head down.)* No, thank you.

GRANDFATHER: How about some orange juice?

TIMOTHY: *(Absent-mindedly eating.)* I'm fine.

GRANDFATHER: *(Slowly leans over the table to get a closer look, then falls back in his seat.)* Ho-ho! You little devil.

TIMOTHY: *(Raising his head.)* What? What'd I do?

GRANDFATHER: *(Laughing.)* You almost had me believing it.

TIMOTHY: *What?*

GRANDFATHER: I was sitting here, thinking I'd hurt your feelings.

TIMOTHY: Why'd you think that?

GRANDFATHER: Because your face hung so low, it was sweeping the floor with your *hair*, that's why. Come to find out you've just got your nose stuck in a *book* again. *(He picks up the book from* TIMOTHY's *lap, and puts it on the counter.)* From now on we'll have both feet on the floor and both hands on the table. There won't be any more reading during breakfast. (TIMOTHY *props his chin in his hand.)* Don't think you'll change my mind, either. I spent all last week staring at *Jacob's Two-Two,* and I don't plan to do it again. It got to the point I didn't even know if you was still sitting there. Thought maybe you'd propped the book up on the

table and snuck off somewhere.
TIMOTHY: *(Into his food.)* You left out "the Hooded Fang."
GRANDFATHER: I what?
TIMOTHY: The name of the book was *Jacob Two-Two and the Hooded Fang.* You left out the...
GRANDFATHER: What kind of a book could it be with a name like that *anyway?*
TIMOTHY: I was reading it over. I liked it when I was younger.
GRANDFATHER: Well, it won't make much difference then. If you read them all twice, I guess you can lay off one summer without losing anything. Now, let's change the subject.
TIMOTHY: *(Dejected.)* To what?
GRANDFATHER: *(After a pause.)* Where'd you find that blunderbus?
TIMOTHY: *(Not playing.)* It's a BB gun.
GRANDFATHER: I know it's a BB gun. I bought it for your mother when she was eight years old. *(He picks it up fondly.)* I can't remember the last time I saw it. It's spotted with rust.
TIMOTHY: It was in the garage.
GRANDFATHER: *(Examining it.)* Needs oiling. They don't make them like this anymore. Hmph. *(He sets it down.)*
TIMOTHY: Your oatmeal's getting cold. (GRANDFATHER *sits at the table.)* You want some more?
GRANDFATHER: *(Subdued.)* No. You finish it. (TIMOTHY *goes to the counter, scoops the last of the oatmeal into his bowl. He turns to start back to the table but stops, looking at his* GRANDFATHER. *He smiles with an idea, goes back to the counter. He very loudly scrapes and clinks the spoon in the pan.)* What the heck is all that racket? You're going to wear the pot clean out with... (TIMOTHY *is laughing.)* What's so funny?
TIMOTHY: Mom says you used to drive her crazy in the mornings by always eating your oatmeal out of the pan. She says you'd *clang-clang-clang* all morning long, until every dog in the neighborhood was barking, and people were calling up to complain.
GRANDFATHER: *(Laughing to himself, he begins to eat his oatmeal.)* She said that, huh?
TIMOTHY: *(Still laughing.)* She sure did.
GRANDFATHER: *(Shaking his head.)* Your mother had a few bad habits herself, as I recall.
TIMOTHY: Like what?
GRANDFATHER: Never you mind. If she'd wanted you to know, I'm sure she'd have told you...She say anything else about me?
TIMOTHY: Not much. Except that, when she was a girl, you wouldn't

tell anyone she was part Indian. Like it was a secret or something.
GRANDFATHER: I reckon maybe it was.
TIMOTHY: Why?
GRANDFATHER: *(Eating his oatmeal.)* Reasons you wouldn't understand.
TIMOTHY: Mom says it was because you were embarrassed.
GRANDFATHER: Well, your mother doesn't always remember things the way they were.
TIMOTHY: She remembers when you knocked Grandma over the back of the couch. *(As soon as he's said it, he realizes he shouldn't have.* GRANDFATHER *sets down his spoon deliberately.)*
GRANDFATHER: *(Not facing him.)* Did she tell you that? (TIMOTHY *nods, unable to talk.)* Well?
TIMOTHY: Yes, sir.
GRANDFATHER: *(Shaking his head.)* The heck! What kind of a thing is that to... *(He stands up from the table.)* We all do things we regret later. Your mother would have a tough time denying that. Oh, well, I got to get ready or I'll be late for work. *(He starts out.)* You know, she tends to forget a few things. I'll bet she never mentioned how hard I worked for her.
TIMOTHY: She says you went to work when you were ten years old.
GRANDFATHER: I'm glad she remembers *that* much, anyway. *(He leaves the kitchen to get ready.)*
TIMOTHY: *(Coming down to face audience.)* My mother remembered quite a few things, actually. *(He at once seems older—the young man of Scene One as opposed to the twelve-year-old boy in this previous scene.)* For example, how Grandpa took her out shooting almost as soon as she was old enough to walk. *(He smiles.)* Well, maybe a *little* older. But not much, to hear her tell it. And how they were the *Talk* of the *Town* at one point, having won every shootin'-match in the county three years in a row. She even has some of her old medals. Not that she's proud of them, we just came across them in an old shoe-box one day. She wanted to throw them out, but I wouldn't let her. There was also a very funny picture of the two of them all dressed up in baggy hunting clothes, like they were going on a safari in the jungle or something. She looked so silly, it made her blush. I kept that, too. *(He hesitates, moving restlessly.)* My own memories were quite a bit different. For one thing, I can't really remember much about my grandfather before Grandma died. I mean, I spent the summer with them several times, but up until then, Grandpa never stuck out in my mind. It was kind of like he was just a stranger living in

Grandma's house: he'd sit with us for meals, read the newspaper, and never really say much. It's funny, thinking back, but the summer I turned twelve was a big change for both of us. Grandma had died, my mom was on her second honeymoon, celebrating her second marriage, and all of a sudden we were just kind of stuck with each other. *(He sits at the table.* GRANDFATHER *enters the kitchen. He is now wearing his work-shirt, but it hangs open, unbuttoned; his hair is combed; and he carries his shoes.)*

GRANDFATHER: *(Setting down his shoes.)* Speaking of memories, you must think mine is slipping. *(He sits down to button his shirt.)*

TIMOTHY: *(Finishing his breakfast.)* Why do you say that?

GRANDFATHER: Well, I can't think of any other reason for the big star someone put on my calender.

TIMOTHY: *(Avoiding* GRANDFATHER.*)* A star?

GRANDFATHER: That's right. Somebody drew a great big star, smack dab in the middle of today. You can't miss it, that's for sure. *(He chuckles to himself, gets to his feet.)* What's the matter? You think I'd forget your birthday? *(Pouring himself a cup of coffee.)* You don't have much faith in your old granddad, do you?

TIMOTHY: *(Looking into his bowl.)* It wasn't that...It was so *I* wouldn't forget. I'm not very good with dates or numbers.

GRANDFATHER: *(Stirring in sugar).* Uh-huh.

TIMOTHY: It's true. Math is my worst subject. *(Changing the subject.)* Could I have a cup of coffee?

GRANDFATHER: *(Looks at him.)* I guess it wouldn't hurt anything. Just don't tell your mom. *(He comes over to the table with the coffee pot.)* And it's only because it's your birthday.

TIMOTHY: *(Watching him pour it.)* Okay.

GRANDFATHER: You want some sugar?

TIMOTHY: *(Nodding.)* And cream.

GRANDFATHER: *(Shaking his head.)* Why don't you just run down to the drugstore and have yourself a *milkshake*?

TIMOTHY: This is the way my father always drank it.

GRANDFATHER: That's true. I had forgotten. *(Pause.* TIMOTHY *reaches across the table for the cream.)* Oh, the milk. Sorry. (GRANDFATHER *returns the coffee pot to the kitchen counter.)*

TIMOTHY: *(Stirring his coffee.)* Am I much like my father?

GRANDFATHER: *(Sitting at the table.)* In some ways, I guess so. *(He puts on a shoe.)* You can tell *me* later. *(He laces the first shoe.)* I can tell you one thing about him: he wasn't any good with guns. In fact, he had the worst luck of any man I ever met.

TIMOTHY: In what way?

GRANDFATHER: *(Settling in for a story.)* Well, all right. One time he and I drove up to Dundas for an auction. Some poor old fellow had died up there and his relatives were selling everything in the house, including some very nice firearms he had collected over the years. Well, we looked through what they had to offer. And I pointed out one gun to your father that was a *real beaut.*

TIMOTHY: Did he buy it?

GRANDFATHER: Nope. When the time came to start the bidding, your father put his money on an antique Army-surplus, bolt-action Japanese rifle from the Second World War.

TIMOTHY: Was it a good gun?

GRANDFATHER: It was probably among the worst guns I'd ever seen. It had a cracked stock and was so full of dust and grit that you couldn't see sunshine through the barrel. We spent the rest of that day trying to polish it up, *then* came to find out I didn't have a bullet in the house that'd fit it.

TIMOTHY: What'd you do?

GRANDFATHER: Well, we went down to O'Callaghan's, showed him the gun, asked him what he suggested. Said he didn't have anything *exactly* like that, but thought that a Swedish bullet might fit her. By now, I didn't have much confidence in the old gun, and I thought we'd better test it. So we drove out until we found a deserted spot, and I lashed that rifle to the trunk of a big oak tree with some baling wire your father had in the car. Then we took cover. With some strong string I'd tied to the trigger, I fired that old gun.... *(Building suspense with each word.)* and it went off like a *cannon.* The sound shook the trees, knocking acorns down for a mile around us. It had such a terrible kick, it snapped all three feet of wire I'd used on it. And the barrel—well, you couldn't even recognize it. It had blown up like an exploding cigar, sending pieces in every direction. Why, I'll bet a couple pieces made it all the way back to Dundas. *(He laughs at the idea.)*

TIMOTHY: *(Enthralled.)* Were you hit?

GRANDFATHER: Us? Oh, we were *fine.* What we didn't realize, though, was that we'd parked the car too close. And when that old gun blew up, it knocked the windshield *clean out* of your father's car! *(He is howling with laughter now.)* When we drove back into town that night, we had the wind in our faces. I swear, it was the high point of the day. *(His laughter settles into a great relish of that afternoon. Finally, he puts on his other shoe and begins to lace it.)*

TIMOTHY: *(Sipping his coffee.)* That's a funny story.

GRANDFATHER: I reckon your father didn't find it funny. But then, he wasn't famous for his sense of humor either.

TIMOTHY: Mom must have been mad.

GRANDFATHER: *(Laughing again.)* Ho-ho! When she saw that car, she was fit to be tied! I'll bet your father never heard the end of it. *(Standing up and clearing the table.)* I always liked your dad, though. He was a good man. *(He smiles, shaking his head.)* He just wasn't any good with a gun, that's all.

TIMOTHY: Did you ever see any of his pictures?

GRANDFATHER: Oh sure. I liked his outdoors stuff, he could draw them real well. Wildlife, you know, things like that. *(He shrugs his shoulders.)* But they always made me itchy to get out and see the real thing.

TIMOTHY: Some people say pictures are *better* than the real thing.

GRANDFATHER: You must have read that in a book; I never heard anyone say it around here.

TIMOTHY: I've heard it said that a good book is better than real life.

GRANDFATHER: No doubt you could find at least *one* fool willing to say *anything* if you waited long enough.

TIMOTHY: I read once...

GRANDFATHER: You read too darn much, if you ask me! Everything you say comes out of one book or another. A man can't hold a decent conversation with you!

TIMOTHY: *(Hurt.)* I thought we were having a good talk.

GRANDFATHER: *(Calming down.)* Well...we *were*. Till you ruined it. *(In frustration.)* For cripes sakes, I can't stand around arguing all day. I got to get to work. Are you coming now or do you want to meet me later?

TIMOTHY: I'll come later. I've got to go to the... *(He catches himself.)* I've got to...do some things first. Before my dad gets here.

GRANDFATHER: *(Putting on his cap.)* Suit yourself. I'll be on the third floor of the music building. Don't be late, or I'll eat my dinner without you.

TIMOTHY: Okay, Grandpa.

GRANDFATHER: *(Grabbing his sack lunch.)* Lock up when you leave.

TIMOTHY: I will.

> GRANDFATHER *walks out of the house, down the walk, and disappears from sight.* TIMOTHY *has sat at the table, biting his thumbnail, until he is certain his* GRANDFATHER *is gone. Then he slumps low in his seat.*

SCENE THREE

TIMOTHY: *(Rises from the table to address the audience.)* I felt bad having to lie to my grandfather. But it would've been worse if I'd told him I was going to the library. *(He pulls his pajama top off and drapes it over the back of the chair. From where it hangs on a peg, he gets a denim shirt that's too big for him, and puts it on.)* The thing was, Grandpa and I were people from completely different times. Whole different *worlds.* He didn't see how certain things could be important to me, when they weren't important to him in his day. *(He buttons the shirt and tucks it in but it still hangs baggy. The sleeves are rolled up.)* And I'm *sure* he never had an overdue book when he was a kid. *(He gets a large book from its hiding place: a drawer in the kitchen counter.)* So how could I explain why I had to go to the library?

TIMOTHY *goes outside of the house. With the book in one hand and the other arm outstretched, he steps up onto the wooden fence and walks the length of it like a tightrope walker. Three* YOUNG MEN, *in their early teens, run in from the opposite direction. They are kicking a can as though in a soccer game, and calling to each other:* "Over here!"—"Good block!"—"No fair!" *The* FIRST YOUNG MAN *notices* TIMOTHY, *who has started back along the fence.*

FIRST YOUNG MAN: *(Quietly.)* Hey, guys. Get a look at this. *(They giggle to each other.)* All together. *(He starts and they join in.)* "He flies through the air with the *greatest* of ease, *(Startled,* TIMOTHY *almost loses his balance.)* The daring young man *on* the flying trapeze!"

TIMOTHY: *(Turning around on the far end.)* Shows how much you know. *(He continues walking the fence.)* It's a tightrope.

FIRST YOUNG MAN: *(Facetiously.)* Oh, it *is*? Silly me. *(The other two laugh.* FIRST YOUNG MAN *walks up to the fence.)* Did you guys know that?

SECOND YOUNG MAN: Not me.

THIRD YOUNG MAN: I didn't know.

FIRST YOUNG MAN: What are you doing on this tightrope?

TIMOTHY: *(Ignoring them.)* Going for a new world's record.

FIRST YOUNG MAN: Oh yeah? Well, isn't that dangerous? I mean, what if you... *(He gives the fence a shove with his foot, causing it to wobble.)* fall off?

TIMOTHY: *(Losing his balance.)* Hey! *(He falls on the opposite side.)*

FIRST YOUNG MAN: *(His foot on the fence.)* There goes your world's record. *(All three laugh, return to their game.)* He goes for the point!

TIMOTHY *gets up from the ground. He steps through the gate and goes to exit the way they came in. The* FIRST YOUNG MAN *gestures for the others to keep quiet. He picks up the can and carefully tosses it so that it bounces lightly off of* TIMOTHY'*s back.*

TIMOTHY: Ow! *(The three* YOUNG MEN *again laugh. He looks back at them.)*
SECOND YOUNG MAN: What you looking at?
TIMOTHY: *(Turning to go.)* Nothing.
FIRST YOUNG MAN: Hey, kid! What's your name?
TIMOTHY: *(Hesitates, then answers.)* Timmy, Tim, Timothy— take your pick.
THIRD YOUNG MAN: What's the matter? Can't you make up your mind? *(They laugh.)*
TIMOTHY: At least I've got one. *(He again turns to go.)*
FIRST YOUNG MAN: Hey, Timmy-Tim-Timothy! Don't go yet.
TIMOTHY: What do you want?
FIRST YOUNG MAN: We want to be your friends, Timmy-Tim-Timothy. *(They walk up to him.)*
SECOND YOUNG MAN: Your buddies.
FIRST YOUNG MAN: You play soccer real good. That last block...
SECOND YOUNG MAN: You really used your head. *(They laugh.)*
FIRST YOUNG MAN: We want you to stick around. You can play soccer with us. Right, guys?
THIRD YOUNG MAN: Sure, we'll let you play.
SECOND YOUNG MAN: You can be the ball. *(They laugh.)*
FIRST YOUNG MAN: No, I'm serious. I think you're good.
THIRD YOUNG MAN: A regular *Pele.*
FIRST YOUNG MAN: What do you say, Timmy-Tim-Timothy? You want to join our team?
TIMOTHY: I don't think so.
THIRD YOUNG MAN: What's the matter? Afraid you'll get hurt?
TIMOTHY: No. I've got other things I have to do.
SECOND YOUNG MAN: *(Derisively.)* Like your homework? *(They all laugh.)*
TIMOTHY: It's not homework.
SECOND YOUNG MAN: *(Closing in.)* Then what is it?
TIMOTHY: It's a book. I was reading it.
FIRST YOUNG MAN: *(Holding out his hand.)* What's the name of the book?

TIMOTHY: Why?
FIRST YOUNG MAN: *(Waiting for the book.)* Maybe I'll read it.
TIMOTHY: *(Backing away.)* I have to go.
THIRD YOUNG MAN: *(Pushing him forward.)* Don't you like our company?
FIRST YOUNG MAN: What's the book, Timmy-Tim-Timothy?
TIMOTHY: I'm late. Leave me alone.
FIRST YOUNG MAN: *(Reaching for it.)* Just let me see the book.
TIMOTHY: *(Pulling it back.)* Keep your hands off! *(Brief pause.)*
SECOND YOUNG MAN: *(Pushing him forward.)* He's scary when he gets mad.
FIRST YOUNG MAN: Let me see it.
THIRD YOUNG MAN: What's the matter? Chicken?
FIRST YOUNG MAN: *(Grabbing it.)* What's the name of it!
TIMOTHY: *(Holding it firm in both hands.)* Read it yourself! *(He shoves the flat of the book into the FIRST YOUNG MAN's face. He falls back, hurt and surprised. TIMOTHY starts to run off, but is grabbed by the other two YOUNG MEN, who wrestle him to the ground.)*
SECOND YOUNG MAN: You're not going anywhere!
FIRST YOUNG MAN: *(Holding his nose.)* He *hit* me! The creep hit me. *(He looks at his hand to see if he's bleeding.)*
TIMOTHY: Let me up!
THIRD YOUNG MAN: *(On top of him.)* Shut up, creep! *(FIRST YOUNG MAN picks up the book.)*
SECOND YOUNG MAN: *(Also on top of him.)* Who do you think you are, hitting people?
FIRST YOUNG MAN: Let him get up! *(The other two get off, the THIRD YOUNG MAN kicking him once as he rises.)* You should have given me the book when I asked you. *(Opening the book, he takes it in both hands and, struggling, tears it down the binding.)* Now *nobody's* reading it! *(He throws the two halves down.)* Let's get out of here.

The three YOUNG MEN *leave in the same direction they entered.* TIMOTHY *gets to his feet, looking very bedraggled: his shirt is untucked and torn and his clothing is covered with dust. He slowly picks up the pieces of the library book, looks at them, and tucks them under his arm.*

SCENE FOUR

GRANDFATHER *is first heard whistling, and then seen moving downstage with his metal bucket on wheels, pushing it along with his mop. He continues whistling as he squeezes the water from the mop and goes to work on the floor. All lighting should suggest the narrow confines of a hallway.* TIMOTHY *enters the hallway from the end nearest the audience. He stoops, with the book behind his back and concealed from his* GRANDFATHER, *and unobtrusively drops the book on the floor. He then moves up to his* GRANDFATHER. *He stands uncertainly for some time before he is noticed.*

GRANDFATHER: *(Mopping.)* There you are. I was wondering where you'd... *(Looking up, he stops.)* What the heck happened to you?
TIMOTHY: I kind of got in a fight.
GRANDFATHER: From the looks of your clothes, I guess you kind of did. *(He laughs quietly to himself.)* What did you do to the other guy?
TIMOTHY: I gave one of them a bloody nose.
GRANDFATHER: One of them? How many were there?
TIMOTHY: Five. (GRANDFATHER *raises his eyebrows.)* Well, counting me. Five of us in all.
GRANDFATHER: I see. What started it?
TIMOTHY: Oh, I don't know. They were just looking for someone to pick on.
GRANDFATHER: It figures. Where'd you run into these hoodlums?
TIMOTHY: They were... *(Waving it off.)* You know, down the street.
GRANDFATHER: Remind me not to come that way to work *(Pointing to* TIMOTHY's *shirt.)* What's that say?
TIMOTHY: *(Looking down over his pocket.)* That? "Indian Power." I sewed that on myself.
GRANDFATHER: You did, huh?
TIMOTHY: Yep. *(Seizing on this.)* In fact, that's why they were picking on me. Because I'm an Indian.
GRANDFATHER: They could tell that?
TIMOTHY: *(Nodding.)* They sure could.
GRANDFATHER: *(Going back to his mopping.)* The heck.
TIMOTHY: Said they didn't want no Indians in their neighborhood.
GRANDFATHER: If that don't beat all.
TIMOTHY: And I said, "Tough! Because I'm staying all summer."
GRANDFATHER: Good for you.
TIMOTHY: That's when I had to hit the one in the nose. *(His* GRANDFATHER *is again laughing to himself. Pause.)* Is that why you

couldn't tell anyone Mom was part Indian?
GRANDFATHER: *(After some hesitation.)* You know? I think I liked you better when you used to wear that shirt that said "Little Stinker" on it. That was a good shirt. You never got in fights wearing that one. *(Placing the mop in the bucket.)* And you didn't ask so many questions. *(He squeezes the water out of the mop, and moves on to a new area. At the end of the hallway nearest the audience,* MARGARET HARTLEY, *a woman in her early fifties, steps out of her classroom by miming the opening of a door.* TIMOTHY *and his* GRANDFATHER *continue without noticing her.)*
TIMOTHY: Grandpa, how am I suppose to learn anything if I can't ask questions and I can't read?
GRANDFATHER: *(Mopping.)* Oh, you can ask questions. Just don't ask *me* any. *(*MARGARET *mimes closing the door and steps back. As she does so her heel strikes the library book. She stoops down to pick it up.)*
MARGARET: *(Calling to them.)* Afternoon, Mr. Christensen. Hard at work, I see. *(She looks at the book, tucks it under her arm.)*
GRANDFATHER: Hard as ever. I've got my grandson here to help me, though.
MARGARET: *(Walking up to them.)* That's nice. How do you do?
GRANDFATHER: His name's Timothy. Say hello to the professor, Timothy.
MARGARET: *(Holding out her hand.)* Timothy, hmm?
TIMOTHY: That's what Grandpa calls me. My mom calls me Timmy, but my friends call me Tim.
MARGARET: Quite a selection, isn't it?
GRANDFATHER: His father, on the other hand, hasn't called him in years. Must be a shortage of dimes I don't know about. *(He laughs at his joke.)*
TIMOTHY: My father's very busy.
MARGARET: He doesn't live with you?
GRANDFATHER: His folks are divorced. But his dad's coming up to see him, isn't he?
TIMOTHY: *(Nodding.)* This evening.
MARGARET: Well, that should be nice.
GRANDFATHER: You aren't working today, are you?
MARGARET: Oh, no, I'm off for the summer. I just stopped by to water my plants and pick up my mail.
GRANDFATHER: *I* could water the plants.
MARGARET: No, it gives me an excuse to get out and around. *(To* TIMOTHY.*)* Have you had a chance to see much of our fair city?

TIMOTHY: *(Laughing.)* No, not yet.
GRANDFATHER: He'll be out on the town tonight, though.
MARGARET: Oh?
GRANDFATHER: Today's his birthday.
TIMOTHY: *(Embarrassed.)* Grandpa...
MARGARET: Well, congratulations. Is that why your father's coming up?
TIMOTHY: *(Shrugging.)* I guess.
GRANDFATHER: They'll probably be out till all hours, you know, dancing and celebrating and chasing wild women.
MARGARET: *(Laughing.)* Oh, my. Around here? I didn't know we had any.
GRANDFATHER: Well, if we do, here's the man to find them. He's from *Out West,* you know.
MARGARET: I *didn't* know that.
TIMOTHY: Just kind of.
GRANDFATHER: Don't let him fool you! Why, you should see him out there on the range. He's an Indian, you know. They're pretty tough characters, those Indians.
MARGARET: Oh really? (GRANDFATHER *does a silly imitation of an Indian dance from an old movie, and then laughs.)* Somehow I get the impression that *you're* the one who's trying to fool me, Tim Christensen.
GRANDFATHER: It's the truth! Tell her, Timothy.
TIMOTHY: I'm only part Indian.
GRANDFATHER: He doesn't like me to tell people about it.
MARGARET: You should be proud of your heritage. The Indians made many important contributions to the early settlers' way of life.
GRANDFATHER: That's what I try to tell him, Professor, but he turns a deaf ear to his old granddad. He'd much rather be home on the range, riding bareback and hunting buffalo.
MARGARET: Go on. Now I know you're joking with me. You don't, do you?
TIMOTHY: *(Smiling.)* No, ma'am. I live in a city. I've never even been on a ranch. I would like a horse, though.
GRANDFATHER: A horse? Ho-Ho! What would you do with it? As it is, I can't get him to take his nose out of a book long enough to go out shooting with me!
TIMOTHY: That's different.
MARGARET: You like to read?
TIMOTHY: Yes, very much.
GRANDFATHER: *Too* much, you mean.

MARGARET: *(Taking it out from under her arm.)* Well, then, maybe this is *your* book I found down the hall. *(TIMOTHY's eyes go big at the sight of it.)* I thought perhaps someone was throwing it away. But it's a library book, as you can see. It's also in desperate need of a new binding, I'm afraid. Is it yours? *(She holds it out to him. Pause.)*

TIMOTHY: *(Slowly taking it.)* Yes, ma'am, it is. Thank you.

MARGARET: *(Cheerfully.)* Well, you'd better get it back to the library. *(She laughs.)* It was due three days ago!

TIMOTHY: Yes, ma'am.

GRANDFATHER: *(Looking down at it.)* You take better care of your books than that.

TIMOTHY: I was on my way to the library when I got in that fight.

GRANDFATHER: They did that?

TIMOTHY: Yeah. And there were only three of them. Four, counting me.

MARGARET: Some other boys did this?

GRANDFATHER: Why didn't you tell me that's what happened?

TIMOTHY: I couldn't, Grandpa. I was afraid you'd be angry.

GRANDFATHER: I guess I *ought* to be! You lied to me.

MARGARET: Tim, that's no way to...

TIMOTHY: *(Upset.)* I had to. You didn't like me reading. And I figured you wouldn't let me go to the library.

GRANDFATHER: Go to the library? What's that got to do with...

MARGARET: Please, now, he's upset enough...

TIMOTHY: I knew the book was overdue, and I had to take it back, but I was afraid to tell you.

GRANDFATHER: Afraid? Afraid of what? What kind of damn...

MARGARET: *(Topping him, interrupting.) Tim Christensen!*

GRANDFATHER: *(Hesitates, softens his choice of words.)* Darn fool nonsense is that anyway?

MARGARET: I hope you don't talk to the boy that way at home.

GRANDFATHER: Since when are *you* a member of this family? And what's more, Margaret Hartley, I will talk to my grandson *any way I...* *(He looks to both of them, frustrated.) Darn* well want to. And without any coaching from you. *(He jams the mop in the bucket.)* Timothy? If you get hungry, you'll find me down in the basement. If I don't see you by dark, I'll figure you went home with the professor. She's obviously more your speed than I am. *(He exits upstage, pushing the bucket.)*

MARGARET: *(With hands on hips.)* What a *wicked* old man!

TIMOTHY: *(Wiping his nose on his sleeve.)* He's not, really.

MARGARET: *(Laughing to herself.)* Oh, I know, dear. *(Puts her arm around his shoulders.)* I've known your grandfather quite some time now—long enough to see through his moods. He doesn't fool me for a second. *(She looks down at him. He sniffs.)* But I think *someone* could use a kleenex. I should have one...Hmm. *(She stops, looks around.)* What did I do with my purse. Must have left it in the classroom. *(She heads back to her room with* TIMOTHY *following. She opens the door.)* Wouldn't you know it? Sitting right there where I left it. *(She crosses to her purse which sits on a single empty chair. She takes out a kleenex, hands it to* TIMOTHY.*)* There you are.

TIMOTHY: *(Sitting in the chair.)* I'm sorry for the trouble.

MARGARET: Don't be silly? You saved the day. If it hadn't been for your runny nose, I'd have gone all the way home before I'd realized I didn't have my house-keys or anything else with me. And I would *not* have been happy walking back here for my purse, either. *(She steps up to and addresses her hanging plants.)* Don't worry, dears. It's only me, come back to say good-by. Don't you just love plants, Timothy?

TIMOTHY: Sure. Plants are neat, Professor.

MARGARET: That's true, never a mess. But you could use a little more water. couldn't you? *(To* TIMOTHY.*)* Would you hand me that spray-bottle? Next to the chair? *(He finds it, brings it to her.)* Thank you. And you don't have to call me "Professor." Margaret is fine.

TIMOTHY: Okay.

MARGARET: *(Spraying the plant.)* There you are. Got to take care of them. They're the only family I've got. (TIMOTHY *returns to the chair.)* Were you named after your grandfather, Timothy?

TIMOTHY: Sort of. But his name isn't really Tim.

MARGARET: *(Turning to him, surprised.)* It isn't?

TIMOTHY: Nope. That's just what people call him.

MARGARET: Then what *is* his name?

TIMOTHY: His real name is Forrest. But people got to calling him Tim, because it was short for *Timber*. I guess it was kind of a joke.

MARGARET: To think he's gone all this time without telling me. *(She shrugs, goes back to her spraying.)* Oh, well. Maybe he feels the need to keep some mystery about him.

TIMOTHY: Don't you have any children?

MARGARET: Me? Oh dear, no. What brought that up?

TIMOTHY: You were talking about your plants.

MARGARET: I see.   No, my late husband and I had talked about having children. But, with all the talk, we never quite managed to get around to it. It's just as well. Raising children is such a difficult job. You want to do everything perfectly. No, I have more than my hands full just taking care of my plants. I don't know *what* I'd do with children. Although, I will admit, there are those times when I miss having a family around. *(Pause.)*

TIMOTHY: *(Rising awkwardly.)* Well, I better get downstairs.

MARGARET: True! I'm sure you must have better things to do than listen to an old woman going on about her past.

TIMOTHY: You're not *that* old.

MARGARET: I'm almost as old as your grandfather—but don't you dare tell him.

TIMOTHY: That's a pretty good age.

MARGARET: *(Smiling.)* I'm glad you think so. *(She offers her hand.)* It was very nice talking to you, Timothy. You're a very good listener.

TIMOTHY: *(Shaking hands.)* Thank you.

MARGARET: *(Walking him to the door.)* I hope you have a happy birthday. And don't forget that book.

TIMOTHY: I won't.

MARGARET: Alright. Well, perhaps I'll see you again before the summer's out.

TIMOTHY: I hope so, ma'am.

MARGARET: Good! Then I'm sure we will. 'Bye. *(She returns to the classroom.* TIMOTHY *watches for a moment as she resumes watering her plants, humming to herself. The classroom fades to black as* TIMOTHY *slowly moves away from the doorway.)*

SCENE FIVE

TIMOTHY: *(Moving down to the audience.)* I think one of the hardest things of all is just figuring out how you really feel about something. Not what people want you to feel, or *expect* you to feel, but how *you yourself* feel underneath everything. Talking to the professor, I thought a person should be thankful to have *any* family, even one you didn't always agree with, and I was all set to tell my grandfather that. *(He has moved into an isolated, square area that represents the elevator in the building.)* But by the time I'd gotten in the elevator, I'd changed my mind, and I was scared of him again. *(He mimes closing the elevator's sliding accordion door. During the following, he mimes the actions of operating the elevator.)* The old elevator that ran down to the basement wasn't like the ones back home. I was used to elevators where you simply pushed a button and the numbers lit up to tell you what floor you were on. Here there weren't any lights or buttons. You ran the elevator by pulling thick ropes that lifted and lowered it—while you were *in* it. I always wondered what happened if your arms gave out, but ours never did. We got where we were going. There were times, of course, when it seemed like forever just getting from one floor to another. And there was even the one time I wished it *would* take forever and that I'd never have to reach the bottom. *(He stops the activity of the elevator.)* But, naturally, I did. And my grandfather was there, waiting for me. *(*TIMOTHY *slides open the door.)*

GRANDFATHER: *(Eating his sandwich.)* A minute later, I'd have eaten *your* sandwich, too. *(He continues eating.)*

TIMOTHY: *(Addressing the audience.)* The janitor's closet was just a small room in the basement, but I remember it full of mysterious things. Every box held a treasure from the past, each item more wonderful than the last. There was so much there waiting to be discovered.

GRANDFATHER: *(Eating his sandwich.)* Nothing personal, but I started without you.

TIMOTHY: *(Addressing the audience.)* This was my grandfather's world. And if he'd been like a stranger in Grandma's house, he was certainly at home here.

GRANDFATHER: Pull up a seat. Got the best boxes money can buy.

TIMOTHY *pulls over a cardboard box, sits on it.* GRANDFATHER *is similarly seated on a box and is using a third box as an impromptu table. Lunch is spread out on a handkerchief. The room itself is cluttered with odds and ends, either sitting out open or stacked on the shelves that comprise one corner of the room.*

GRANDFATHER: I wondered how long it would take.
TIMOTHY: For what?
GRANDFATHER: For you to get bored with the professor.
TIMOTHY: I thought she was interesting.
GRANDFATHER: Ho-Ho!
TIMOTHY: She kind of reminded me of Grandma. *(*GRANDFATHER *stops in mid bite.)*
GRANDFATHER: Well, you can't remember your grandmother very well, then.
TIMOTHY: I remember she never let you swear. *(*TIMOTHY *laughs.)*
GRANDFATHER: Eat your dinner.
TIMOTHY: *(Pointing to a sandwich.)* Is that mine?
GRANDFATHER: I've got mine in my mouth; whose else would it be?

TIMOTHY: *(Taking it.)* Thank you. *(He unwraps it, takes a bite.)* Can I have some potato chips?
GRANDFATHER: Eat them all, what do I care? *(TIMOTHY takes a couple of chips from the bag, puts them on his side of the box. GRANDFATHER takes the bag, pours a pile of chips on TIMOTHY's side.)* There. You're too big for children's portions.
TIMOTHY: Thanks, Grandpa. *(He takes a chip and eats it.)*
GRANDFATHER: *(Unable to contain it.)* Margaret Hartley is nothing like your grandmother! Her husband was an old coot! She's an old biddy! A marriage made in Heaven, if ever there was. The kindest thing Old Man Hartley ever did was to kick off and give this town a rest! I only wish the professor would find herself equally kind-hearted, keep her nose in her own affairs, and give *me* a rest! *(He takes an angry bite of his sandwich. They eat on in silence for a moment, although TIMOTHY is on the verge of laughing.)* When's your father coming in?
TIMOTHY: I don't know. Sometime this evening.
GRANDFATHER: That much I know. Did he say anything about taking you out for supper?
TIMOTHY: *(Smiling.)* Well, we can't go out for *dinner*. I just ate *that* for *lunch*.
GRANDFATHER: What's that supposed to mean?
TIMOTHY: *(Still smiling.)* Nothing, grandpa. It was a joke.
GRANDFATHER: If you don't like the food I serve, there are plenty of restaurants that'll take your money.
TIMOTHY: The food's fine. *(He take a big bite.)* Mmm-mmm, good! It's just confusing when you call lunch dinner.
GRANDFATHER: What would you call it?
TIMOTHY: I'd call it lunch! And dinner I'd eat at night.
GRANDFATHER: No, you eat *supper* at night.
TIMOTHY: *You* eat supper at night. *I* eat *dinner*.
GRANDFATHER: You don't know what you're talking about! Breakfast's in the morning, dinner's in the afternoon, and supper you eat at night.
TIMOTHY: Not where I come from.
GRANDFATHER: For cripes sake, you're from Minneapolis! That's not a hundred miles from here! And in Minneapolis they eat their meals the same time we do here.
TIMOTHY: That was a long time ago. I'm not there anymore.
GRANDFATHER: You still come from Minneapolis! A man might move somewhere else, but he always comes from the same place, no matter where he's living!

TIMOTHY: Okay.
GRANDFATHER: Now eat your...your *food*. Your sandwich'll go stale in a minute. *(They eat quietly for a moment.)*
TIMOTHY: *(To himself.)* I'll bet even in *Minneapolis* they don't eat cereal for dessert.
GRANDFATHER: What did you say?
TIMOTHY: Nothing.
GRANDFATHER: I heard you say something.
TIMOTHY: Just that you're the only person I know who eats their breakfast for dessert...
GRANDFATHER: *(Throwing down sandwich.)* Holy Mackerel!
TIMOTHY: *(Continuing.)* At *night* instead of in the morning, like the rest of the world.
GRANDFATHER: You're getting *too darn smart* for your britches, you know that?
TIMOTHY: Do *you* know anyone else who eats cereal for dessert?
GRANDFATHER: I thought you liked breakfast food!
TIMOTHY: I do, in the *morning*. But I feel *funny* eating Cheerios before I go to *bed*.
GRANDFATHER: We wouldn't want you to feel *funny*.
TIMOTHY: Oh, Grandpa...
GRANDFATHER: Maybe you ought to go live with your *father*. He'd probably let you eat *ice cream* every meal of the day. Is that what you want?
TIMOTHY: Well, I don't want to *argue*.
GRANDFATHER: Ho-ho! I wonder sometimes! *(Pause.)*
TIMOTHY: Maybe I *should* go live with my father.
GRANDFATHER: That's what I said! Put your suitcase in the back of the car, it won't take long to get there. *(Pause.)*
TIMOTHY: I don't need your help. There's always the bus.
GRANDFATHER: Fine! It makes my life easier. Just don't go calling me if you get lost somewhere.
TIMOTHY: I won't. *(Pause.)*
GRANDFATHER: You going to finish your dinner?
TIMOTHY: I guess.
GRANDFATHER: You'd better! You got a long trip ahead of you.
TIMOTHY: *(Getting his sandwich.)* I didn't think I'd leave for a little while yet.
GRANDFATHER: Whenever you want, just say the word. *(He collects the pieces of his sandwich from various parts of the "table" and puts the sandwich back together.)* But as long as you're here, you'll have to eat by my time-table. I learned that schedule at ten

years old, when I had to go to work to support three sisters and a younger brother. At that age I never complained about what they called a meal—I was just darn thankful to have a little food in my stomach. So if you're staying on, you'd better get used to it! I will eat my dinner in the afternoon, my supper at night, and, yes, when I feel like it, I'll even have my breakfast for dessert! That's the way I've done it most my life. I see no earthly reason to change my ways now. *(He eats his sandwich.)* And what's more, stay away from the library. No good'll come to you hanging out with those hooligans. *(He continues eating. Pause.)*

TIMOTHY: *(Quietly.)* Is that how you drove Mom away? By making her do things she didn't want to?

GRANDFATHER: *(Staring at him.)* Ho-ho! You're a *prize*, aren't you? *(He sets down his sandwich, wipes his hands and mouth with a hanky.)* I'll tell you something: I never made your mother do anything. She was head-strong from the start and always did what she wanted no matter what I told her.

TIMOTHY: That's not what she said.

GRANDFATHER: *(Continuing.) As for your father,* he was not a strong man. Do you have any idea why they got divorced?

TIMOTHY: Because they weren't happy. (GRANDFATHER *looks at him, unbelieving.)* It seemed like a good reason to me.

GRANDFATHER: Why do I bother?

TIMOTHY: You're just saying that because you don't want me to leave.

GRANDFATHER: Go on! What do I care? I'm done trying to point you in the right direction.

TIMOTHY: Mom told me...

GRANDFATHER: *(Interrupting.)* According to your mother, the man gave up!

TIMOTHY: That's not true!

GRANDFATHER: I know it, but try tellng her! When they got married he was going to spend his life drawing pictures. Well, it don't take long to discover you can't make a living at that. So the man got a job to support his family. A man's got to work! A body's got to eat, doesn't it? But your mother never forgave him.

TIMOTHY: You made that up.

GRANDFATHER: God's truth, so help me! Your mother claimed he'd given up and he believed her. I warned her what would happen but she never listened to me. That's when things went wrong. And it didn't take a great mind to see it coming. *(Pause. He calms down.)* So don't go telling me about your mother and how I made her do things. She hasn't heard a word I've said since she left home. *(Long pause. Both* TIMOTHY *and* GRANDFATHER *seem isolated and lonely in the cluttered room.)* I'm sorry, boy. But I reckon you ought to know all sides of the story. *(He fidgets uncomfortably.)* How about a little music? Quiet things down a little. *(From one of the boxes he takes an early record-player and several cardboard tubes containing cylinder-shaped records.)* Let's see what we've got here. *(He reads the bottoms of the tubes.)* Here we go. *(He slips out the hollow cylinder, sets it on the record-player.)* One of my favorites. *(He cranks up the record-player.)* This is "Wine on the Rhine." Your grandma liked it once. *(An old song starts to play; pause.)* Can't say as I blame you, wanting to go live with your father.

TIMOTHY: *(Quietly.)* Maybe I will.

GRANDFATHER: Well, maybe you should. I'm no company for you, I admit that. But don't be thinking it's 'cause I don't care. It's just... *(Fiddling distractedly in a box, he finds a large feather.)* Hmph. Here's a feather. You want it?

TIMOTHY: *(Without looking at him.)* What kind is it?

GRANDFATHER: *(Examining it.)* Looks like chicken. But, for the sake of argument, let's pretend it's an eagle. What do you say?

TIMOTHY: *(Accepting it.)* Sure, I'll take it. It'll make a great bookmark.

GRANDFATHER: *(He hesitates, staring.)* I've got a better idea: Why don't you put it in your hair when you cut my *heart* out! *(He shakes his head in resignation.)* You're a hard one to get on with, you know that? You remind me of your mother in a lot of ways—both stubborn as sin. Funny thing is, I miss your mother. I never thought it'd happen but now that your grandmother's gone I miss your mother... *(He puts on his cap, grabs his mop and bucket.)* Aw, the heck with it. I should finish up around five. I won't expect you to wait for me, just...say hello to your father for me. *(He exits.* TIMOTHY *sits until the music runs its course, then removes the needle from the record.)*

SCENE SIX

TIMOTHY *steps forward to address the audience. He moves quickly, obviously in a hurry.*

TIMOTHY: I didn't wait until grandpa was done. I left the college early and ran all the way home, because I didn't want to miss my father. *(He rushes through the gate and into the house.)* I changed my shirt... *(He pulls off the shirt, throws it over the chair that already holds his pajama top, and puts on a new shirt.)* And I combed my hair... *(He does so, looking at his reflection in the side of the toaster.)* Then I waited for him to arrive. *(He takes a deep breath, and sits down in the kitchen chair. The telephone rings.* TIMOTHY *hesitates, letting it ring, then rises to answer it.)* Hello?...Oh, hi, Professor. My grandfather isn't here right now, do you want me to take a message?...No, I haven't left yet. Yes, I am, very much...Do you want me to say you called?...Okay. I won't. Goodbye. *(He sets down the receiver and returns to the chair. He waits.)*

KARL KURTZ, TIMOTHY'*s father, enters and walks up to the gate. He looks tentatively towards the house, checks a small notepad from his pocket, and steps through the gate. He is in his midthirties, is dressed conservatively, and carries his sports-coat over his arm.* TIMOTHY *hears his approach, rises to meet him. As* KARL *steps up to knock,* TIMOTHY *appears at the threshold, and opens the door. Pause.*

KARL: Timmy?
TIMOTHY: Hi, Dad.
KARL: You've changed.
TIMOTHY: Maybe a little.
KARL: No, you have. You've grown.
TIMOTHY: *(Smiling, embarrassed.)* I guess.
KARL: How've you been?
TIMOTHY: Fine. And you?
KARL: Great, really great. *(Pause.* KARL *extends his hand. They shake hands.)* It's so good to see you.
TIMOTHY: *(Backing into the house.)* Come on in.
KARL: *(Entering the kitchen)* Sure, no sense in standing outside, is there? Is your grandpa Tim here?
TIMOTHY: *(Shaking his head.)* He's still working. You want to sit down?
KARL: No, I've been sitting for the last hour and a half. It's a long drive. I was lucky they let me off work a little early, it would've been dark already. *(He looks around the kitchen.)* So, what have you been doing?
TIMOTHY: Not much.
KARL: The neighborhood sure looks different.
TIMOTHY: Yeah.
KARL: Of course it's been a while since I was here. *(*TIMOTHY *pulls out a chair, sits down.)* How's your mom?
TIMOTHY: She's fine.

KARL: Does she like living out there in the desert?
TIMOTHY: I think so.
KARL: Good, that's good. She was never afraid of snakes or lizards, so I guess the desert wouldn't bother her.
TIMOTHY: Where we live you don't see many snakes.
KARL: I thought the desert was full of them.
TIMOTHY: Nope.
KARL: Just crawling with them.
TIMOTHY: Not where we live. I haven't seen a single one yet.
KARL: Oh. Well, it's just as well. *(He pulls out the other chair, sits.)* How's school?
TIMOTHY: It's okay.
KARL: You get good grades?
TIMOTHY: Sure. *(Pause.)*
KARL: I'm sorry I haven't written you.
TIMOTHY: I figured you were busy.
KARL: I have been! There's a lot of work now. They laid off some people and the rest of us try to pick up the slack. But you just get further behind.
TIMOTHY: What do you do?
KARL: I'm a draftsman.
TIMOTHY: Is that like an artist?
KARL: Sort of. I still draw. But not really, no. It's more mathematical.
TIMOTHY: I'm not good at math.
KARL: Just between us, neither am I. *(They both laugh.)* But I have to do it.
TIMOTHY: Do you like it?
KARL: *(Shrugs.)* It's work. *(He smiles.)* I just can't get over how big you've gotten. You'll be taller than me before too long.
TIMOTHY: Not for a while.
KARL: Oh, not too much longer. You're shooting right up there. Height you get from your mother's side of the family, you sure don't get it from me. How *is* Grandpa Tim?
TIMOTHY: He's fine.
KARL: Feeling okay?
TIMOTHY: Sure.
KARL: I came up after Grandma died, spent the afternoon with him. We didn't have a lot to say, of course. But he seems to be getting along real well. *(He takes his wallet out of his coat pocket, opens it to some pictures.)* Speaking of family, you haven't seen mine yet, have you? *(He moves closer to show* TIMOTHY *the photographs.)* These are your sisters, Timmy.

TIMOTHY: They're just babies.

KARL: That's true, they're young yet. But they'll grow. This one is Emily. And Rachel is the oldest, she's three now. We took the picture right at the hospital, after she was born.

TIMOTHY: Mom told me I had a couple of half-sisters. I asked her if two half-sisters would add up to one *whole* sister, but she said no. *(He looks at his father, shrugs.)* Maybe that's why I'm not any good at math. *(He hands back the wallet.)* They're very nice. I wish I could meet them.

KARL: *(Avoiding* TIMOTHY'S *eyes as he puts the wallet back.)* Yeah. We'll have to try and do that some time.

TIMOTHY: *(Hesitantly.)* Would you like me to come down to the city and visit with you for a while? Grandpa would drive me down. I've got the whole summer.

KARL: I don't know...

TIMOTHY: I could meet your family.

KARL: Sure, that'd be great. But I don't know if it would work out very well.

TIMOTHY: Why not?

KARL: You see, my new wife hasn't told her folks that I was married before. They don't know that I have a boy, we've never told them. And it might make things a little difficult for everybody. *(He stands up from the table.)* I know it sounds funny—silly—but that's the way her family is. You have to work you way up to things. See, they don't know about you, Timmy. And it wouldn't be fair to...surprise them. I just don't think it's a very good idea.

TIMOTHY: Okay.

KARL: But, you know, eventually...Sure! Maybe you could come and stay with us for a while. After everything's straightened around.

TIMOTHY: Sure. *(Pause.)*

KARL: What do you say? You want to walk down to Ben Franklin's and get a chocolate milkshake?

TIMOTHY: *(Still avoiding his eyes.)* I can't. I...promised Grandpa I'd go out to dinner with him tonight. He wanted to try a new restaurant.

KARL: Where's that?

TIMOTHY: Out by Fairboult. Just off of the highway.

KARL: Oh? I didn't see any place out there.

TIMOTHY: Well, it's new.

KARL: I see. That should be fun. They still have Ben Franklin's Five and Dime downtown, don't they?

TIMOTHY: Yeah. but they don't make milkshakes anymore. There's a drugstore now.

KARL: *(Laughing to himself.)* Things certainly do change fast, don't they? *(Pause.)* Well, I'd better head for home. My family'll worry if I'm *too* late. It's already getting dark. *(He puts on his coat.)* You going to walk me out?

TIMOTHY: Sure.

KARL: *(Looking at him.)* What is that?

TIMOTHY: What do you mean?

KARL: On your cheek. It looks like the beginnings of a shiner. Did somebody give you a black eye?

TIMOTHY: Oh, that. I had an overdue book.

KARL: I didn't realize the librarian was that tough.

TIMOTHY: She's not. But she has a lot of friends.

KARL: *(As they both laugh quietly.)* I see. Gosh, I just can't get over how tall you've gotten. You've really grown up. *(Almost as an afterthought he again offers his hand and they shake.)* I can't tell you how good it is to see you. I wish we had more time to talk, but...

TIMOTHY: *(Walking him out to the yard.)* I understand. Would it be alright if I write to you?

KARL: Well, sure. That would be nice.

TIMOTHY: Okay.

KARL: Tell your grandpa Tim hello for me.

TIMOTHY: I will. *(Pause.)*

KARL: *(Turning to go.)* Well, good-bye!

TIMOTHY: So long, Dad.

KARL: *(Stopping at the gate.)* Say, isn't your birthday coming up pretty soon?

TIMOTHY: Yes, it is.

KARL: I'll have to try and get back up for that. Take care!

TIMOTHY: *(As KARL exits.)* 'Bye. (TIMOTHY *returns to the kitchen and sits quietly.* GRANDFATHER *enters, carrying a small bundle, which he sets on the kitchen counter.)*

GRANDFATHER: *(Seeing him for the first time.)* What are *you* doing here?

TIMOTHY: Just sitting.

GRANDFATHER: *(Turning on a light.)* Shouldn't sit in the dark. Bad for your eyes. *(He looks around the room.)* Where's your dad?

TIMOTHY: He went home.

GRANDFATHER: Already?

TIMOTHY: Family and all. You know.

GRANDFATHER: Yeah...You left your book at the college.

TIMOTHY: I know. I forgot.

GRANDFATHER: It's alright. I dropped it off at the library on my way home. Librarian said it wasn't as bad as we thought, they can fix it. So I paid the difference. You're clear.

TIMOTHY: *(For the first time in the scene, looking at him.)* Thanks, Grandpa.
GRANDFATHER: Anytime. *(He smiles.)* It's your birthday, isn't it? *(*TIMOTHY *nods, turns away again.)* I'm sorry about the fight we had.
TIMOTHY: It's okay.
GRANDFATHER: I guess maybe I started feeling a little *lonely* for the first time in my life. Your grandma's gone...Your mom and me ain't exactly close. It's my first summer alone! *(He laughs to himself.)* It's not easy getting by without women in your life. *(He stops, watches for a reaction. He can't see that* TIMOTHY *has started to cry. He continues uncertainly.)* The librarian was nicer than I expected. I figured if anyone knew what a young man should be reading, it'd be a librarian. We got to talking, and she told me about one book that sounded kind of interesting. All about this fellow named Nick Adams who lives up in Michigan, I think. Does a little hunting and fishing. Gets to know some people. Travels around. It kind of appealed to me. *(He takes the small bundle, sets it on the table next to* TIMOTHY.*)* Anyway...Happy Birthday. If I was going to read anything, I think that's the one... *(*TIMOTHY *suddenly throws his arms around his* GRANDFATHER*'s neck, hugging him and crying.)* Good Lord! I didn't know it was *that* good a gift!
TIMOTHY: *(Locked in the hug.)* It's a *wonderful* gift!
GRANDFATHER: *(Laughing.)* Score one for me! Wait a minute. Are you crying?
TIMOTHY: *(Obviously he is.)* No.
GRANDFATHER: *(Still laughing.)* Well, loosen up a little! You'll drag us both down! *(*MARGARET HARTLEY *appears at the door, holding a bakery box.)*
MARGARET: *(Calling inside.)* Knock, knock! Anybody home?
GRANDFATHER: Yes!
MARGARET: Open the door! I've got my hands full.
GRANDFATHER: *(Breaking the hug.)* Much as I hate to!
TIMOTHY: *(Quietly.)* I love you, Grandpa. *(Pause.* GRANDFATHER *stands still, unable to find words to say. He is deeply moved.)*
MARGARET: Hurry up in there!
GRANDFATHER: That woman has a talent for timing. *(He goes to let her in.)* Come on, now that you've announced yourself to the neighborhood. *(She enters the kitchen, sets the box on the table, and opens it.)*
MARGARET: I saw the light and came right over. You can't have a birthday without a cake, can you?
GRANDFATHER: *(Shaking his head.)* Will you look at that?

MARGARET: Well, can you?
TIMOTHY: But it's only got ten candles.
MARGARET: Ten was all I could find, I'm afraid.
TIMOTHY: But I was ten *two years* ago.
MARGARET: I hoped, dear, that with your new maturity you might find it in your heart of hearts to forgive me the two missing candles.
TIMOTHY: *(Kissing her on the cheek.)* Thank you, Professor.
GRANDFATHER: Well, light the things and make a wish.
MARGARET: *(With matches.)* I'll do the honors since I've never had the chance before. *(She lights the candles.* GRANDFATHER *turns out the light.)* There you are! All together!
ALL: One! Two! Three! *(TIMOTHY blows out the candles. The kitchen goes dark.)*

SCENE SEVEN

The stage is still except for the playing of "The Old Rugged Cross" in the background. TIMOTHY *appears, approaches the audience and an isolated area, lit rectangularly, on the forestage. He now wears a dark blue suit-coat over his clothing.*

TIMOTHY: *(To the audience.)* My grandma was a small, delicate woman, as I remember. Her house was full of small, delicate things: mementoes and bric-a-brac; little statues and faded pictures. She walked to church almost every Sunday. Grandpa always stayed home. I cried at her funeral...Because I'd never really taken the time to know her. *(Pause.)* At my grandfather's funeral, they played "The Old Rugged Cross." I didn't cry that time. I *felt* like crying, but I think there were just too many things to remember. *(Pause.)* There were a lot of questions Grandpa never answered, of course. But that's pretty much how life is. It's like traveling on a bus or a plane: everything's going by so quick, you can't see it all, so you settle for those details that jump out at you. The summer of my twelfth birthday, there were plenty. *(Pause.)* My grandfather once told me I reminded him of my mother. But *she* always claimed I reminded her of *him*. I tend to believe they were both right, that a person can't help being made up of everyone in his family, all rolled into one. And I don't mean like being part Indian, or part *anything*. Those things don't exist unless you study them, I'm convinced. But your family's part of you and you can't get rid of that, no matter how you try. Death tries. But even death can't do it. *(Pause.* TIMOTHY *takes from his pocket the large feather. He drops it onto the lit area before him. As it falls, he turns and exits. Lights slowly fade to black.)*

Sand Castles
Adele Edling Shank

Sand Castles was first presented at the Magic Theatre, San Francisco, on October 5, 1982, with the following cast:

STEPHEN	Michael O'Rourke
IRIS	Mary McKeon
CAROL	Conner Steffens
THE AUSSIE	Robert Calvert
KIM	Leslie Grinspan
ANDY	Blair Tatton
GLEN	Jerry Donchin
GINGER	Carol Shoup-Sanders
LINDA BLUE	Terez Tunder
ANEMONE	Jane H. Macfie

Directed by Theodore Shank
Set design by John Ammirati
Light design by Patty Ann Farrell
Costume design by Deborah Capen D'Oran
Sound design by Kurt Graffy
Properties by Steve Scheitlin

Sand Castles was revised by the author and presented at the Actors Theatre of Louisville, Kentucky, on February 23, 1983, with the following cast:

IRIS, PREGNANT WOMAN, SAILOR	Mary Seward-McKeon
STEPHEN	John C. Vennema
CAROL	Conner Steffens
AUSSIE, FAST FLOYD, PHOTOGRAPHER, BOOKWORM	William Mesnik
KIM, BIKER CHICK	Stephanie Saft
ANDY, FRITZ, POLICEMAN, TEXAN	Scott Phelps
GLEN, RETIRED MAN, ANDY'S FATHER	Frederic Major
GINGER, RETIRED WOMAN	Carol Shoup-Sanders
LINDA BLUE, AUSSIE'S WOMAN	Becky Mayo
ANEMONE, JOGGER	Sally Faye Reit

©1983 by Adele Edling Shank
CAUTION: All rights strictly reserved. Professionals and amateurs are hereby warned that *Sand Castles* is subject to a royalty. It is protected under the copyright laws of all countries covered by the International Copyright Convention. Permission in writing must be secured before any kind of performance is given. All inquiries should be addressed to the author's agent, Michael Imison Playwrights, Ltd., 150 West 47th Street, Suite, 5F, New York, NY 10026.

Directed by Theodore Shank
Set design by Paul Owen
Costume design by Karen Gerson
Sound design by Richard L. Sirois
Lighting design by Jeff Hill
Property masters, Sam Garst and Sandra Strawn

Place: A southern California beach.
Time: The following summer.

NOTE

The text has been newly revised by the author for this edition.

CHARACTERS

CAROL: 39, wife of Stephen and mother of two young children. She is a private secretary in a large corporation.
STEPHEN: 42, husband of Carol and father of her children. He is an M.D., internal medicine his specialty.
IRIS: 29, a beautiful enigma.
PAUL: 26, an addict and a poet.
THE AUSSIE: a wasted 30ish scrambled surfer.
KIM: 17, youngest child of Glen and Ginger. A university freshman in the fall, she dreams of space.
ANDY: 22, a nice kid whose goal in life is the perfect wave.
GLEN: 55, husband of Ginger and father of Kim. His "hobby" of building houses has taken off.
GINGER: 53, wife of Glen and Kim's mother. She uses her job as an administrative assistant in the same corporation where Carol works as an escape from her family.
LINDA BLUE: 36, a working woman.
ANEMONE: 18, a beach smart realist.

In addition, several actors cast in above listed roles will play additional roles:

GLEN also plays the RETIRED MAN (a 70ish recycler), ANDY'S FATHER (a 45 year old businessman), and the DEALER'S MUSCLE.
PAUL is the TEXAN.
ANDY also appears as IRIS'S attendant FRITZ (a young stud in leather and chains), the DEALER, and as a POLICEMAN.
THE AUSSIE also plays FAST FLOYD (a construction worker), the PHOTOGRAPHER TOURIST, the BOOKWORM, and the SAILOR.
ANEMONE also appears as a JOGGER.
KIM is also the BIKER CHICK.
GINGER also appears as the RETIRED WOMAN.
LINDA also plays THE AUSSIE'S WOMAN (a 30ish left-over hippy).
IRIS also appears as the PREGNANT WOMAN.

SETTING

The audience is where the ocean would be. The sand beach extends up to a retaining wall at the back of the acting area. The wall should be not less than three nor more than eight feet high. On the embankment there is a walking path, a trash can, a park bench, a street lamp, and a telephone booth. There is a path or steps from the embankment to the beach. On the beach there is a concrete fire pit.

What is said on the embankment cannot be heard by the audience. A taped sound of the ocean should run throughout the performance. The volume should be increased when the focus is on the embankment action.

Sand Castles
Adele Edling Shank

ACT ONE

It is late afternoon, about 5:30, on a July day. It is still hot, bright. When the lights come up IRIS *is leaning back and reading in a low canvas beach chair, a towel over her legs. She is wearing a bathing suit and is surrounded by a radio/cassette player, suntan lotion, champagne glass, magazines, books, a large tote bag, and an open champagne bottle in a wine cooler. She is perfectly tanned, very expensive, and extremely beautiful. Also on the beach are* CAROL *and* STEPHEN. *They are in swimming suits and lie on beach towels—* CAROL *on her stomach apparently asleep,* STEPHEN, *on his back, eyes closed but awake. They are an attractive couple, handsome and fit.* PAUL *sits on an old sleeping bag, upstage and apart from the others, using the embankment as a back rest. He is thin and tired. He wears Levis and a long sleeved shirt. His face is to the sun, his eyes are closed.*

On the embankment the AUSSIE'S WOMAN *in long-skirted hippy garb stands near the bench staring out to sea. For a time there is no movement and the only sounds are the ocean and contemporary jazz piano music coming from* IRIS's *cassette player.*

IRIS *turns a page in her book.* STEPHEN *sits up and leans on his elbows. He frowns, perhaps because of the sun. He rolls on his side away from* CAROL *and leans on one elbow. He looks at* IRIS. IRIS *raises her sunglasses and looks at* STEPHEN. STEPHEN *pushes his sunglasses low on his nose and looks over them at* IRIS. *She smiles. He returns the smile.*

The AUSSIE'S WOMAN *sits on the bench on the embankment and mends a piece of clothing. A* RETIRED COUPLE *appear on the embankment. He carries a large plastic trash bag. They move to the trash can and the old woman picks through the trash taking out aluminum cans and putting them in the plastic bag her husband holds open for her.*

IRIS *takes a second champagne glass out of her carrier and pours two glasses of champagne. She holds one out to* STEPHEN *who gets up, goes to her, and takes the glass.* STEPHEN *sits down and picks up the contemporary novel (perhaps* The White Hotel*)* IRIS *has been reading and turns it over to read the title.* STEPHEN *does not speak until the* RETIRED COUPLE *has moved slowly off down the embankment path.*

STEPHEN: Good?
IRIS: Very. (STEPHEN *looks at the titles of the other books.*)
STEPHEN: You're a serious person.
IRIS: You might say that.
STEPHEN: A professor?
IRIS: No. I have nothing to profess.

The AUSSIE *has come out of the water. He is wet and carries his surf board (an old-fashioned long board, no leash). He walks across the beach and goes up the path to the embankment. His* WOMAN *stands up when she sees him coming. The* AUSSIE *forgets where he is and stands dazed, looking at her with confusion and apprehension. His* WOMAN *tries to comfort him and after pulling back he suddenly recognizes her. She leads him off toward the parking area where their van/home is apparently parked as are other cars and vans.*

The JOGGER *jogs along the embankment.*

STEPHEN: (*Has been reading from a book of poetry.*) Nice. Are you reading all of these?
IRIS: I like variety.
STEPHEN: (*Ignoring the innuendo.*) Are you a writer?
IRIS: No. I'm a reader.
STEPHEN: (*Looks her over thoroughly—personally but asexually.*) That's your profession?
IRIS: No. I don't *do* anything.
STEPHEN: Oh.
IRIS: And you're a...let me guess...a lawyer?
STEPHEN: Doctor.
IRIS: Yes. Yes of course you are.
STEPHEN: OK if I borrow this?
IRIS: If you promise to read number twenty-seven.
STEPHEN: Thanks for the champagne.
IRIS: My pleasure.

> STEPHEN *returns to his beach towel, lies down and reads. The* AUSSIE *appears on the embankment with a can of Foster's beer and a towel. As* CAROL *and* STEPHEN *talk, he scowls out to sea.*

CAROL: *(Without moving.)* She's beautiful.
STEPHEN: Interesting.
CAROL: *(Rolls over and sits up. She looks at* STEPHEN.*)* Oh?
STEPHEN: She's a reader.
CAROL: What do you mean?
STEPHEN: She reads.
CAROL: What does she read?
STEPHEN: Books.
CAROL: *(Puzzled)* Oh.

> STEPHEN *reads poem number twenty-seven. After reading a few lines he looks with surprise at* IRIS *who smiles at him.* CAROL *looks out to sea.*

> *The* JOGGER *jogs on again and jogs away. The* AUSSIE *looks around confused and helpless. He has a conversation with an imaginary person. The* AUSSIE'S WOMAN *appears from the direction of the parking area. She leads him off toward their van in the parking area.*

CAROL: Stephen?
STEPHEN: Um?
CAROL: Jeff's tough. But I'm worried about Heather.
STEPHEN: I know.
CAROL: She adores you.
STEPHEN: Oh come on.
CAROL: It's true. (STEPHEN *goes back to his book. Silence.*) She still needs a night light.
STEPHEN: I know.

> KIM *and* ANDY *have come out of the water.* ANDY *has been surfing and carries his board.* KIM *has been swimming.* ANDY *is sunbleached, mindless, nice.* KIM *is sunburned, bright, and fresh.* ANDY *goes up to the embankment and off toward the parking area as* KIM *goes to her beach towel. She dries off as she talks.*

KIM: Hi
CAROL: Hi Kim.
STEPHEN: Who's your friend?
KIM: Ahhh, that's Andy.
STEPHEN: Where'd you find him?

KIM: In the ocean.
STEPHEN: Is he man or fish?
KIM: A dolphin. I can't tell whether he's dumb or we just don't speak the same language. Actually, the words are familiar, it's the concepts that are alien.
STEPHEN: You have the instincts of an anthropologist.
KIM: He's kind of sweet really. *(Noticing the book, surprised.)* Poetry?
STEPHEN: *(Indicating* IRIS.*)* It's hers.
KIM: Oh. Where're Mom and Dad?
CAROL: They went to change and pick up the drinks. They'll be down soon.

> ANDY *reappears on the embankment with two beers.* KIM *sees him.*

KIM: Oh. Well, see you later.
STEPHEN: Right.

> KIM *goes up to the embankment to join* ANDY. *They sit on the bench with their backs to the ocean and drink beer, trying to break through the concept barrier.*

STEPHEN: I wonder if Heather will turn out that well.
CAROL: She's a nice girl isn't she?
STEPHEN: Yes.
CAROL: I know it's hard to believe, but I was actually that young once. *(*STEPHEN *smiles at her.)* By the way.
STEPHEN: Um?
CAROL: Jeff's keeping a pair of panties under his mattress.
STEPHEN: Whose?
CAROL: I don't know! They aren't mine and they aren't Heather's. Thank god.
STEPHEN: You haven't asked him have you?
CAROL: Should I?
STEPHEN: No.
CAROL: Should you?
STEPHEN: No.
CAROL: I wonder how he got them.
STEPHEN: *(Laughs.)* I wonder.
CAROL: Did you do that? When you were twelve?
STEPHEN: What?
CAROL: You know.
STEPHEN: Never mind. *(Silence.* STEPHEN *reads.)*
CAROL: Maybe I should go and change too.

STEPHEN: Are you cold?
CAROL: No. *(Pause.)* I'm getting too old to sit around in a bathing suit.
STEPHEN: Are you?
CAROL: You think I'm all right?
STEPHEN: Why not?
CAROL: Damn you.
STEPHEN: What's the matter?
CAROL: You give everyone else what they need! Why hold out on me?
STEPHEN: *(Surprised.)* You don't need reinforcement on the quality of your body. I'm sure David takes care of that. *(He rolls away from* CAROL *leaving her lying silent.)*

GLEN *and* GINGER *have appeared on the embankment from the direction of the parking area. They are dressed in slacks and shirts and* GLEN *carries an ice chest and a blanket.* GINGER *has a picnic basket. They stop on their way down to the beach and speak briefly to* KIM *who introduces them to* ANDY.

IRIS: *(Looks up at the embankment, turns back, and calls from her chair.)* Excuse me. Do you have the time?
STEPHEN: No. Do you?
IRIS: I have lots and lots and lots of time.
STEPHEN: *(Finds his watch.)* It's ten to six.
IRIS: That's what I thought. Three. Four. Five. Six.
STEPHEN: What happened to one and two?
IRIS: I don't remember.
STEPHEN: You're a native, aren't you?
IRIS: Does it show?
STEPHEN: Well you didn't get that tan in a week.
IRIS: I live in the condominiums.
STEPHEN: Great view.
IRIS: I keep the camera ready.
STEPHEN: You're a whale watcher.
IRIS: No, the catastrophe. Haven't you heard? California's going to fall into the ocean. I'm going to watch it all come down.
STEPHEN: But it will stop just in front of your place, right?
IRIS: Of course. Catastrophes only happen to other people. What's your name?
STEPHEN: Stephen.
IRIS: I'm Iris.
STEPHEN: Long stemmed.
CAROL: *(Snorts.)* With a purple head?!

KIM and ANDY sit down on the bench again, their backs to the beach. GLEN and GINGER come down to the beach. GLEN feels a bit out of his element with STEPHEN. GINGER always feels a kind of tingling excitement in STEPHEN's presence which she cherishes.

GLEN: Hope nobody here has died of thirst.
STEPHEN: We're hanging on.
CAROL: But not much longer. Hi, Ginger.
GINGER: Hello.
GLEN: Heather said to tell you she's going to win.
CAROL: Oh ho! Sure.
GLEN: That's what Jeff said.
CAROL: Thanks for dropping them off.
GLEN: Don't mention it. I was tempted to go with them. Mini-golf and McDonald's is my kind of evening.

PAUL gets up, looks around, then goes up the steps to the embankment. GINGER spreads their blanket out near CAROL and STEPHEN's towels. She unpacks potato chips and a can of dip.

GINGER: *(To GLEN.)* Are you going to tend bar?
GLEN: *(Opening ice chest containing canned cocktails.)* Sure thing. What'll it be folks? We've got daiquiris, dry martinis, mai tais, and beer.
CAROL: Any white wine?
GLEN: No, I'm sorry. I'll go up and get some.
CAROL: Oh no Glen. That's OK. I'll have a martini.
GLEN: You sure?
CAROL: Yes.
GLEN: You got it. *(He pours a canned martini nito a plastic glass and gives it to CAROL. He pours a daiquiri for GINGER and gives it to her.)*

The AUSSIE appears from the parking area wearing ragged cut-off jeans and drinking Foster's beer. ANDY is focusing on KIM and doesn't see the AUSSIE. PAUL stops to watch as the AUSSIE becomes suddenly angry and lunges at ANDY, grabbing his arm. ANDY jumps up and for a moment there is a standoff as ANDY appraises the AUSSIE's state of mind. ANDY decides he'd better split and runs off toward the shops. KIM watches in astonishment. The AUSSIE pushes her out of his way as he clumsily runs off after ANDY. PAUL and KIM exchange a look, KIM shrugs and goes down to the beach. PAUL looks down the path in both directions before going off toward the shops. Those on the beach are oblivious to the action above.

GLEN: Steve, how about you?
STEPHEN: I'll have a beer thanks.
GLEN: *(Opens cans of beer for* STEPHEN *and himself.)* I thought doctors always drank martinis.
STEPHEN: What?
GLEN: Nothing. A little joke. Very little.
CAROL: Here's to a safe trip home.
GLEN: I'll drink to that.

They all drink. KIM *has come down from the embankment to join them.*

GLEN: *(Teasing.)* Hi bikini girl. Must be feeding time.
KIM: *(Laughs.)* Hi Pop.
STEPHEN: What happened to the dolphin?
KIM: I don't know. He left. The long hair is mad at him about something.
STEPHEN: Have you cracked the concept barrier?
KIM: *(Laughing.)* Not yet. We're still working on it. *(Looking with disappointment at the chips and dip.)* This is dinner?
GINGER: We thought we'd have our drinks first, and then go and get the food.
KIM: Go and get? Whatever happened to home cooking?
GINGER: It stayed at home. We're on vacation remember.
KIM: But Mom, I'm so sick of take-out junk.
GLEN: Kim.
KIM: I just thought maybe on our last night we'd have real food.
GINGER: If you want to cook, the motel kitchenette is at your disposal. But this is the first vacation I have had in twelve years and I am not cooking anything.
CAROL: Isn't this what vacations are for?
GLEN: What?
CAROL: Eating all the stuff you deny yourself the rest of the year.
KIM: Hey doc, it's not good for you, is it? All this junk.
STEPHEN: I'm on vacation. Pass me a potato chip.

CAROL *smiles and passes him the bag.* GINGER *holds the can of dip out to him.*

GINGER: You might as well go all the way.
STEPHEN: *(Laughs.)* Thanks.
CAROL: Is this really your first vacation in twelve years?

STEPHEN *gives the dip back to* GINGER.

GINGER: Yes.
GLEN: Well no, not really. We used to have a place on the American River.
GINGER: That was never a vacation. We camped out for two summers while he built the place. Then every summer he added more onto the damned thing until we sold it. His idea of a vacation is twelve hours a day with a hammer in his hand.
GLEN: We're here right? We've been here ten whole days. And look, no hammer.
STEPHEN: How many houses have you built Glen?
GLEN: Oh, I don't know. I've sort of lost count.
GINGER: Twenty-one.
STEPHEN: By yourself!
GLEN: Well it started out that way. Now I have a couple of guys who help me out.
GINGER: He has a crew of eleven.
STEPHEN: I thought you worked for the state?
GLEN: I took an early retirement last year.
GINGER: Some retirement.
GLEN: It's just a hobby really.
STEPHEN: Isn't it a bad time for the building trades?
GLEN: We're small, we just build things one at a time and sell 'em. Ginger keeps the books and she tells me we're doing OK.
KIM: I sure hope so. My tuition bills are going to be exorbitant.
GLEN: Oh?
KIM: Mom didn't tell you?
GLEN: How much?
KIM: Nine thousand a year.
GLEN: What!
GINGER: We can afford it.
GLEN: Nine thousand dollars a year!
GINGER: It's important.
GLEN: She could go to the state university and live at home.
GINGER: No! I mean, she needs to be on her own. You spoil her.
KIM: Hey, I'm here, right? I'm not her, I'm me!

An awkward silence. A TEXAN *in a ten-gallon hat appears from the parking area. He sits on the bench and looks out to sea while he eats his McDonald's hamburger and Coke.*

GLEN: Anybody ready for a refill?
STEPHEN: I'm fine.
CAROL: Not yet, thanks. Kim? What are you going to study?

KIM: Astrophysics. And astronautics.
STEPHEN: You want to be an astronaut?
KIM: Yes and no. Astro means star of course, and nautic comes from the word for sailor. It's a beautiful concept, but really astronauts are just sky jockeys. I'm going to be an astroexplorer.
CAROL: I don't think I understand.
KIM: I'm going to land, explore other spaces. Walk on virgin turf.
GLEN: My daughter's a dreamer.
KIM: My father's earth-bound.
CAROL: Is this really a...practical idea?
KIM: Very. In fact, it's going to become high priority. Things are getting crowded here.

PHOTO: ALLEN NOMURA

STEPHEN: I notice that when I try to park the car.
KIM: Do you know what happens to an overpopulated group of rats?
CAROL: Gee, I never thought about it.
KIM: When the population density reaches a certain level the rats start to eat each other—even if they have all the food they need.
CAROL: Terrific.
KIM: It's true. They eat each other. To control the population.
STEPHEN: And you want out of here before that starts?
KIM: Haven't you noticed? It already has.
GLEN: Ridiculous.
KIM: He wants me to be an architect. Yuck. Architects design walls around things.

STEPHEN: You'll need what, a PhD in...
KIM: Probably celestial mechanics. I haven't decided for sure.
STEPHEN: It's a long haul.
KIM: Yup. That's OK. We're rich. Besides, they aren't ready for me yet. But by the time I'm all educated up they will be. Can you imagine what it must be like out there?
STEPHEN: Send us a post card, eh?
KIM: Sure. Having a wonderful time in the wide open spaces.
GLEN: *(Has picked up a frisbee and toys with it.)* This is the only flying saucer you're going to see.
KIM: *(Laughs.)* Poor Dad.
GLEN: Anybody feel like throwing this thing?
KIM: *(Jumping up.)* Sure.
STEPHEN: *(Also getting up.)* Why not? Carol?
CAROL: No thanks. (KIM *and* GLEN *move off down the beach.*)
STEPHEN: Iris? Would you like to join us in a frisbee toss?
IRIS: Thank you, but no. I don't...I don't toss frisbees.
STEPHEN: OK. See you later.
IRIS: Yes. Later.

STEPHEN *follows* KIM *and* GLEN. CAROL *and* GINGER *feel awkward alone together.*

CAROL: They seem to get on very well together really.
GINGER: Who?
CAROL: Glen and Kim.
GINGER: Oh. Yes. They've always been close. He spoils her. I suppose that's inevitable with the youngest. *(Silence.)* Would you like another drink?
CAROL: Sure, why not? (GINGER *gets* CAROL *another martini.*)

LINDA BLUE *appears on the embankment from the parking area. She is an attractive, lively woman. She carries a large model's tote bag. She notices the* TEXAN *sitting on the bench and sits down beside him. She helps herself to a sip of his Coke which is on the bench between them.* LINDA *whispers something to the* TEXAN *who stands up hurriedly, then gives* LINDA *his Coke before going off toward the parking area.*

CAROL: *(Taking the drink.)* Thanks. I haven't had a martini for a long time.
GINGER: Carol. I wanted to say...it's good to see you and...you and Stephen...I mean, together.

CAROL: Together?
GINGER: Yes. I mean I had thought that you...well, I guess I misunderstood.
CAROL: Misunderstood what?
GINGER: Never mind. I'm sorry...I didn't mean to...
CAROL: Oh it's all right. Never mind. In fact, you might as well know. We're getting a divorce.
GINGER: You are?
CAROL: As soon as we get home.
GINGER: Poor Stephen!
CAROL: What?
GINGER: Oh. But...but then what are you doing here?
CAROL: We decided a month ago, but we didn't want to disappoint the kids. So here we are...one last family vacation.
GINGER: I see.
CAROL: Do you?

ANEMONE *appears on the embankment from the parking area. She wears a back pack and is dressed in sports clothes and running shoes. She has a whistle around her neck and a can of mace on a belt around her waist. A walkie-talkie is attached to the belt. Her hair is tied back. She is ready for combat. She gives a walkie-talkie to* LINDA, *then gives her the van keys, and a lunch pail.*

GINGER: Carol, is David...
CAROL: So tell me, have you enjoyed your vacation?
GINGER: Very much. The beach is crowded in the afternoon, but when you lie in the sun with your eyes closed everyone disappears. (*The "beeper" on* STEPHEN's *towel starts beeping.* CAROL *turns it off.*)
CAROL: I'm glad it worked out.
GINGER: Thanks for giving me the name of the motel. I didn't have any idea where to go.
CAROL: How did you get Glen to agree to take a vacation?
GINGER: That's a long story. (*Helps herself to another daiquiri from the ice chest.*) Ready for a refill?
CAROL: No thanks.

ANEMONE *arrives on the beach. She is a healthy, composed, and unemotional young woman. She takes a beach towel out of her back pack and spreads it next to* IRIS's.

ANEMONE: Hi, Iris. How goes it?
IRIS: *(Puts down her contemporary novel.)* I'm renouncing the modern world.
ANEMONE: How come?
IRIS: There's no hope in it. *(Picks up a copy of* Paradise Lost.*)*
ANEMONE: What's that?
IRIS: Ancient wisdom.
ANEMONE: Oh?

> ANEMONE *sets up her station. She takes the walkie-talkie off her belt and puts it on the towel. She takes out of her back pack a brown paper lunch bag, a flashlight, an address book, an accounts ledger, a pen, and a calculator and arranges them on her towel.* PAUL *returns from the shops with a can of beer. He stands on the embankment and watches* ANEMONE.
>
> STEPHEN *enters on the beach.* GINGER *can't look at him.*

CAROL: Beeper.
STEPHEN: *(Drops the frisbee and checks his pocket for a dime and gets his address book from among his things on his towel.)* Thanks.
CAROL: Don't mention it. Where are Glen and Kim?
STEPHEN: They went for a walk.
CAROL: Seems strange to me.
STEPHEN: What?
CAROL: That that thing would work so far from your hospital.
STEPHEN: *(On his way up to the embankment.)* They relay calls through the local hospital.
CAROL: Must be awfully important.
ANEMONE: *(To* IRIS.*)* Have you got something?
IRIS: Yes.
ANEMONE: Hot?
IRIS: I think so. *(Hands* ANEMONE *a notebook.)* Here.

> ANEMONE *copies the name and phone number into her address book.* STEPHEN *goes into the phone booth and makes a call.* CAROL *watches him.*

GINGER: It must be difficult being a doctor.
CAROL: Why?
GINGER: Well, I guess you can probably never relax completely. There's always somebody who needs you.

CAROL: Oh yes. There's always somebody. He loves it.
GINGER: He's very...very good isn't he?
CAROL: How would I know? You tell me, you're one of his patients.
GINGER: That was years ago.
CAROL: I'm sure he hasn't changed.
GINGER: No. I'm sure he hasn't.
ANEMONE: *(Gives the notebook back to* IRIS.*)* Would now be a good time to try him?
IRIS: No, later. I've never seen him get home before nine.
ANEMONE: OK Thanks a lot Iris.
IRIS: I hope he works out.
ANEMONE: Me too. That last suggestion you gave us? I think he's going to become a regular.
IRIS: Good.

> ANEMONE *starts doing warm-up exercises in preparation for her daily run.* IRIS *returns to her book.* CAROL *is leafing through a magazine.* GINGER *is staring out to sea. Their positions make a static, formal composition. Silence.*

GINGER: *(To* CAROL.*)* Sometimes I almost understand Kim's thing about space.
CAROL: What?
GINGER: Look at all that out there, all that...nothing. If I could choose my place to die, I think I'd pick a life boat in the middle of the ocean.

> STEPHEN *comes out of the phone booth and starts back down to the beach. As he passes* LINDA *she speaks to him. He stops and exchanges a few words with her.*

CAROL: And who for company?
GINGER: Company?
CAROL: Yeah, you know, Robert Redford or someone.
GINGER: Oh. No. Alone.
CAROL: I think you're forgetting the considerable discomfort involved.
GINGER: You're right. That's the trouble with fantasies. They all have considerable discomfort lurking underneath.
CAROL: *(Surprised.)* Oh? (GINGER *lies down, looks out to sea.)*
ANEMONE: Iris?
IRIS: Yes?
ANEMONE: That guy up there?
IRIS: *(Turns to see* PAUL *on the embankment.)* What about him?
ANEMONE: He keeps looking at me.
IRIS: I'll call Fritz.

ANEMONE: No, don't do that. It's OK.
IRIS: He's been hanging around all day.
ANEMONE: Oh yeah?
CAROL: *(Teasing a smiling* STEPHEN *as he arrives on the beach.)* Must have been an entertaining consultation.
STEPHEN: You see that woman? *(He is speaking to* CAROL *and* GINGER, *but all turn to look at* LINDA.*)*
CAROL: What about her?
STEPHEN: She's a prostitute.
GINGER: A prostitute!
STEPHEN: Her name is Linda Blue. She operates out of her van in the parking area.
CAROL: You're kidding.
STEPHEN: That telephone booth is her headquarters.
GINGER: I didn't know this was...It doesn't look like that kind of neighborhood.
ANEMONE: It isn't.
STEPHEN: Do you live around here?
ANEMONE: Yes.
STEPHEN: Is she here every day? I mean, it's her territory?
ANEMONE: *(Half joking.)* Say what are you, vice squad?
STEPHEN: Just a curious tourist.
IRIS: He's all right. His name is Stephen.
ANEMONE: Oh.
STEPHEN: Are you a friend of hers?
ANEMONE: Sort of. She's my mother.
STEPHEN: Really?
ANEMONE: What's the matter, prostitutes aren't supposed to have daughters?
STEPHEN: Don't be offended. I was just surprised.
ANEMONE: Oh.
STEPHEN: What's your name?
ANEMONE: Anemone.
STEPHEN: I beg your pardon?
ANEMONE: Anemone. You know. *(Wiggling ten fingers in the air like ten tentacles.)* Poke me.
STEPHEN: *(Laughs delightedly.)* It's a beautiful name.
ANEMONE: Yeah? Well, she's a real romantic my mom. Anemone Rose. It doesn't suit me.
STEPHEN: Why not?
ANEMONE: What's it to you?
STEPHEN: Nothing. I just wondered.

> FAST FLOYD *appears on the embankment path. He is a construction worker.* LINDA *greets him as a friend.*

ANEMONE: Oh damn.
IRIS: What's the matter?
ANEMONE: Fast Floyd is early again today.

> *They watch as* LINDA *and* FAST FLOYD *disappear toward the parking area.*

ANEMONE: What a beaver.
STEPHEN: Is there a problem?
ANEMONE: I was hoping to get my run in before he showed up.
STEPHEN: He's a regular?
ANEMONE: Yeah. Once a week. *(To* IRIS.*)* What's with this guy?
IRIS: He's just...just a collector. (STEPHEN *looks surprised.*)
ANEMONE: What's he collect?
IRIS: Curiosities.
ANEMONE: Yeah? Well, look. Don't get the wrong idea about Mom. She's in a transition period.
STEPHEN: Going straight?
ANEMONE: Nooooo. She's moving up to call girl.l.
STEPHEN: Oh, I see.
ANEMONE: But it takes a while to build up a book.

> FRITZ, IRIS'*s attendant, appears on the embankment from the direction of the condominium. He is dressed in leather and wears a studded collar and wrist bands. He stands near the bench watching* IRIS. CAROL *stands up and sees* FRITZ *as she turns.*

CAROL: *(To* GINGER.*)* Well, well.
GINGER: *(Looking at* FRITZ.*)* Oh my!
CAROL: Imagine going to bed with that! (GINGER *is shocked.* CAROL *laughs and turns to leave. To* STEPHEN.*)* I'm going to the motel and change.
STEPHEN: OK.
GINGER: We'll go and get the food as soon as Glen and Kim get back. We need to decide what to eat.
CAROL: Whatever you want is fine with me. Except chicken.

> CAROL *goes up to the embankment and disappears down the path toward the motel.* GINGER *looks at* STEPHEN *who has turned his attention back to* ANEMONE, *then pretends to read* CAROL'*s magazine.*

STEPHEN: Anemone, tell me. Why the call girl aspirations?
ANEMONE: The income is steadier. See, she does OK in the tourist season, but the winters are real slow. Mostly I've been pushing her because it's just a whole lot safer.
STEPHEN: How's that?
ANEMONE: The pick-up trade is very dicey. I never know when she's going to get a real sicko.

STEPHEN: Aren't there uh...sickos amongst the men who call?
ANEMONE: We screen them first. And you know, we've got their addresses. A john's not so likely to come on kinky when he knows that we know where he lives.

The walkie-talkie on ANEMONE's *towel starts broadcasting.* ANEMONE *sits down to listen.*

PAUL *paces on the embankment, looks off in both directions, then goes off toward the motel. The voices of* LINDA *and* FAST FLOYD *are heard through the walkie-talkie.*

FAST FLOYD: Hurry up.
LINDA: OK OK. Just let me get my shoes off.
FAST FLOYD: Forget the shoes. I only got five minutes!
LINDA: How come?
FAST FLOYD: I gotta pick up my kid at the dentist. forget that! Just lay down.
LINDA: You're the boss.

STEPHEN *has gone to sit near* GINGER *who is very conscious of his presence, but continues to look at the magazine.* IRIS *discovers the champagne bottle is empty. She signals to* FRITZ *on the embankment. He comes down to the beach and takes the empty bottle and goes off toward the condominiums.* ANEMONE *looks at the embankment.*

ANEMONE: He's gone.
IRIS: He'll be back.
ANEMONE: How do you know?
IRIS: He's waiting.
ANEMONE: *(With some regret.)* Oh. I see.
GINGER: *(Finally looks up at* STEPHEN, *looks away, then looks back at him. She must speak although she knows she shouldn't.)* Carol's right. You haven't changed.
STEPHEN: How's that?
GINGER: The concern. The caring.
STEPHEN: Caring?
GINGER: About people. The little beach girl, just now. You are so... interested in everyone. So kind.
STEPHEN: I don't think you'd get a unanimous opinion on that. *(Pause.)* So, has the vacation been a success?
GINGER: Oh. Yes.
IRIS: *(Produces a fashion magazine. To* ANEMONE.*)* There are some dresses in here I want you to consider.

ANEMONE: OK. (IRIS *flips through the magazine looking for the right page.*)
STEPHEN: (*With professional concern.*) Ginger? How are you, really?
GINGER: I'm all right. I keep busy.
STEPHEN: Busy?
GINGER: I forget who, but somebody said that an unhappy person is someone with the leisure to consider the issue. I keep busy.
STEPHEN: Are you still taking the Librium?
GINGER: (*Quietly.*) No.
STEPHEN: Good. Did you see the doctor I recommended?
GINGER: No.
STEPHEN: (*Gently.*) Why not?
GINGER: (*Looking at him.*) I didn't want another doctor. (STEPHEN *looks away. There is a pause.* GINGER *looks at the ocean.*) I'm all right, really. I am. Fine.
IRIS: (*Gives* ANEMONE *the fashion magazine.*) Here.
ANEMONE: (*Puzzled.*) You really think so?
IRIS: I really think. (ANEMONE *studies the magazine seriously.*)
STEPHEN: (*Uncomfortable in the heavy silence.*) Carol said you got a promotion. Are you enjoying your work?
GINGER: Oh, it's all right. Glen wants me to quit.
STEPHEN: Why?
GINGER: He wants me to work full-time with him on the construction business.
STEPHEN: Are you going to?
GINGER: I don't know.
STEPHEN: I guess I don't see the problem.
GINGER: Well for one thing I'd never leave the house.
STEPHEN: Why not?
GINGER: The office is there.
STEPHEN: I see the problem.
GINGER: You always did.

> IRIS *takes the magazine back from* ANEMONE *and looks through it.* GINGER'*s knowledge that these may be her last moments alone with him gives her the courage to try once more.*

GINGER: Stephen. Carol told me...about the divorce.
STEPHEN: Oh.
GINGER: I just wanted to tell you...I...I'm sorry.
STEPHEN: So am I.
GINGER: Oh.
STEPHEN: It's not my idea.

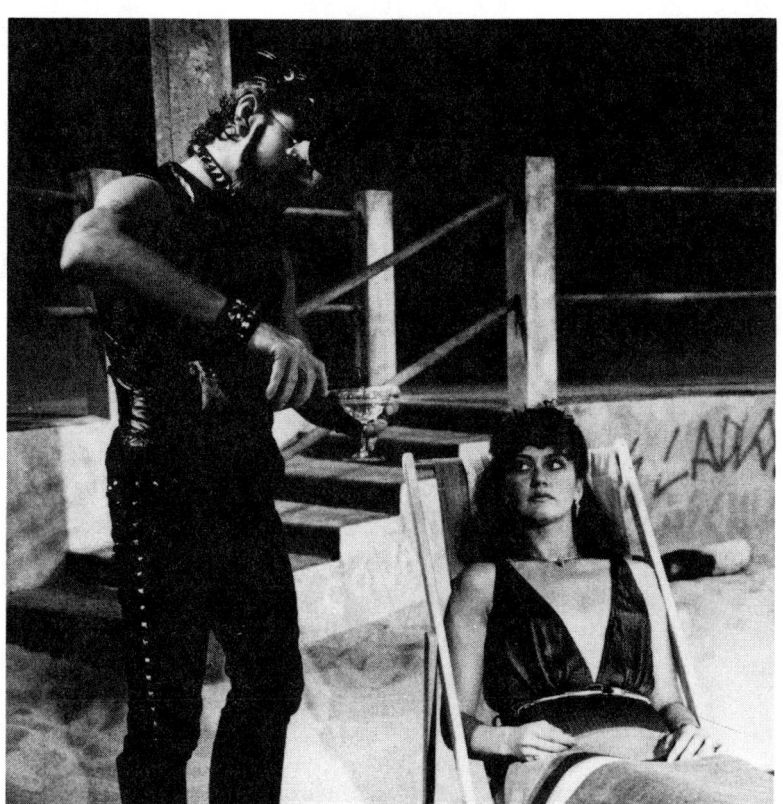

GINGER: I see.
STEPHEN: You know, practically everyone I know has been divorced. At least once. It's surprising that it actually turns out to be a very unpleasant business. It's upsetting. Economically, socially, and emotionally upsetting.
GINGER: You have your work, and you're very...attractive. I mean, you won't be lonely long.
STEPHEN: If you mean I will have company, that is true.
IRIS: *(Returns the magazine to* ANEMONE.*)* This one is even better. Just right for the woman on her way up.

> ANEMONE *studies.* KIM *and* GLEN *return from their walk.* KIM *carries shells they have collected.*

KIM: Mom, I'm absolutely starving.
STEPHEN: What've you got there, earth specimens?
KIM: Have you ever seen one like this?

STEPHEN: No.

> KIM *sits next to* STEPHEN *and shows him the shells.* GINGER *and* GLEN *watch them.* FRITZ *appears on the embankment with a full bottle of champagne. He comes down to the beach and goes to* IRIS *and awaits orders.*

IRIS: Thank you, Fritz. *(*FRITZ *pours champagne into* IRIS*'s glass and puts the bottle into the wine cooler beside her.)*
GLEN: What happened to Carol?
STEPHEN: She went back to the motel to change.
ANEMONE: *(To* IRIS*.)* I don't know. It just...it doesn't look like Mom.
IRIS: My dear, I thought that was the whole point.

> PAUL *appears from the direction of the motel. He looks around, settles to wait near the bench.* FRITZ *stands waiting for further orders.*

IRIS: That will be all, Fritz. *(*FRITZ *goes up to the embankment and disappears toward the condominium.)*
ANEMONE: You were right.
IRIS: About what?
ANEMONE: *(Very sadly.)* He's back. Waiting.
IRIS: Hey...what's going on here, Anemone Rose?
ANEMONE: I don't know.
IRIS: You don't even know him. Or do you?
ANEMONE: No, not really.
IRIS: What's this?
ANEMONE: He...yesterday, he ran a while with me.
IRIS: And?
ANEMONE: Nothing. We just ran. I even slowed down for him. But then he stopped and I kept going.
IRIS: He didn't say anything?
ANEMONE: No. He just...looked at me. Like he's doing now.
IRIS: *(Very seriously.)* Take my advice. Don't look back.
ANEMONE: *(Tearing her eyes away from him.)* Yeah, You're right. *(Returns her attention to the magazine.)*
KIM: I'm going to starve.
GINGER: We can go ahead and get the food. Carol said anything was fine, except chicken.
GLEN: OK, what's it going to be? We can have some of Long John Silver's fish and chips, Big Macs, Smokey Pit ribs...
GINGER: We had ribs last night.

Sand Castles

GLEN: A veto on the ribs. Or there's pizza, tacos, or dogs from the Wienerschnitzel.
KIM: I would rather die than eat a Big Mac.
STEPHEN: A woman of principle.
KIM: You betcha.
ANEMONE: *(To* IRIS.*)* You really think this is good huh?
GLEN: OK. We're down to fish and chips, tacos, pizza, or hot dogs. Do I hear any other vetoes?
IRIS: *(To* ANEMONE.*)* I think it's just right.
STEPHEN: I'm not a fish and chips fan.
ANEMONE: *(Returns the magazine to* IRIS.*)* Is it expensive? *(*IRIS *looks up the price.* ANEMONE *watches* PAUL *watching her.)*
GLEN: Hey, this is going to be easy! It's going to be pizza, tacos, or hot dogs.
STEPHEN *and* KIM: Pizza!
GLEN: You got it. Now, how do we stand on anchovies?
KIM: Boooooo!
IRIS: *(To* ANEMONE.*)* One hundred and thirty dollars.
ANEMONE: *(Horrified.)* For a dress!
GLEN: So what'll I get, an everything, hold the anchovies?
GINGER: And the green pepper.
GLEN: OK. *(He prepares to leave.)*
IRIS: *(To* ANEMONE.*)* It's not expensive.
ANEMONE: It is too!
IRIS: You can afford it.
ANEMONE: I can't. There's practically nothing left by the time I've paid all the insurance premiums and put money in the retirement fund.
IRIS: Think of it as an investment.
GLEN: Ginger? Want to come along?
GINGER: I'm going for a walk.
GLEN: So am I.
GINGER: On the beach.
GLEN: Now?
GINGER: Why not? *(Strides off down the beach.* GLEN *watches her.)*
ANEMONE: *(To* IRIS.*)* I wonder if it's deductible?
IRIS: She pays taxes?
ANEMONE: Sure. You think I want her in jail for evasion?
STEPHEN: *(As* GLEN *turns and starts toward the embankment.)* Do you need another hand, Glen?
GLEN: No thanks. You stay and protect the women.

LINDA *reappears on the embankment from the parking area.* ANEMONE *sees her almost immediately.*

ANEMONE: Terrific! Fast Floyd is getting faster every week. (LINDA *goes into the phone booth as* ANEMONE *picks up the walkie-talkie and speaks into it.)* Mom? Mom?
LINDA: Yes?
ANEMONE: I'm going for a run, OK?
LINDA: Of course.
ANEMONE: I won't be long. And I'll leave the walkie-talkie with Iris.
LINDA: All right. Have a good time.

> LINDA *comes out of the phone booth.* ANDY *appears on the embankment from the direction of the shops. He exchanges a greeting with* LINDA *before coming to the edge of the embankment where he tries to get* KIM's *attention.* ANEMONE *gives her walkie-talkie to* IRIS. *She glances at* PAUL.

ANEMONE: I'll make it fast.
IRIS: No hurry.
ANEMONE: Maybe I should leave the whistle with you.
IRIS: Don't worry, Anemone. Fritz is around. If there's any trouble he'll snarl and bite.

> CAROL *has returned from the motel wearing slacks and shirt. She joins* KIM *and* STEPHEN.

CAROL: Kim. The dolphin's back.
ANEMONE: *(Starts to run in place, moving a bit away from* IRIS *and looking at* PAUL. *To* IRIS.*)* OK. See you later.
IRIS: Run a mile for me.
ANEMONE: Right. *(Runs off down the beach.* PAUL *watches her leave.* ANDY *beckons to* KIM *to join him.* KIM *doesn't move.)*
STEPHEN: Aren't you going up?
KIM: I don't know.
STEPHEN: Annoyed?
KIM: No. But he disappears and reappears as he likes, he can wait if I like.
CAROL: Thata girl!

> ANDY *looks apprehensively behind him, then beckons to* KIM *again more urgently.*

STEPHEN: It seems important.
KIM: Yeah.

> CAROL *laughs.* KIM *stands staring at* ANDY *who stops gesturing*

and just looks at her. He holds out his arms to her. After a pause she holds out her arms to him without moving toward him. With a resigned look ANDY *drops his arms.* KIM *drops her arms. Stalemate. He looks around, then beckons to* KIM *with a very small wave of one arm. She smiles and beckons to him with an even smaller wave.* ANDY *looks around, then comes down to the beach.*

STEPHEN: *(To* KIM.*)* You seem to have broken the concept barrier. (KIM *laughs.*)
CAROL: He's beautiful, Kim.
KIM: Ummmmm.
STEPHEN: Down girl. Kim saw him first.
ANDY: *(Moves to* KIM, *stops three feet from her.)* Hi.
KIM: Hi.
ANDY: I need words.
KIM: *(Making introductions.)* This is Stephen. And Carol. Andy.
STEPHEN: Hello Andy.
CAROL: Hi.
ANDY: Hi.
KIM: Want a beer?
ANDY: Can we walk?
KIM: Nope.
ANDY: OK. I'll have a beer. (KIM *gets a beer out of the ice chest and gives it to him.)*
STEPHEN: So you're a surfer?
ANDY: Yeah.
STEPHEN: You....uh, you're really into it, huh?
ANDY: Yeah.
CAROL: Are you a pro?
ANDY: Sort of.
CAROL: Have you won any prizes?
ANDY: Not yet.
KIM: He's a fake. He masquerades as a surfer, but he's really just a college kid.
CAROL: You go to the university?
ANDY: No.
KIM: You said...
ANDY: I'm enrolled. I don't go *(Noticing* IRIS.*)* Hi Iris.
IRIS: How's it going Andy?
ANDY: So-so.
IRIS: The surf looks good.
ANDY: Hot.

IRIS: Why aren't you out?
ANDY: Trouble.
IRIS: What kind?
ANDY: The Aussie.
IRIS: Oh oh.
ANDY: It's OK for now. Their van's gone. *(Turns back to* KIM.*)* Look, lady, I really need words with you.
KIM: These are friends, you can talk here.

ANDY's look tells her that she is being unbelievably naive. He sits down with a sigh. Looks out to sea. Silence.

CAROL: I guess the surfing's pretty good here.
ANDY: Not bad.
CAROL: Not like Hawaii huh?
ANDY: *(With the first sign of real ife.)* You know about Hawaii?
CAROL: Oh, well. Everybody knows about Hawaii.
ANDY: Yeah. *(Deeply depressed.)* It's not Hawaii.
CAROL: What's different?
ANDY: Waves. Twenty footers. Great green walls of water with white tips.
CAROL: Poetic.
ANDY: Huh?

The telephone rings in the phone booth on the embankment and LINDA *goes to answer it.*

CAROL: Have you ever been?
ANDY: Once. With my folks last year. Two weeks. I almost stayed.
CAROL: Why didn't you?
ANDY: Money. No use in being where the best waves are if you have to spend all your time toting dirty dishes.
CAROL: Your parents support you?
ANDY: As long as I'm in California and in school.
CAROL: Ohhhhh. I see.
ANDY: Yeah.
CAROL: So you make do with the inferior waves.
ANDY: Yeah. Well, I go down to San Miguel or Rosarita Beach when I can.
CAROL: Mexico?
ANDY: Baja.
CAROL: Good waves?
ANDY: Fewer people.

CAROL: Oh.
ANDY: Hardly any tourists.
CAROL: Except you.
ANDY: Huh?
CAROL: Never mind.
STEPHEN: *(Picks up the poetry book and goes to* IRIS. *Handing her the book.)* Thank you.
IRIS: Are you convinced?
STEPHEN: I'm not sure.
IRIS: What will it take?
STEPHEN: Perhaps more of the same.

> LINDA *has hung up the telephone. She takes the walkie-talkie out of her tote bag and speaks into it.*

LINDA: Iris?
IRIS: *(Into walkie-talkie.)* Yes?
LINDA: Sorry to disturb you. I'm going up to the condos.
IRIS: Which one is it?
LINDA: Your neighbor.
IRIS: Good. I'll tell Anemone.
LINDA: I hope this thing won't bother you. Anemone insists I leave it on when I'm out on call.
IRIS: No problem. *(Looking at the book she is holding.)* It'll make an interesting score for *Paradise Lost.*
LINDA: Paradise what?
IRIS: *(Smiling at* STEPHEN.*)* Lost. Have a good time.

> LINDA *puts the walkie-talkie back into her tote bag and goes off down the path toward the condominiums.* STEPHEN *starts to leave.*

IRIS: Wait. I want to give you something. *(*STEPHEN *waits as* IRIS *writes her address and phone number on a piece of paper.)*
ANDY: *(To* KIM.*)* Hey, lady?
KIM: Hum?
ANDY: Are you ready to walk yet?
KIM: Almost.
ANDY: What'a I have to do first?
KIM: Nothing.
ANDY: OK. *(Sits in a frozen position, motionless and expressionless.)*
CAROL: Andy. Ready for another beer? *(She is getting herself another martini.)* Kim? You want anything?
KIM: No thanks.
CAROL: Andy? *(Turning around.)* Andy? *(*ANDY *is motionless.)* What's with him?

KIM: He's into the positive contemplation of nothingness.
CAROL: *(Pretending to understand.)* Oh.
KIM: It's a joke.
CAROL: *(Pretending to get the joke.)* Oh.
IRIS: *(Gives* STEPHEN *the piece of paper.)* Here's my address. Eleven o'clock. I'll be waiting.
ANEMONE: *(Returns from her run. She is hardly winded.)* Where's Mom?
IRIS: Plying her trade in condoville.
ANEMONE: Great.
IRIS: You can finish your run. I'm on duty.
ANEMONE: Later. *(She sits down on her towel.)*
STEPHEN: Well, thanks again for the loan of the book.
IRIS: Any time. There's plenty more where that came from.
STEPHEN: I look forward to seeing your library. *(*IRIS *smiles.* STEPHEN *rejoins* CAROL, KIM, *and* ANDY.*)*
ANEMONE: *(To* IRIS.*)* Which one is it?
IRIS: My neighbor.
ANEMONE: Terrific. He's hooked, don't you think?
IRIS: The habit seems to be forming.

The walkie-talkie starts broadcasting. We hear the sound of a door opening.

CONDO JOHN: Come in.
LINDA: Thanks. *(Sound of door closing.)* Hey, you look tired.
CONDO JOHN: I am.
LINDA: How about a nice massage, huh? You'll feel better.
JOHN: Sounds great.

ANEMONE, *having satisfied herself that her mother is safe, turns down the volume. She glances at* PAUL *who is looking at her.*

The AUSSIE *appears from the parking area and moves to the edge of the embankment.* KIM *looks up and sees him.*

KIM: Hey Andy. The long hair's back. *(*ANDY *jumps up.)* What's the matter?
ANDY: I've got to split. *(Starts moving off.)* Are you coming?
KIM: What's the matter?
ANDY: Are you coming!?
KIM: I don't know! What's the matter?! *(*ANDY *runs off down the beach. On the embankment the* AUSSIE *follows him off.* KIM *starts to follow* ANDY.*)*

CAROL: Kim!
KIM: What?!
CAROL: Be careful! You don't know what you might be getting into.
KIM: I know! *(She runs off after* ANDY.*)*
CAROL: We should have stopped her.
STEPHEN: She'll be all right.
CAROL: I don't know.
STEPHEN: It's a public beach for heavens sake. What can happen?
ANEMONE: Well for openers she can get raped. Or beat up. Or sliced up.
IRIS: Anemone.
ANEMONE: Well it's true. It happens. I mean this place looks all right, but it's a slaughterhouse.
IRIS: Andy's all right.
ANEMONE: Sure Andy's all right. But you never know about the AUSSIE!

    IRIS *is silent.* STEPHEN *moves toward* ANEMONE.

STEPHEN: What's this about the Aussie?
ANEMONE: Oh, he's got this thing with Andy.
STEPHEN: What thing?
ANEMONE: It's an old beef. They... *(She glances at the embankment. She sees* PAUL *who is looking at her.)*
STEPHEN: Are you saying there's going to be trouble?
ANEMONE: *(Still looking at* PAUL.*)* Who's to say? You can't tell in advance.
STEPHEN: *(To* IRIS.*)* Should I go after her?
IRIS: She'll be all right. Our little friend here is a bit of an alarmist.
ANEMONE: You mean a realist. People do the most absolutely shitty things to each other. Always have. Ever since we started walking on two legs we've been killing each other. That's what those history books are full of, you know. They're the record of us killing each other.
STEPHEN: You have a point there.
ANEMONE: Yeah. Well. Everybody's dying and some people are going to do it sooner than they'd have to because they don't keep their eyes open.
STEPHEN: You're right about your name. It doesn't suit you.
ANEMONE: Well. You get soft and start thinking people are loving animals and you end up fucked over.
STEPHEN: What's that? Mace?
ANEMONE: Yeah. And if that doesn't stop them karate and jujitsu

will. *(She points to* KIM's *high-heeled sandals.)* And I don't wear those!
CAROL: What's the matter with them?
ANEMONE: Rape shoes. You wear things like that, you give the edge to the rapist.
STEPHEN: I'm surprised you don't carry a gun.
ANEMONE: I trust myself more than I trust machinery. Say I'm grabbed from behind. I can throw the jerk and break his neck long before I'd get a gun out.
IRIS: You should see her practicing with Fritz. Quite a sight.
ANEMONE: Besides, I don't like the idea of a gun. Creeps have guns.
STEPHEN: I think I'll just take a little walk and check things out.
ANEMONE: Better let me. You might get hurt.
STEPHEN: I don't want to involve you.
ANEMONE: Don't worry! I won't get involved unless I have to. I'll just finish my run...with my eyes open. OK Iris?
IRIS: Yes. *(*ANEMONE *starts to run off down the beach.)* Whistle if you want Fritz.
ANEMONE: Never!
IRIS: *(To* STEPHEN.*)* Fritz believes in machinery. He packs a Mauser.
STEPHEN: I see.

A TOURIST *in an immaculately stylish white suit and straw hat comes on from the parking area. He has an expensive camera around his neck and takes pictures of the sunset.*

CAROL: I wish Ginger and Glen had been here.
STEPHEN: You can't stop a girl from going for a walk with her boyfriend.
CAROL: I wonder if we should have let the kids walk back to the motel alone?
STEPHEN: It's only a couple of blocks.
CAROL: Maybe I should go and check on them?
STEPHEN: You can't treat them like babies. They need self-confidence. Especially now.
CAROL: I suppose so.

On the embankment the DEALER *enters hurriedly from the direction of the shops.* PAUL *sees him immediately. Without looking at* PAUL *and without pausing, the* DEALER *signals* PAUL *to follow him off toward the parking area. Just before they go out of sight, the* AUSSIE'S WOMAN *enters. She tries to retreat when she sees the* DEALER, *but he stops her and asks her an angry question. She shakes her head no insistently. The* DEALER *goes off followed by* PAUL.

Sand Castles

> *The sun is setting. Along the embankment people will gather, as they do every night, to observe the event. Most drink beer and eat junk food. They watch the sun setting behind the ocean, mellow and noncommunicative. The* AUSSIE'S WOMAN *is the first. She looks worriedly around for the* AUSSIE, *then sits on the bench.*

CAROL: Do you want another beer?
STEPHEN: I'll wait for the pizza. *(Pause.)* Carol?
CAROL: Um?
STEPHEN: Rethink the divorce, huh?
CAROL: What?!
STEPHEN: Look. Admit it. We've had fun here. It's been pretty good hasn't it, these past few days.
CAROL: More than pretty good.
STEPHEN: It's been terrific. Like the old days. Only better.

> *The photographer-*TOURIST *goes off toward the parking area. The* DEALER *comes on from the parking area and goes off down the path toward the shops.*

CAROL: Oh Stephen. It's all decided.
STEPHEN: Carol, David won't make you any happier than I do! He won't be faithful to you, you know that. He's got a rotten track record.
CAROL: I know. So do I. And so do you.
STEPHEN: That's not the issue.
CAROL: Oh no, of course not, that's never the issue! I am so damned sick of women salivating all over my husband!
STEPHEN: Salivating?
CAROL: Drooling. Slobbering all over you. It's disgusting.
STEPHEN: You may be exaggerating just a little.
CAROL: No I'm not! Have you seen the way Ginger looks at you?!
STEPHEN: Ginger?
CAROL: Yes, even the icicle lady. She practically came when she passed you the dip! You must have given her a very special treatment.
STEPHEN: What are you talking about?
CAROL: When she was your patient.
STEPHEN: Ancient history.
CAROL: Well she hasn't forgotten. Must have been memorable.
STEPHEN: Perhaps. She was badly in need of a sympathetic shoulder.
CAROL: Why?
STEPHEN: She had just left Glen and her children.
CAROL: She what?!

STEPHEN: She moved to a motel for a couple of weeks. She needed some time by herself, to take the pressure off.
CAROL: And what did you do to relieve it?
STEPHEN: Not much. Tranquilizers. Mild sleeping pills. We talked.
CAROL: I see. And where did you do this talking? In her motel room?
STEPHEN: *(Pause.)* Once or twice.
CAROL: What! *(STEPHEN looks uncomfortably at IRIS who has looked up.)* You went to her motel!?
STEPHEN: She was very close to a nervous breakdown. She called me, hysterical.
CAROL: So naturally you rushed right over and got in bed with her!
STEPHEN: We did not have an affair. You're getting upset over nothing.
CAROL: Nothing! You lied to me.
STEPHEN: Carol, if you don't calm down, I'm going for a walk.

CAROL *glares at* STEPHEN, *then softens.*

A BIKER CHICK *appears on the embankment carrying her helmet. She is wearing boots, leather jacket, and tight jeans. She stands near the edge of the embankment to watch the sunset.*

CAROL: Stephen. We promised. No matter what else, at least we were supposed to be able to depend on each other's honesty.
STEPHEN: I told you, we did not have an affair.
CAROL: No?
STEPHEN: Carol, my dear, I know it will be a strain, but for once please, just try to think. You know she's not my type.
CAROL: If she needed you, she was your type. I have never gone to bed with any man who was a colleague or a friend of yours. Never. And it's not because I haven't been asked.
STEPHEN: That's your code of ethics, not mine.
CAROL: You admit it! You slept with her!
STEPHEN: I'll talk to you when you've calmed down! *(He gets up and as he starts to walk down the beach he sees* GINGER *approaching.)* Damn! *(Returning to* CAROL.*)* Ginger's coming back. Please, let's don't have a scene!

CAROL *gives* STEPHEN *a hard look. She looks smolderingly out to sea as* GINGER *joins them.*

The AUSSIE *enters on the embankment path and goes off to the parking area.*

STEPHEN: *(To Ginger.)* Hi.
GINGER: Hi.

Sand Castles

STEPHEN: Good walk?
GINGER: *(Looking at the sunset.)* It's beautiful isn't it?
STEPHEN: Yes.

> FRITZ *appears on the embankment entering from the direction of the condos. He stands near the bench, looking down at* IRIS.

GINGER: I wonder what's taking Glen so long.
STEPHEN: Must be crowded.
GINGER: I suppose.

> PAUL *comes on from the parking area. He is calm. He sits on the first step down to the beach and watches the sunset.*

GINGER: *(Goes to the ice chest.)* Can I get anybody anything? Carol?
STEPHEN: *(Quickly.)* I'll have a beer.

> *The* AUSSIE *appears from the parking area with his surfboard. He is capitvated by the sunset and stands staring at it.* GINGER *gets a beer for* STEPHEN *and a daiquiri for herself.* ANEMONE *runs on. She is somewhat winded.*

ANEMONE: *(Indicating* AUSSIE.*)* Cool. They lost him.
STEPHEN: Thanks Anemone.
ANEMONE: OK.

> ANEMONE *and* PAUL *look at each other.* PAUL *stands up.*

> *A man dressed in a business suit* (ANDY'S FATHER) *appears on the embankment from the parking area. He looks around as if expecting to see someone, then settles down to wait.* STEPHEN *notices the crowd on the embankment.*

STEPHEN: Don't look now ladies, but it's time to draw the wagons in a circle.
GINGER: What?
STEPHEN: The Indians are massing for attack.
GINGER: *(With unexpected and bashful wit.)* Do you think our courier will be able to get through with the supplies?
STEPHEN: *(Laughs.)* Let's hope so, or they'll starve us out. *(Calling to* ANEMONE *who is still staring at* PAUL: .*)* Anemone?
ANEMONE: Huh?
STEPHEN: Tell me. Why the gathering?
ANEMONE: Oh. The sunset's the big social event around here. *(To* IRIS.*)* Mom?

PHOTO: ALLEN NOMURA

Sand Castles

IRIS: All's quiet on the fornication front.
ANEMONE: Good.

> IRIS *looks up at* FRITZ *who is watching her. She signals to him. He acknowledges her signal and goes off toward the condominiums.*

ANEMONE: Calling it a day?
IRIS: Yes. Why don't you and Linda knock off early tonight and come up to my place. We can have some dinner and play cards or something.
ANEMONE: Not tonight.
IRIS: *(Glancing at* PAUL.*)* Why not?
ANEMONE: Can't afford it. Maybe Sunday?
IRIS: All right. *(She is packing up her gear, putting things in her oversized tote bag.* PAUL *walks down the steps and stands at the bottom.)*

PHOTO: ALLEN NOMURA

ANEMONE: Iris?
IRIS: Um?
ANEMONE: Thanks for the help with Mom.
IRIS: *(With an affectionate pat.)* You're welcome my friend. *(Picks up fashion magazine.)* We'll decide on this tomorrow.
ANEMONE: OK. Something cheaper.
IRIS: Cheap looks cheap.

ANEMONE: Oh.
IRIS: We'll have to do something about her hair.
ANEMONE: No good huh?
IRIS: Too obvious.
ANEMONE: Bring some pictures.
IRIS: I will.

> ANEMONE *glances over her shoulder and sees* PAUL. *She quickly turns away, alarmed by his nearness.* PAUL *goes to his sleeping bag and stands leaning against the embankment.*

GINGER: Carol, can I get you anything? (CAROL *looks at her without speaking.*) Is something wrong?
CAROL: Yes.
STEPHEN: She has a headache.
GINGER: Oh, I'm sorry. I've got some asprin.
STEPHEN: She just took some.
GINGER: Oh.

> FRITZ *appears on the embankment with a wheelchair. He puts on the brake and comes down to the beach.* IRIS *glances at* PAUL.

IRIS: Look here, Anemone Rose. You be careful tonight.
ANEMONE: I will.
IRIS: I'll leave my sliding glass doors open. If you whistle Fritz'll come down.
ANEMONE: I don't need help.
IRIS: Lucky you. (*To* FRITZ *who waits beside her.*) Ready. (FRITZ *picks her up.*) So. See you tomorrow.
ANEMONE: Yes.
IRIS: Stephen. Would you like the remains? (*She holds the champagne bottle out to* STEPHEN *who comes to take it.*) Remember. Eleven o'clock. I'll be waiting. Home, Fritz.

> FRITZ *carries her up to the embankment and puts her in the wheelchair.* FRITZ *starts to wheel* IRIS *off down the embankment path toward the condominiums. She does not turn around.* CAROL *and* GINGER *look at* STEPHEN. CAROL *laughs. Blackout.*

ACT TWO

When the lights come up those on stage are in approximately the same positions as at the end of Act One, except that IRIS *and* FRITZ *are gone. There is almost no time lapse between acts. The sun has set and it is twilight. There is still enough light to see those on the embankment and beach. The street light on the embankment has not yet come on.*

PAUL *sits down on his sleeping bag and leans against the embankment.* CAROL *is laughing as the lights come up.*

STEPHEN: Stop it.
CAROL: That was beautiful!

> GINGER *is shocked.* STEPHEN *says nothing. He looks at* GINGER *who looks away.*

GINGER: Does she do it on purpose do you think?
CAROL: Of course she does it on purpose!
GINGER: I thought it was... (GINGER *shudders.* CAROL *laughs again.*)
STEPHEN: Stop it!
CAROL: Why?
STEPHEN: You aren't really sadistic.
CAROL: No? (*She looks at* GINGER, *then at* STEPHEN, *then turns away and looks at the ocean.*) Maybe not.

> *There is an uneasy silence. The* BIKER CHICK *on the embankment goes off down the path toward the parking area. The* AUSSIE *wanders off toward the parking area.* STEPHEN *goes to* ANEMONE.

STEPHEN: Anemone? Does she do that often?
ANEMONE: Yeah.
STEPHEN: What happened to her?
ANEMONE: I don't know.
STEPHEN: She won't talk about it?
ANEMONE: I never asked.
STEPHEN: Has she been paraplegic long?
ANEMONE: Crippled? I guess that depends on how you look at it. A week'ud seem like a long time to me. She moved here three years ago. All I know is it happened before that.
STEPHEN: Thanks Anemone.

CAROL *helps herself to another drink. On the embankment* ANDY *enters on the path from the direction of the shops. He glances apprehensively at the* AUSSIE'S WOMAN, *but his need to meet his father is greater than his fear of the* AUSSIE. ANDY'S FATHER *(the man in the business suit) comes forward to meet him. They shake hands.* ANDY'S FATHER *takes out his wallet and questions* ANDY *getting a short answer. After a "good boy" gesture* ANDY'S FATHER *hands* ANDY *several bills. On the beach* GINGER *looks up and sees* ANDY.

GINGER: Stephen?
STEPHEN: What?
GINGER: Isn't that Andy?
STEPHEN: Yes.
GINGER: I thought you said Kim was with him.
STEPHEN: She was. *(He goes to the embankment and asks* ANDY *where* KIM *is.)*
CAROL: *(Stiffly, to* GINGER.*)* I'm sure there's nothing to worry about.
GINGER: I'm not worried.
CAROL: *(Goes over to* ANEMONE.*)* Andy's back and there's no sign of Kim. You don't suppose something's happened to her?
ANEMONE: There are about a thousand things that could happen to a puff ball like her. Including nothing.

STEPHEN *returns to the beach. On the embankment* ANDY'S FATHER *gives* ANDY *a departing twenty dollar bill.* ANDY *thanks him, they shake hands, and* ANDY'S FATHER *goes out of sight toward the parking area.*

STEPHEN: *(Arriving on the beach.)* Andy says she went to her motel room to change.
GINGER: Oh.
STEPHEN: I think I'll just go up and walk her back.
GINGER: Why?
STEPHEN: Probably nothing to worry about Ginger. It's just that there's some problem between Andy and this guy they call the Aussie. And the Aussie's a little...
ANEMONE: He's a paranoid schizophrenic nut case. Brain's been scrambled.
GINGER: What's that got to do with Kim?
STEPHEN: Probably nothing. I just thought I'd walk her down to the beach.
GINGER: Oh. Well, if you want to.

The AUSSIE'S WOMAN *gets up and goes off toward the parking area.*

STEPHEN: Where do you suppose she's going?
ANEMONE: Maybe he's in their van.
STEPHEN: *(Starts up the embankment.)* I'll be right back.
CAROL: No hurry. Ginger and I have plenty to talk about.

STEPHEN *stops en route. He turns to* CAROL *and looks at her with great displeasure.* STEPHEN *hesitates, then turns to leave.* KIM *appears on the embankment from the direction of the motel. She is unscathed and virginal. She stops to talk to* ANDY.

CAROL: *(Teasing.)* Ohhhh. Too bad. The rescue mission is off.

STEPHEN *glares at* CAROL, *then purposefully turns and goes up to the embankment and to the telephone booth. He stands facing out making his call, looking down at* CAROL *who is looking up at him.*

ANDY *and* KIM *sit on the embankment and talk.* GINGER *and* CAROL *are both watching* STEPHEN *on the telephone.*

GINGER: I didn't hear his "beeper."
CAROL: He's not calling his hospital.
GINGER: Oh?
CAROL: He's calling his playmate.
GINGER: Oh.
CAROL: One of his playmates. I'm not sure which one. *(Silence.)* Sorry to disillusion you. *(Silence.)* It's probably Fran. I wonder if they'll get married.
GINGER: Oh Carol.
CAROL: Maybe we could have a double wedding.
GINGER: Double wedding?
CAROL: Stephen and Fran and David and me.
GINGER: You're getting married?
CAROL: Just as soon as the blood's been spilled.
GINGER: I don't see...how can you do this?!
CAROL: Divorce god you mean?
GINGER: No, I meant...be here, with him, when you're...
CAROL: It's remarkably easy. The pressure's off.
GINGER: I see.
CAROL: We've been having fun actually. Especially in bed.

GINGER *withers.* PAUL *digs around in his sleeping bag and finds a notebook. He write in it.*

The AUSSIE *appears with a can of Foster's beer. When* ANDY *and* KIM *see him they get up and come immediately down to the beach. The* AUSSIE, *however, is very subdued and smiles at them vacantly.*

KIM: *(To* GINGER.*)* Where's the pizza?
GINGER: Your dad isn't back yet.
KIM: I'm starved. My stomach is eating itself.
GINGER: Have a potato chip.

KIM *gets cans of beer for herself and* ANDY *from the ice chest.* CAROL *looks at* STEPHEN *on the telephone. He is no longer watching her, but focusing entirely on his conversation.* GINGER *has withdrawn into herself.* CAROL *turns her attention to* ANDY.

CAROL: So Andy, what's all this about the Aussie?
ANDY: Oh, nothing much.
CAROL: He seems harmless enough now.
ANDY: Yeah.
CAROL: How come?
ANDY: He forgot. He forgets easy.
CAROL: Will he remember again?
ANDY: Sure.
CAROL: And you don't know when?
ANDY: Nope.
CAROL: Kind of nerve wracking isn't it?
ANDY: Yeah.
CAROL: Is he really dangerous?
ANDY: Yeah. Well. It comes and goes.
CAROL: Is he armed?
ANDY: Knife.
CAROL: Oh!

GLEN *appears on the embankment from the direction of the shops. He carries a cardboard pizza box and a bottle of white wine. He comes down to the beach.* KIM *runs to meet him.* STEPHEN *finishes his telephone call and comes down to the beach.*

KIM: *(Calling like a gull.)* Food! Food! Food!
GLEN: Sorry it took so long. *(He gives the pizza box to* GINGER *who produces paper napkins and serves out slices of pizza.* GLEN *holds*

up a bottle of white wine.) Carol, I got some white wine.
CAROL: Oh. Thanks Glen.
GLEN: Don't mention it.
STEPHEN: *(Arriving on the beach.)* Well, the hunter's home.
GLEN: Sorry it took so long.
STEPHEN: Don't worry about it.
GINGER: *(Offering CAROL a piece of pizza on a napkin.)* Carol?
CAROL: No thanks.
GINGER: What?
CAROL: *(Spelling it out for a two year old.)* No... thanks.
GINGER: You're not eating?
CAROL: No.
GINGER: Oh.
CAROL: It's a personal fast day.
GINGER: Oh.
CAROL: No food shall pass my lips until...
STEPHEN: Great. Leaves more for the rest of us. *(GINGER gives the piece of pizza to STEPHEN. KIM is eating hungrily.)*
GINGER: Andy? Would you like some pizza?
ANDY: Sure. *(GINGER gives him a piece.)*
CAROL: But I will have some of Glen's wine. *(GLEN looks for a corkscrew.)*
STEPHEN: Are you sure you really want to get sick?
CAROL: I do not get sick.
STEPHEN: I have considerable evidence to the contrary.
CAROL: Shut up.
GLEN: We haven't got a corkscrew.
CAROL: Good. I'll have a martini. *(Joins GLEN at the ice chest.)*
GLEN: Sorry, the martinis are gone. How about a mai tai?
CAROL: Fine.
STEPHEN: At least there's some nourishment in the fruit juice.
GLEN: *(Getting her the mai tai.)* Must be great having a doctor in the family.
CAROL: Oh, it's wonderful.
GLEN: Got any secret hangover cures, doc?
STEPHEN: Yup. Don't drink too much.
CAROL: *(Rather drunk and entertaining GLEN.)* My husband is a very temperate man...in most ways. On the other hand, his wife is very intemperate. Now tell me, Glen. Who do you think enjoys herself, or himself, the most?

Silence.

GINGER: Are you sure you won't have some pizza?
CAROL: I really couldn't.
KIM: I can.
GINGER: Help yourself. *(KIM gets another piece of pizza.)*
STEPHEN: It's good pizza, Glen.
GLEN: Yeah, they do a pretty good job. Wood fire.
STEPHEN: Huh?
GLEN: In the oven. They build a wood fire. Gives it a smokey taste.
STEPHEN: Oh.
GINGER: Anemone? Would you like some pizza?
ANEMONE: Oh, no thanks. I've got my dinner.

ANDY *crawls over to* ANEMONE. KIM *hangs nearby.*

STEPHEN: *(Holding out his piece of pizza to* CAROL.*)* Taste? *(*CAROL *shakes her head and tightens her lips.)* You really should eat something you know. *(*CAROL *looks at him, then looks away.)*
ANDY: Nemone, Nemone, Nemone.
ANEMONE: Andy.
ANDY: I got this little problem.
ANEMONE: Money.
ANDY: Yeah. I need a little.
ANEMONE: How much?
ANDY: Six hundred.
ANEMONE: No way.
ANDY: Three hundred.
ANEMONE: Nope.
ANDY: One hundred.
ANEMONE: Why?
ANDY: I gotta get out of here.
ANEMONE: How far are you going to get on a hundred? Tijuana?
ANDY: Don't be smart, lady. I asked for six.
ANEMONE: Hawaii.
ANDY: If you got to lam it, you might as well go with the waves.
ANEMONE: And if you want to lose him you'd be better off in Idaho.
ANDY: Idaho! Jesus!
ANEMONE: What about your puff ball here, why don't you get it from her?
KIM: *(Joins them.)* I don't have any. If I had it, I'd lend it to him.
ANEMONE: That's safe enough to say since you haven't got any.
KIM: *(A little defensively.)* But I don't really see what there is to worry about. He doesn't look dangerous.
ANEMONE: *(Looks up at the* AUSSIE *who is lying down on the*

embankment bench, apparently asleep. With a sigh.) How much does he think you owe him?

ANDY: A hundred and forty.

ANEMONE: If I loan you a hundred and forty will you pay him off and be done with it?

ANDY: No way. I paid him once, I'm not paying him again.

ANEMONE: But he doesn't remember.

ANDY: Yeah. And he probably wouldn't remember if I paid him again. So what's the point? I'm better off stayin' out of sight for a while. Until he moves on, or the cops get him.

KIM: Are they looking for him?

ANDY: Well, it isn't exactly a full-scale man hunt. But he's in the computer.

KIM: What for?

ANDY: Smuggling.

KIM: Dope?

ANDY: *(Teasing.)* No, diamonds.

ANEMONE: You never should have bought from him.

ANDY: Yeah. I know. Now. But he had this really good stuff.

ANEMONE: I hope it was worth it.

ANDY: Fourth generation Mendocino out of Kona Gold seeds. So how about it, I could sure use the six.

ANEMONE: You'll have to stay off the beach.

ANDY: Be serious!

ANEMONE: OK, so go up north.

ANDY: *(Appalled at the thought.)* Lady, I've got standards.

ANEMONE: How much have you got?

ANDY: Just the hundred and twenty my dad gave me. And that'll be the last I get if I'm not here a week from today to collect it.

ANEMONE: Decision time, little boy.

ANDY: Hey!

ANEMONE: Time to grow up.

ANDY: Hey, lady! Ease up.

Linda returns from the condominiums. GLEN, STEPHEN, *and* GINGER, *watch and listen as* LINDA *takes her walkie-talkie out of her tote bag and goes into the telephone booth.* KIM *and* ANDY *move away by themselves as* ANEMONE *talks to* LINDA.

LINDA: *(Over walkie-talkie.)* Anemone?

ANEMONE: *(Looks up and waves at her mother. Into walkie-talkie.)* Hi, Mom. How'd it go?

LINDA: Fine.

ANEMONE: What've you got on you? Ninety?
LINDA: A hundred and ten.
ANEMONE: What!
LINDA: A tip.
ANEMONE: Damn it, Mom! You promised you wouldn't do any kinks.
LINDA: Anemone, honey, it was only a cold towel trick.
ANEMONE: *(With a sigh.)* Oh Mom. You don't know where that kind of thing is going to lead.
LINDA: It leads to a tip.
ANEMONE: And it can lead to the hospital.
LINDA: You have to take some chances in this business, Anemone. It's the nature of the game.
ANEMONE: *(Depressed.)* Yeah. *(Brightening.)* Iris gave us a new number. You want to try it now?
LINDA: Sure. What's the number?
ANEMONE: Just a second. *(She looks in the address book for the phone number IRIS gave her.)*

CAROL *stands and starts toward the steps to the embankment.*

STEPHEN: Carol? Where are you going?
CAROL: To check on the kids.
STEPHEN: Good idea. I'll come with you. *(They look at each other until CAROL turns away.)*
CAROL: No. I need to go alone.
STEPHEN: All right.

CAROL *goes up to the embankment and off down the path toward the motel.*

GLEN: Steve? How about another beer?
STEPHEN: Sure, thanks. *(GLEN gets two beers out of the ice chest.)*
ANEMONE: *(Into walkie-talkie.)* 557-2314.
LINDA: Got it.
ANEMONE: Hold on a second. I'll come and get the cash.
LINDA: All right.

ANEMONE *goes up to the embankment where her mother gives her a hundred and ten dollars in cash.* ANDY *is a bit depressed.* KIM *has been studying the* AUSSIE.

KIM: Hey, Andy. What are you afraid of? I mean, you're not exactly a wimp. You can take care of yourself, right?
ANDY: Lady, there's a lot here you don't understand.

KIM: *(Skeptically.)* Oh come on.
ANDY: He's pretty fried. His brain short circuits see, and then he just sort of goes berserk. Does weird stuff.
KIM: Such as?
ANDY: Surfs at night.
KIM: So what?
ANDY: It's real dangerous. And sometimes he gets this thing about going home. Says he's going to get on his board and ride to Australia.
KIM: But he would drown!
ANDY: Yeah. He's a regular lemming. And sometimes he thinks he's a dingo.
KIM: OK. So he's a little crazy.
ANDY: He's a lot crazy. And getting worse. He used to lose it just every once in a while, but it's getting so he's out of it more than he's with it. And it isn't just the spook stuff.
KIM: What do you mean?
ANDY: He's got some pretty heavy...associates.
KIM: Associates?
ANDY: *(Almost impatient with her naivete.)* He's a dope dealer, right? Well, those aren't exactly pollyanna people he's hooked up with.
KIM: *(Impressed.)* Oh.
ANDY: And he hasn't been tending to business.
KIM: Is he in trouble?
ANDY: Sure he's in trouble. You don't mess around with the heavy men.
KIM: What about his woman?
ANDY: What about her?
KIM: Can't she do anything?
ANDY: Do? Nothing anybody can do.

The street lights come on on the embankment.

The AUSSIE *sits up, stretches, and gets unsteadily to his feet.* ANEMONE *has collected the cash and turns to come back down to the beach. She can't avoid the* AUSSIE *who is in her path. He makes an aggressive movement toward her.* ANEMONE *pulls her mace off her belt and threatens him with it. He shrugs, then moves off and disappears toward the parking area.* ANEMONE *looks after the* AUSSIE, *then returns to the beach as* LINDA *goes to the telephone booth and makes a call.*

ANEMONE: *(To* ANDY.*)* You'd better hussle that decision, Andy. The sleeping dog has risen. *(She starts back to her towel.* PAUL *stands up and comes towards her. She pulls back. He laughs.)*
PAUL: I'm going up to get a beer, can I bring you something?
ANEMONE: I don't drink beer.
PAUL: I know. Fruit juice.
ANEMONE: OK.

PAUL *goes up the steps to the embankment and off down the path toward the shops.* ANEMONE *watches until he is out of sight, then sits down, and, by flashlight, fills out a bank deposit slip, counting the cash twice. She then makes an entry in her account book and puts the money and deposit slip in a bank envelope for night deposit.*

KIM: *(To* ANDY.*)* You'd better get out of here.
ANDY: Yeah. The big question is where.
GINGER: *(To* GLEN.*)* Did you put the wood in the car?
GLEN: Sure. You want a fire?
KIM: *(To* ANDY.*)* Can't you just go home?
GINGER: *(To* GLEN.*)* It would be nice.
ANDY: No. He knows where I live. He broke in last week.
KIM: Really?
GLEN: *(To* GINGER.*)* OK. I'll get the wood.
STEPHEN: I'll give you a hand. *(They go up to the embankment and off toward the parking area.)*
ANDY: *(To* KIM.*)* I got out the bathroom window. He trashed the place, but it didn't matter much. *(Laughs.)* Fact, you could hardly tell the difference.
KIM: I've got an idea.
ANDY: So?
KIM: You could go to my room.
ANDY: Come again?
KIM: My motel room. You can stay there.
ANDY: Yeah?
KIM: Yeah.
ANDY: Your folks...
KIM: I've got my own room, it doesn't connect with theirs or anything. You want to?
ANDY: Uh...Yeah...Sure.
KIM: *(Takes a motel room key out of the pocket of her shorts.)* Here's the key. Room twenty-four.

ANDY: OK.
KIM: You'll have to let me in when I come up.
ANDY: Sure.
KIM: So don't fall asleep.
ANDY: Hey, lady. You sure you want to do this?
KIM: Why not?
ANDY: *(Touching her.)* You know why not.
KIM: Yeah. I want to. *(ANDY kisses her.)* You'd better hurry.
ANDY: Yeah. *(Gets up, turns to go, then turns back and squats down beside her.)* You...uh...you don't stay out too late. Ok?
KIM: OK?

> ANDY *slips away toward the motel. It is quite dark and, while figures can be made out on the beach, faces are somewhat in shadow.* KIM *sits without moving, looking out at the dark ocean.* LINDA *has finished her telephone call.* ANEMONE *has put on her back pack.*

LINDA: *(Over walkie-talkie.)* Anemone?
ANEMONE: *(Into walkie-talkie.)* Yeah Mom?
LINDA: Got him.
ANEMONE: Hey, that's great Mom!
LINDA: I'm going up at one o'clock.
ANEMONE: That's too late.
LINDA: He wouldn't make it earlier.
ANEMONE: But you're supposed to quit at midnight!
LINDA: Look Anemone, if you want me to move up in the world, I'm going to have to be a little flexible. Overtime once in a while won't do me any harm.
ANEMONE: I suppose not. I'm going to the bank to deposit the cash. I won't be gone long.
LINDA: All right.
ANEMONE: Maybe you should take your dinner break now.
LINDA: Yes dear.

> ANEMONE *takes her walkie-talkie and goes up to the embankment. She waves to her mother and goes off toward the shops.* LINDA *sits on the bench and takes the brown paper bag out of her tote bag and eats a sandwich.*

GINGER: *(Her voice comes out of the darkness. She speaks flatly, not accusingly.)* You gave him the key to your room.

KIM: *(Freezes, her back is to her mother. She speaks after a pause.)* How do you know?
GINGER: I saw you.
KIM: Does Dad know?
GINGER: No.
KIM: *(Turns toward her mother.)* Don't tell him.

GINGER: Why would I tell him? It's your business.
KIM: You don't...mind?
GINGER: I assume you are...protected.
KIM: Protected?
GINGER: Birth control.
KIM: *(Embarrassed and defensive.)* Mom!
GINGER: I only...
KIM: I'm not completely stupid you know!
GINGER: Kimberly...
KIM: Don't call me that! Kim is bad enough, but Kimberly! What did you think, I would be going to grow up to be a leggy blond and go to Vassar? I must be a terrific disappointment. *(Silence.)* By the way, Mom. Speaking of rooms. Does Dad know about 2417 El Camino Drive? Apartment 6B?

Silence.

GINGER: I don't know what you're talking about.
KIM: You've got a key.
GINGER: How do you know?
KIM: I followed you.
GINGER: Followed me!
KIM: You were a little careless one afternoon with your cover story. I got suspicious.
GINGER: *(Quietly.)* Have you told anyone?
KIM: No. Do you meet your lover there?
GINGER: I don't have a lover.
KIM: Oh sure.
GINGER: I don't!
KIM: Then what do you need an apartment for?
GINGER: It's just a room. A studio apartment.
KIM: With a double bed I'll bet.
GINGER: Kim. When you tell me something, I believe you. Please have the courtesy to treat me the same way. I tell you, I do not have a lover.
KIM: OK. OK. But I don't get it. What's it for?
GINGER: Just a place where I can be by myself.
KIM: Dad doesn't know?
GINGER: No one knows. *(Bitterly.)* No one knew.
KIM: Weird.
GINGER: I don't use it often. Once or twice a week.
KIM: You just go and, what? Listen to music or something?
GINGER: No. There's nothing there.

KIM: What do you mean?
GINGER: It's unfurnished.
KIM: You just go and sit on the floor in an empty room?! *(GINGER is silent.)* Man, that's ultimate weird. *(Silence.)* Mom?
GINGER: What?
KIM: *(The possibility has occurred to her for the first time.)* Are you... are you unhappy or something?
GINGER: *(Pause.)* It's a difficult question.
KIM: You don't know if you're unhappy?
GINGER: What if I said I was? It wouldn't change anything.
KIM: You and Dad...you...
GINGER: Your father and I are fine.
KIM: I don't know. You always seem to hold out on him.
GINGER: What do you mean?
KIM: It's like you're always keeping something back. You're sort of stingy.
GINGER: Stingy!
KIM: Yeah. I mean, he wants you to do something and you won't do it. Like the construction business. You won't join in.
GINGER: Oh that.
KIM: And I don't see why not.
GINGER: Kim, I...

GLEN *and* STEPHEN *appear on the embankment from the parking area. They are carrying a few pieces of wood and some kindling. They stop to talk to* LINDA.

KIM: *(Gently.)* What is it, Mom?
GINGER: It seems to me that things have always just happened to me. I never had any say in anything. I got married without really deciding I wanted to be married, and then I got pregnant without deciding I wanted to have children. Everything's been like that. I started keeping Glen's books without deciding that I wanted to run a construction company. Things have sort of...happened to me. Without my consent.
KIM: Well Mom, if you don't make decisions they get made for you.
GINGER: Maybe so.

GLEN *and* STEPHEN *say goodbye to* LINDA *and start down to the beach.* GINGER *sees them coming.*

GINGER: Kim. Please don't tell your father about the room.
KIM: Mom, I wouldn't do that.
GINGER: And look Kim, about Andy...

Sand Castles

KIM: Don't worry about Andy. I've got things under control.
GINGER: I hope so.
KIM: In fact I'm going to solve his little problem for him.
GINGER: Don't get involved in something you don't understand.

GLEN and STEPHEN put their wood in the fire pit and GLEN sets about building a fire.

GLEN: Get involved with what?
GINGER: Andy's problems.
KIM: Andy's not going to have any more problems.
GLEN: Oh?
KIM: Nope.
STEPHEN: Any sign of Carol?
GINGER: No. Maybe she's reading to the kids.
STEPHEN: Carol doesn't read. Not even to the kids.
GINGER: Really?
STEPHEN: Maybe that's her problem. She's got no ready-made fantasies to escape into. She has to make her own.
KIM: *(Looking out at the black sea.)* Those lights out there? I wonder what they are.
GINGER: Maybe a ship.
GLEN: I think it's an oil drilling rig.
KIM: Really? Funny. It looks pretty.

GLEN lights the fire using lighter fluid. KIM looks at GINGER who returns her look and smiles shyly. KIM returns the smile.

GLEN: There we are.
STEPHEN: You're quite a fire builder Glen.

KIM, GINGER, STEPHEN, and GLEN sit around the fire which lights their faces.

GLEN: Funny about fire.
STEPHEN: How's that?
GLEN: Small ones are comforting. Big ones eat everything up. When I was a kid we had a fire on the ranch. Damnedest thing I ever saw.
KIM: Did your house burn down, Daddy?
GLEN: No. A hay stack.
KIM: Oh.
GLEN: The thing was huge. You could see the fire for miles. The foreman called my dad in the middle of the night. When we got there it was too late, the whole stack was blazing.

KIM: Didn't the fire department come?

GLEN: By the time they got out from town there was nothing they could do.

KIM: What happened?

GLEN: Nothing. We all stood around and watched it burn...and joked. Might as well, nothing else to be done. We watched it go. It was kind of beautiful in a way. I remember the way people's faces were lit up. My dad and the foreman, and the firemen. And then back further, in the shadows under the eucalyptus trees, the Mexican farmhands watched. Soft brown faces.

Silence. On the embankment the BOOKWORM *enters reading. When* LINDA *approaches him he is surprised and starts to leave, then stops and turns back. She comes to him and takes his book and goes off to her van. He follows.*

STEPHEN: So you were raised on a ranch.

GLEN: Yes.

KIM: Dad was a cowboy.

STEPHEN: Really? Horse and all?

GLEN: Sure. *(As* KIM *starts to go up to the embankment.)* Kim, where are you going?

KIM: I've got something to take care of. *(She goes up to the telephone booth. She looks up a number in the book, then makes a call.)*

STEPHEN: How'd you end up behind a desk for the state?

GLEN: Dad wanted me to go to college so I could talk to the banker for him. His folk grammar embarrassed him. Never had much time for school.

STEPHEN: Where was this?

GLEN: Nebraska. He came to California and worked in a gold mine for a while, then homesteaded.

STEPHEN: You're kidding.

GLEN: No.

STEPHEN: It seems like that all happened a long time ago.

GLEN: Parts of California weren't homesteaded until 1920, even 1940. As the irrigation canals dug further into the deserts. It's all a question of water.

GINGER: I don't imagine Stephen is very interested in the history of California.

GLEN: Sorry.

STEPHEN: Do you regret leaving the ranch?

GLEN: God no! The valley is a piece of hell. Hot, dry, and full of wretched souls.

Sand Castles

PHOTO: ALLEN NOMURA

ANEMONE *returns from the bank. She notices* KIM *in the telephone booth on her way down to the beach. She takes off her back pack.*

STEPHEN: Hey, Anemone, your mother has a customer.
ANEMONE: *(Indicating her walkie-talkie.)* I heard.
BOOKWORM: *(Voice over walkie-talkie.)* Start on page one-seventy-one. *(*ANEMONE *laughs.)*
STEPHEN: You know who it is?
ANEMONE: It's the Bookworm. He's a tourist, been here a couple of weeks and every other night he comes down. Always pretends he's never been before. He wants Mom to read to him.
STEPHEN: While he's...
ANEMONE: Yeah.

LINDA: *(Over walkie-talkie.)* Who's this Jack London?
BOOKWORM: Start here.
LINDA: "An hour went by, and a second hour. The pale light of the short sunless day was beginning to fade, when a faint far cry arose on the still air. It soared upward with a swift rush, till it reached its topmost note, where it persisted, palpitant and tense, and then slowly died away. It might have been a lost soul wailing..." *(*ANEMONE *sits on her towel, listens, is content that things are proceeding normally, so turns volume off. She prepares another bank deposit slip.)*

STEPHEN: *(To* GLEN *and* GINGER.*)* I'm going to go see what's keeping Carol.
GINGER: If her headache is worse, tell her I've got some Darvon.
GLEN: Seems like a case of coals to Newcastle.
GINGER: What do you mean?
GLEN: Offering pills to a pill pusher's wife.
STEPHEN: I'll see you later.

STEPHEN *goes up to the embankment and off toward the motel. At her station* ANEMONE *makes an entry in her account book by flashlight.* KIM *is still on the phone.*

A PREGNANT WOMAN *carrying a bag of groceries comes along the embankment path from the direction of the shops. She puts down the bag and sits on the bench to rest.*

GINGER: *(To* GLEN.*)* Who on earth can she be telephoning?
GLEN: I don't know.
GINGER: She doesn't know anybody around here except Andy.
GLEN: Maybe she's calling a friend at home.
GINGER: Why would she do that? We're going home tomorrow.
GLEN: I think I'll have another beer. You want anything?
GINGER: No thanks.
GLEN: Sure?
GINGER: Yes. *(Pause.)* Glen.
GLEN: What?
GINGER: You haven't minded the vacation too much, have you?
GLEN: Oh, it hasn't been so bad. You know, this afternoon I talked to a guy up the street from the motel. He's adding a room onto his house and he says down here they...
GINGER: I'm sorry I asked.
GLEN: *(Pause.)* Ginge. About your quitting your job...
GINGER: *(Defensively.)* What about it?
GLEN: I'm not going to push anymore. If you don't want to, then that's that. *(Silence.)* OK?
GINGER: OK.
GLEN: It's not that I've changed my mind. I still think it's a hell of a good idea.
GINGER: Glen. You don't need me to talk to the banker.
GLEN: I'm not so sure about that. You speak his language.
GINGER: You do too, when you want to.
GLEN: But I'd rather not.
GINGER: Why can't we just go on the way we are?

GLEN: I suppose we can. It's just that I'd kind of like to see what would happen if we really cut loose with it.

GINGER: I do plenty now.

GLEN: Yeah, with half your head. You're...Ginge, you get damned good ideas. But I'll tell you the truth. A few of those ideas, for instance that little mini-shopping center we did over on Del Norte Drive? When you first talked about that, I thought...well.

GINGER: Why didn't you say so?

GLEN: Because I've learned. You always know what's going to go and what isn't.

GINGER: I'll make a mistake one of these days.

GLEN: I'm not worried. You have a real knack. And I really admire you.

GINGER: Why this...this pep talk?

GLEN: I just wanted to tell you, in case you didn't know, that... *(He gives her a playful punch on the arm causing her to spill her drink.)* I think you're terrific kiddo.

GINGER: *(Rises to move away.)* Thanks.

GLEN: Think nothing of it.

Silence. GLEN *lies down and looks up at the stars.* GINGER *moves away. She looks at* KIM *in the telephone booth.*

The AUSSIE *appears on the embankment from the parking area. He goes to the bench and stares at the* PREGNANT WOMAN *who picks up her grocery bag and hurries away. The* AUSSIE'S WOMAN *comes on from the parking area. She carries a shopping bag. She asks the* AUSSIE *to come with her, he refuses, she goes off toward the shops.*

GINGER: Glen?

GLEN: Yeah?

GINGER: I would need a secretary.

GLEN: *(Hopefully.)* Yeah...

GINGER: And a bookkeeper.

GLEN: And what are you going to do?

GINGER: What *would* I do.

GLEN: *(Carefully.)* OK. What would you do?

GINGER: Plan. And do research.

GLEN: *(Pause.)* Maybe a half-time bookkeeper.

GINGER: OK. That would do it, for now. And a full-time secretary.

GLEN: Right.

GINGER: And a suite of offices.

GLEN: A suite!

GINGER: A suite. Minimum of three rooms.

GLEN: Jeez, Ginger!
GINGER: Minimum. Four would be better.
GLEN: We've got a perfectly good office right there in the house.
GINGER: I've had it with the cottage industry. That piece over on La Mesa would be just right for an office complex.
GLEN: What piece?
GINGER: I bought it last winter.
GLEN: Oh.
GINGER: You build it. *(Pause.)* I'll quit my job when it's finished.
GLEN: *(Tentatively.)* You quit your job when we break ground.
GINGER: All right.
GLEN: *(Happy sigh.)* All right.

> KIM *hangs up the telephone. She comes out of the booth and looks around, hesitates, then goes to the* AUSSIE *and sits down on the bench with him.*

GINGER: But you hire and fire your own men. I won't have anything to do with that.
GLEN: Good, you're too soft.
GINGER: Soft! Me?!
GLEN: Sure. You should have held out for a full-time bookkeeper.

> *They laugh together.* GLEN *looks up and sees* KIM *sitting by the* AUSSIE. STEPHEN *enters from the direction of the motel. When he sees* KIM *with the* AUSSIE *he goes over to the bench.*

GLEN: Hey! What's she doing with that freak!
GINGER: I don't know.
GLEN: I don't like it.
GINGER: Stephen said something about him. I think he's a friend of Andy's.
GLEN: What is he, some kind of ecology bum?

> STEPHEN *says something to the* AUSSIE *who looks at him in horror and scuttles away hurriedly.*

GLEN: *(Chuckling.)* Steve seems to have lit a fire under him. (STEPHEN *comes down to the beach.* KIM *follows but stays by herself.)*
GINGER: But Glen, don't pressure Kim, about the architect thing.
GLEN: I suppose you're right. *(To* STEPHEN.*)* What's it take to make his hair curl like that?
STEPHEN: I told him I know a good drug rehabilitation clinic. *(They laugh.)* Carol isn't here?

GINGER: No.
STEPHEN: The kids are asleep. I guess I must have missed her.
GINGER: She probably just went for a walk.
STEPHEN: *(Worried.)* Ummm.
GLEN: There's another beer, Steve, if you want one.
STEPHEN: No thanks, Glen.

> PAUL *appears on the embankment from the direction of the shops carrying a small carton of orange juice and a can of beer. He comes directly down to the beach.*

KIM: *(Privately.)* Anemone?
ANEMONE: Hi.
GLEN: *(To* GINGER *and* STEPHEN.*)* We should be drinking champagne.
STEPHEN: Champagne?
GLEN: Ginger's agreed to become a tycoon.
STEPHEN: Really? Well, congratulations.

> GLEN, GINGER, *and* STEPHEN *sit around the fire, absorbed in their own worlds. The* AUSSIE *reappears on the embankment. He looks around.* KIM *sees him and is relieved.* PAUL *gives* ANEMONE *the fruit juice.*

PAUL: Here.
ANEMONE: Thanks.
PAUL: You're welcome. *(Goes to sit on his sleeping bag.* ANEMONE *watches him go.)*
KIM: Anemone, can I ask you something?
ANEMONE: What's on your mind?
KIM: Do you know any drug store around here that's open this late?
ANEMONE: Noooo. I don't think so. What do you need?
KIM: Condoms.
ANEMONE: What?
KIM: Condoms.
ANEMONE: Oh.
KIM: You know anywhere I can get them?
ANEMONE: Tonight?
KIM: Yeah. Like now. Any ideas?
ANEMONE: Well, I think some of the men's toilets at gas stations have them in machines.
KIM: I can't go into a men's room!
ANEMONE: Oh.
KIM: Can't you think of anywhere else?

ANEMONE: The grocery store's still open, but I don't think they sell them.
KIM: I thought maybe...doesn't your mom have some?
ANEMONE: Maybe you should just forget the whole thing. It's overrated.
KIM: Yeah?
ANEMONE: I tried it once.
KIM: You didn't like it?
ANEMONE: I don't see what the big deal is. But I might try it again sometime. It might be an acquired taste. You know, like artichokes.
KIM: Maybe it wasn't with the right guy.
ANEMONE: Does that make a difference?
KIM: It's supposed to.
ANEMONE: You ever done it before?
KIM: *(Hesitating.)* Not exactly.
ANEMONE: What's that mean?
KIM: No.

A siren is heard in the distance, getting closer. The AUSSIE *disappears toward the parking area.* PAUL *starts to get up, then decides to stay where he is.* KIM *moves away from* ANEMONE, *listening to the siren.*

ANEMONE *turns up the volume on the walkie-talkie to check on* LINDA *who is still reading. She turns the volume back down.*

CAROL *has entered on the enbankment path and now comes down to the beach. She has sobered up.*

STEPHEN: Where have you been?
CAROL: I went for a walk.
STEPHEN: I've been worried.
CAROL: *(Surprised.)* Really? The kids are fine. Sleeping.
STEPHEN: I know. I went to look for you.
CAROL: You did? *(The siren sound gets closer.)*
GINGER: What's that? Fire?
STEPHEN: Sounds like police.

A flashing red light can be seen from the parking area. The AUSSIE *runs on from that direction and runs off toward the shops.* ANEMONE *looks at* PAUL *who doesn't move.*

GINGER: Something's going on. *(The siren winds down in the parking area.)*

BOOKWORM: *(Over the walkie-talkie.)* Hey, it's the police! What are we going to do?!
LINDA: Quiet.

A POLICEMAN *appears on the embankment with a flashlight. He goes to the phone booth and compares the number on the telephone with that in his notebook. He looks around, looks down at the beach, then signals an unseen policeman in parking area to search there.*

ANEMONE: *(Into walkie-talkie.)* Mom?
LINDA: *(Whispering into walkie-talkie.)* I'm here.
ANEMONE: Cops.
LINDA: I know that.
ANEMONE: Stay low.
LINDA: What did you think I was going to do, proposition them?
ANEMONE: And keep the Bookworm quiet.
LINDA: I'll try.

The POLICEMAN*'s flashlight illuminates faces on the beach.*

GLEN: He's looking for someone.
STEPHEN: Yes.
ANEMONE: *(Goes to* KIM.*)* Hey, what've you done?
KIM: *(Bluffing.)* Me?
ANEMONE: You called the cops on the Aussie, didn't you?
KIM: What if I did?
ANEMONE: You dingbat!
KIM: He's a menace.
ANEMONE: Go back to suburbia little girl, you don't belong here. Sticking yourself into something you don't understand. Man, you can't live like that. You gotta deal with things yourself.
KIM: He's dangerous. He needs to be locked up.
ANEMONE: He's a pathetic, sick, damaged person. Most of the time. And when he's crazy we can deal with him. We don't need no cops.

ANEMONE *returns to her towel when she hears* LINDA*'s voice over the walkie-talkie. The* POLICEMAN*'s flashlight hits* PAUL*'s face, lingers, moves away, returns.* ANEMONE *watches.*

LINDA: *(To* BOOKWORM *over the walkie-talkie.)* Hey, what are you doing?
BOOKWORM: Start over again.

LINDA: Oh, all right. But I charge twice for a double header. "An hour went by, and a second hour. The pale light of the short sunless day was beginning to fade..." (ANEMONE *turns the volume down. The* POLICEMAN *moves off down the embankment path, still searching with his flashlight.*)

ANEMONE: *(Calling to the tourists.)* Hey look, folks. Will you just sit down and act like everything's normal. You make me real nervous.

STEPHEN: Is it a raid or something?

ANEMONE: *(Glaring at* KIM.*)* No. It's not. *(She and* PAUL *look at one another.* KIM *joins her parents and they sit down around their fire.)*

STEPHEN: *(To* GLEN.*)* So are you going to get an early start in the morning?

GINGER: Much too early.

GLEN: We don't have to leave that early.

PAUL *goes to* ANEMONE.

GINGER: It's all right.

GLEN: I figure we're always up anyway. We might as well get going.

PAUL: *(To* ANEMONE.*)* What's going on?

ANEMONE: The cops are after the Aussie.

PAUL: Oh.

ANEMONE: I was afraid it might be you.

PAUL: Were you?

ANEMONE: Yeah.

The AUSSIE *runs in from the direction of the shops. He is confused and desperate. He starts to go to the parking area, sees the flashing red light, stops.*

GLEN: I'd kind of like to go back to the motel and turn in. But I don't want to get mixed up in the middle of something.

GINGER: Let's wait.

STEPHEN: Good idea.

The AUSSIE *comes down to the beach. He is heading for the ocean when* PAUL *stops him.*

PAUL: Hey, no man, come here!

The tourists shrink back watching in fascinated horror as PAUL *helps the* AUSSIE *into his sleeping bag, then lies down across it so that it only looks like a lumpy bag.*

Sand Castles

GLEN: Hey, wait a minute, you can't...
ANEMONE: Stay out of this, mister. This is our problem, not yours.

The POLICEMAN appears from the direction of the shops and looks around. He again checks the beach with his flashlight.

GINGER: I'm glad they don't have dogs.
CAROL: Dogs?
GINGER: To smell him out.
CAROL: Good god.
GLEN: *(To STEPHEN.)* Maybe we should do something.
STEPHEN: What?
GLEN: Tell the police where he is.
GINGER: No! Don't do that!
GLEN: Why not?
GINGER: Just stay out of it.

The POLICEMAN gives up and goes off toward the parking area.

STEPHEN: Well, that was a nasty bit of local color.
GINGER: Thank god they didn't find him.
GLEN: What's going on with you?
GINGER: I don't know.

The flashing red light in the parking area goes out.

ANEMONE: *(Into walkie-talkie.)* Mom?
LINDA: *(Over walkie-talkie.)* What?
ANEMONE: Have the cops gone?
LINDA: You're not supposed to interrupt me.
ANEMONE: This is important. Are they gone?
LINDA: Yes. Now leave me alone. This is his time, he's paying for it.
ANEMONE: Sorry. *(She turns down the walkie-talkie volume and goes to PAUL.)* All clear.
PAUL: *(Gets up and helps the confused AUSSIE out of his bag.)* It's OK, man. You're all right now. *(The AUSSIE is out of the sleeping bag, and looks around in helpless confusion, then looks to PAUL not knowing what to do.)* OK. Come on, let's go up to your van. You need to cool down.

PAUL and the AUSSIE go up to the embankment and off toward the parking area. PAUL is very gentle with him. ANEMONE watches with admiration.

KIM: *(To her parents.)* I gotta go.

GLEN: *(Starts picking up the picnic debris.)* So do we. You'd better come with us.
KIM: I'd rather walk back.
GLEN: You are *not* walking around here alone at night.
STEPHEN: She can walk back with us later.
KIM: *(Gives up as it looks she will have a chaperon whichever way she plays it.)* I guess I might as well go now.
STEPHEN: *(To* GLEN *who is folding up the blanket.)* Well, I hope you have an uneventful trip.
GLEN: Thanks. *(Shaking hands.)* Well, Steve, Carol. You guys have a good time, huh, for a few more days. *(*CAROL *laughs.)*
GINGER: Glen!
GLEN: What's the matter?
GINGER: Nothing.
STEPHEN: Well, Kim. Good luck in outer space.
KIM: Thanks.
STEPHEN: Watch out for the black holes.
KIM: I'll do that.
STEPHEN: What happened to the dolphin?
KIM: I uh...don't know. He disappeared.
STEPHEN: The end of a summer romance.
KIM: Yeah.
GINGER: Goodnight, Carol. Thanks for everything.
CAROL: I didn't do anything.
GINGER: Recommending the motel, you know.
CAROL: Oh that. You're welcome. Thanks for dinner.
GINGER: Dinner?
CAROL: Well, thanks for the drinks anyway.
STEPHEN: Yes, thank you. *(They are picking up their gear.* KIM *goes to* ANEMONE. *She is carrying her high-heeled sandals.)*
KIM: Anemone, maybe you were right. But it seems to me a person has to get involved with things. Help out.
ANEMONE: Oh yeah?
KIM: Your mother couldn't spare a...
ANEMONE: Better forget it. And do yourself a favor. Get some new footwear, huh? You'll live longer.
KIM: Thanks for nothing. *(Rejoins her parents.)*
GINGER: Goodnight everyone.
CAROL: Night. Safe trip.
GINGER: Thanks. *(They start towards the embankment.)*
KIM: *(Stops her father.)* Daddy, why don't we stop now and gas up the car?

GLEN: I already did it this afternoon.
KIM: *(Sighing.)* Oh.
STEPHEN: *(To* KIM.*)* Pleasant dreams.
KIM: Thanks. *(They go up to the embankment and off toward the parking area,* KIM *reluctantly following behind.)*
STEPHEN: *(To* CAROL.*)* Do you want to go back to the motel?
CAROL: *(Sitting down by the fire.)* Not yet. OK?
STEPHEN: Sure. *(He moves his towel to the firepit and sits down across from* CAROL.*)*
LINDA: *(Appears on the embankment and goes to the telephone booth. She speaks over walkie-talkie.)* Anemone?
ANEMONE: *(Into walkie-talkie.)* Yeah, Mom?
LINDA: Just checking in.
ANEMONE: OK. *(Looking at her watch.)* It's almost time for your appointment in apartment three-ten.
LINDA: I'm on my way.
ANEMONE: Wait a minute. I'll walk you over.
LINDA: Fine.

ANEMONE *goes up to the embankment and she and* LINDA *go off toward the condominiums.*

PAUL *comes on from the parking area, looks around for* ANEMONE, *sits on the bench.*

CAROL: *(To* STEPHEN.*)* Nice Fire.
STEPHEN: Yes.

Silence. Sea gulls cry. A SAILOR *walks slowly along the embankment path. He pauses from time to time and looks out at the ocean.*

CAROL: Stephen?
STEPHEN: Um?
CAROL: Just supposing...I mean, just say that...What if we were starting over?
STEPHEN: How do you mean?
CAROL: If we'd just gotten married. And we knew what we know now. Do you think things would turn out differently?
STEPHEN: Who knows?
CAROL: Suppose...what if...What if we didn't get the divorce. What if we...
STEPHEN: What?
CAROL: Stayed together.
STEPHEN: I'd like that very much.

CAROL: But would you...change?
STEPHEN: I could say that I would. But it probably wouldn't be the truth.
CAROL: No. Probably not.
STEPHEN: And you won't change either.
CAROL: Oh yes I will!
STEPHEN: My poor romantic optimist.
CAROL: It will be better, this time, with David. I know it will.

STEPHEN is silent. They watch the ocean, alone. The SAILOR moves slowly away. ANEMONE returns from the condominiums.

PAUL goes to meet her and they talk.

CAROL: Well. I guess we'd better go back to the motel.
STEPHEN: All right.

They stand up and gather their things. IRIS appears in her wheelchair, rolling on the embankment path from the direction of the condominiums. She stops and looks out at the ocean.

CAROL: I'll help you find an apartment if you like.
STEPHEN: That won't be necessary.
CAROL: You can see the children whenever you want.
STEPHEN: Good.
CAROL: *(Looks up and sees IRIS.)* She's back. I wonder what she's doing here.
STEPHEN: Asking for trouble.
CAROL: Fritz must be around somewhere.
STEPHEN: I doubt it. *(CAROL starts toward the steps.)* Carol. *(CAROL returns to him. He kisses her lightly on the mouth.)*
CAROL: What's that for?
STEPHEN: For luck. And for sorrow. Please excuse me. *(He goes up to the embankment. The sound of the ocean increases. STEPHEN says something to ANEMONE who nods, then he goes to IRIS and wheels her chair off toward the condominiums as she looks at him with astonishment.)*
CAROL: Stephen! Oh Stephen!

ANEMONE and PAUL come down the steps.

ANEMONE: He asked me to walk you back to the motel.
CAROL: Motel hell! Where's the nearest bar?
ANEMONE: *(Pointing in the direction of the motel.)* Take the first right. But it's not...

CAROL: Thanks. *(She goes up the steps and off in the direction of the motel.* ANEMONE *and* PAUL *look at one another.* ANEMONE *turns away.)*
ANEMONE: Are you going to stay around here long?
PAUL: I don't know. Maybe.
ANEMONE: You been sleeping on the beach?
PAUL: Yeah.
ANEMONE: It's illegal.
PAUL: I know. So they roust me.
ANEMONE: No money?
PAUL: My expenses are high. Leaves very little for nonessentials like room and board.

Silence.

ANEMONE: What's your name?
PAUL: Paul.
ANEMONE: I'm...
PAUL: Anemone. You're Anemone Rose.
ANEMONE: Sounds pretty good when you say it. *(*PAUL *takes her hand.)* I feel funny.
PAUL: What's the matter?
ANEMONE: I'm sort of dizzy. *(She sits down.)* Maybe I'm getting the flu.
PAUL: I doubt it. *(He goes to his sleeping bag to get his notebook. He returns to* ANEMONE, *sits beside her, and makes a note.)*

On the embankment the DEALER *and his* MUSCLE *come along the path from the direction of the shops. They look around briefly, then the* DEALER *gestures toward the parking area and leads his* MUSCLE *off in that direction.*

ANEMONE: What are you doing?
PAUL: Making a note.
ANEMONE: How come?
PAUL: I write.
ANEMONE: Yeah? Like what?
PAUL: Poetry.
ANEMONE: You're kidding.
PAUL: No.
ANEMONE: Why?
PAUL: Why do I write?
ANEMONE: Yeah.
PAUL: *(Pause.)* I uh...I don't think you'd understand.

ANEMONE: Try me.

PAUL: It's...well it's just a way of dealing with things. Makes the world less painful.

An anguished howl like a dog in pain is heard from the parking area.

ANEMONE: What's that?!
PAUL: I don't know. It sounds like a hurt dog.
ANEMONE: Yeah. Paul?
PAUL: What?
ANEMONE: I've got part of a sandwich left. You want it?
PAUL: Not now.

The DEALER *and his* MUSCLE *come onto the embankment from the parking area and go off toward the shops.*

PAUL *moves toward* ANEMONE *to kiss her.*

ANEMONE: Hey, what are you doing?
PAUL: I'm going to kiss you.
ANEMONE: Better not. I might be getting the flu.
PAUL: I'll risk it. Relax. You'll like it.

PAUL *kisses her. The sound of the ocean gets louder. On the embankment the* AUSSIE *appears from the parking area. He is bloody and limping. He is carrying his board and wearing an ancient army surplus back pack. He stops, looks at the ocean, then comes down the steps. He howls in anguish as he disappears toward the water. Blackout.*

What Is A Play Anyway?
Raising Some Initial Questions
Bernard Weiner

Imagine yourself as a daily newspaper theater critic opening the mail on any particular day. Thirty press releases arrive announcing new shows, at least three of which are for performances that fall "between the cracks," as it were, of the various disciplines covered by the paper, and for which reviewers have been hired. Here's a release that calls itself a "theater/dance/performance art event." Is this show for the dance critic? The music critic? The art critic? The theater critic? The "events" editor?

You leave your desk and traipse on over to the dance critic, the music critic, the art critic. "Is this yours?" They shake their heads in puzzlement as well. Who reviews the show? Too often, nobody. (Not incidentally, I know of only one publication, the *Village Voice*, that has hired a reviewer precisely for these "between-the-cracks" shows.)

Alternate scenario: You're an editor of a new-plays journal, anxious to bring to the attention of your readers—who are primarily theater directors, managers, producers, agents, actors, writers, etc.—the best of the original works currently being produced. Scripts pour in, but some of the most interesting theatrical shows you've seen in recent months are not scripted, or cannot be scripted, or, if they can be scripted, can hardly be remounted by another producing outfit. (Thanks to the daring and commitment of the editors of *West Coast Plays*, the first attempts along these lines have been made, with the publication of *Surface Tension* and *Renaissance Radar*.) But the basic question remains: What is a "play" these days?

In the olden days—that is, only a few years ago—plays had logical beginnings, middles, and ends, even if they explored the reaches of surrealism and absurdism. They also had language, motivation, identifiable characters, points of view.

Nowadays, according to many avant-garde producers, plays are anything put on in theaters. Remove your traditional blinders, they say, and see how the frame of theatrical presentations turns any performance into a "play."

Bernard Weiner, a playwright and director, is Theater Critic for the San Francisco *Chronicle*.

There are certain problems with this definition, however. For one, as more and more theaters have gone dark in search of successful commercial "product," producers, desperately in search of the magic formula to draw the public in, have tended to put *anything* on stage. And so, we've seen a spate of shows in large and small houses that in other times would be identified as little more than glorified nightclub acts or magic shows or music recitals or clown sketches. Also, because there are, in relative terms, fewer theater shows than, say, music or dance presentations, quite a few artists have tried to slide their music and dance shows over into the theater area by calling what they do a "play with music (or dance, or whatever)"—sometimes with little or no justification—in order to get the all-important newspaper review, useful for their next grant application.

But, those commercial and self-aggrandizement problems aside, how DO we assess the new plays, and distinguish between, say, so-called "performance art" and a genuine play? Or, as some would have it, why should we bother at all? Why try to define something that is there merely for edification, enjoyment, itself? Well, either out of stubbornness, the old-fashioned desire to know and classify and examine and analyze, or the practical consideration of trying to divide up the assignments, I find myself at times obsessed with—and confused by—the question of definition.

Let me be more specific. I went to see *Tango Glaciale*— presented in the Bay Area by Italy's hot new-wave troupe Falso Movimento for the San Francisco International Theater Festival—and thought to myself as I watched it: "coffeetable theater...pretty pictures, but so what?" But George Coates' *are are* also could be accused of the same "crimes," yes?

Question to myself: Why do I consider one a theater piece and the other a kind of disco design show? If I can answer that, perhaps rules for definitions will follow.

Tango was, for the most part, all flash and no content. Oh, there was the usual attempt to paste some on: new wave punkers acting out roles of those dancing on the lip of the apocalyse. But that simplistic "message" could have been handled on a sign-card. No, this was high-tech for its own sake, with one scene equaling another. No doubt, the pop borrowings from American films went over big back home in Naples, but they seemed old-hat over here.

are are, on the other hand, used the new technology and new musical forms in the enhancement of a point of view. One scene built onto another, and the complex construction led somewhere: to a demonstration of the value of artistic cooperation, which took the three aesthetic astronauts to a beatific "liftoff" into the cosmic ether.

I don't mean to suggest that there has to be an uplifting (no pun intended) message—or any Message, for that matter—to qualify a performance-art piece as a play. Some performance-art plays, after all, are little more than one-person character sketches (David Schein's remarkable *Out Comes Butch,* for example). But for them to be anything more than graphic displays, they need have some "build," some development of character or point of view, some unfolding in the service of momentum. An image laid on top of another image laid on top of another image simply won't make it.

They also need, it seems to me, some relation to text. This is not to say that a mime piece (say, Beckett's *Acts Without Words*) must be considered a non-play; it's simply one the audience doesn't hear. But I think a performance-art piece—or dance-theater piece or whatever—does have to have some relationship to a text, preferably with spoken words. Not that these words need be totally decipherable (certainly they were not in *are are*) but, in a perversely traditional way, because use of language tends to indicate a piece based on some considered sense of development. The tongue leads to the ear leads to the brain.

Now, having spent so much time arguing for a more traditional view of avant-garde theater, as a way of aesthetic cataloguing, let me say that when I go to see these performance-art shows, I most often throw all my mental dictionaries and divisions out the proverbial *fenster,* and simply enjoy—or, as the case may be, not enjoy. Stuart Sherman's *Hamlet* is not Shakespeare's—which is to say that it is more graphic art than theatrical art—but it still resonates as a *kind* of a play performed in a theater, and I enjoy it on that level. (About his *Spectacles,* and such, I have other feelings, of watching a personal collage-ist at work; it moves me not. But I admire the intelligence, if not the ego, behind it.)

The key question for me, then, in performance, boils down, as it always does for a theater critic, to: Does it work? Call it "performance-art" or "movement/theater/film event" or "play with music" or whatever: Does it work as theater?

Oh my God! I've just opened up a new can of worms: What is "theater" anyway?

ORDER FORM

SINGLE ISSUES

West Coast Plays 1 _____ copies at $ 5.00 $_____
West Coast Plays 7 _____ copies at $ 6.00 $_____
West Coast Plays 8 _____ copies at $ 6.00 $_____
West Coast Plays 9 _____ copies at $ 6.00 $_____
West Coast Plays 10 _____ copies at $ 6.00 $_____
West Coast Plays 11/12 _____ copies at $ 9.95 $_____
West Coast Plays 13/14 _____ copies at $12.50 $_____
West Coast Plays 15/16 _____ copies at $12.50 $_____

THE COMPLETE SET
West Coast Plays 1-16 _____ sets at $80.00 $_____
    note: volumes 2-7 and 9 are available only in the complete set.

Subtotal $_____
Calif. orders add 6% tax $_____

SUBSCRIPTIONS
One Year (4 volumes, 2 double issues) $25.00
West Coast Plays subscription _____ at $25.00 $_____
Total $_____

STANDING ORDERS ARE AVAILABLE TO LIBRARIES AND THEATERS AND ARE BILLED AT CURRENT COVER PRICE.

Please make check or money order payable to *West Coast Plays*.

NAME _____

ORGANIZATION _____

ADDRESS _____

CITY _____ STATE _____ COUNTRY _____ ZIP _____

West Coast Plays back issues available:

#1 **Ashes** by David Rudkin $4.95
    Cross Country by Susan Miller
    Daddies by Douglass Gower
    Passing Shots by Steven Yafa
    The Mark Taper Forum's New Play Program (an interview)

#2 (Available only in full set orders.)
    And by Robert Gordon
    Goethe: Ein Fragment by Michael McClure
    The Last of the Marx Brothers' Writers by Louis Phillips
    Wolves by John Robinson
    Giving Playwrights Experience (an article) by Matin Esslin

#3 (Available only in full set orders.)
    Animals are Passing From Our Lives by Robert Eisele
    Safe House by Nicholas Kazan
    St. George by J. Paul Porter
    Maud Gone Says No to the Poet by Susan Rivers
    And if That Mockingbird Don't Sing by William Whitehead

#4 (Available only in full set orders.)
    Sunset/Sunrise: A Hyperreal Comedy by Adele Edling Shank
    Hyperrealism in the Theatre: Shank Interviews Shank
    Skaters by Ted Pezzulo
    Two O'Clock Feeding by Madeline Puccioni
    Earth Worms by Albert Innaurato

#5 (Available only in full set orders.)
    Judas by Robert Patrick
    The Bathtub by Lisa Shipley
    Imitations by Nancy Larson
    Autobiography of a Pearl Diver by Martin Esslin

#6 (Available only in full set orders.)
    Pizza by Michele Linfante
    Dinosaur by Glenn Hopkins and Wayne Lindberg
    Silvester the Cat Vs. Galloping Billy Bronco
      by Michael Lynch
    Jacob's Ladder by Barbara Graham

#7 **The Chicago Conspiracy Trial** by Ron Sossi $6.00
      and Frank Condon
    Camp Shepard: Exploring the Geography of Character
      (an article) by Scott Christopher Wren
    From the Coyote Cycle by Murray Mednick

#8 **Three Acts of Recognition** by Botho Strauss $6.00
    Tequila by Bennett Cohen
    Intrigue at Ah-pah by The Dell 'Arte Players
    Essays:
    Botho Strauss in America by Robert Goss
    The Ah-pah File by Stephen Most

#9 **Jo Anne!** by Ed Bullins $6.00
    Coyote IV: Other Side Camp by Murray Mednick
    Back to Back by Al Brown
    The "True West" Interviews: Sam Shepard and Others

#10 **Hotel Universe** and **Ghosts** by $6.00
        The San Francisco Mime Troupe
    The Day Roosevelt Died by Barry Pritchard
    An Evening in Our Century by Drury Pifer
    Inching Through the Everglades by The Provisional Theatre
    Essays:
    Playwrights' Polemic: A Shortage of Themes by
    Martin Esslin and others

#11/12 (Special double issue) $9.95
    The Shrunken Head of Pancho Villa by Luis Valdez
    Chekhov in Yalta by John Driver and Jeffrey Haddow
    And the Soul Shall Dance by Wakako Yamauchi
    Surface Tension by Laura Farabough
    Catholic Girls by Doris Baizley
    The Reactivated Man by Curtis Zahn
    Home Free by Robert Alexander
    And a Special Section on Playwright Development

#13/14 (Special double issue.) $12.50
    Yellow Fever by R.A. Shiomi
    The Fox by Allan Miller
    The Widow's Blind Date by Israel Horovitz
    Estonia You Fall by Martin Weetman
    Your Place Is No Longer With Us by Ellen V. Sabastian
    Hoss Drawin' by Leon Martell
    Coyote V: Listening to Old Nana by Murray Mednick
    One Step Beyond the Absurd/Tangled Up In Blue
        by Hal Gelb
    Renaissance Radar: A Performance Landscape
        by Alan Finneran
    An Interview With Alan Finneran
    Playwrights in England: Development and Survival
        by Theodore Shank

ATA Is American Theatre Today!

ATA Is the American Theatre Association, and we've been contributing to American theatre life since 1936.

ATA is 7500 theatre professionals who share a common goal: to develop the highest quality of theatre in America for all audiences and at all levels. And ATA is reaching that goal in many exciting ways.

ATA is involved in everything from the latest performance trends to research in theatre history. Our programs and activities focus on nearly every aspect of the contemporary theatre scene, from women's theatre to Black theatre, children's theatre to performance training. Our publications range from the internationally-respected quarterly of criticism and research **Theatre Journal** to the lively membership publication **Theatre News**. We're actively serving today's theatre community, and committed to training tomorrow's performers, designers, directors, and playwrights.

We'd like to tell you more about membership in the American Theatre Association. Write us at 1010 Wisconsin Avenue, NW, Washington, DC, 20007 for complete information about how you can become part of ATA, and the many benefits and bonuses that are part of that professional affiliation.

ATA reflects the many faces of theatre today... won't you join us as a member of the American Theatre Association?

ATA Is The American Theatre Association

APPLAUSE
THEATRE BOOKS
100 West 67 St. • New York • N.Y. • 10023 • (212)496-7511

Now You don't have To live in New York to shop at the Finest Theatre Book Shop in the World.

Announcing the winter 1984 **APPLAUSE** catalog

Over 3100 new and recent titles
On every aspect of the theatre
From all publishers

WE SHIP WORLDWIDE

Of course I want the free Applause 1984 catalog!

Name_____
Address_____
_____ Zip _____

WE ARE STRONG

A GUIDE TO THE WORK OF POPULAR THEATRES ACROSS THE AMERICAS

... with over one hundred photographs, essays, list of festivals and support groups, and a directory profiling seventy-two companies and solo performers at work across the Americas.

243 pages: $14.95 perfect-bound paperback. In the U.S. include $1.00 postage and handling for the first copy and .30 for each additional copy. We will ship books by book rate. Allow six to eight weeks for delivery. **TERMS:** Prepayment is preferred, but billing is available on orders of more than one copy. Net in thirty days. **LIBRARIES:** We will bill libraries at the net plus library rate. **BOOK-SELLERS:** Inquire about discount rates. **ABROAD:** For shipping outside of the U.S. include $1.50 for the first book and .50 for each additional copy for postage and handling. Payment should be in U.S. funds. Make checks payable to **THEATERWORK,** 120 South Broad Street, Mankato, Minnesota 56001. ISBN 0-912197-00-5

DATE DUE

PRINTED IN U.S.A

GAYLORD